Engagement in Teaching History

Theory and Practices for Middle and Secondary Teachers

Second Edition

Frederick D. Drake
Illinois State University

Lynn R. Nelson
Purdue University

Merrill
is an imprint of

Upper Saddle River, New Jersey
Columbus, Ohio

Library of Congress Cataloging in Publication Data
Drake, Frederick D.
    Engagement in teaching history : theory and practices for middle and secondary teachers /
Frederick D. Drake, Lynn R. Nelson.
        p. cm.
    Includes bibliographical references and index.
    ISBN-13: 978-0-13-158673-4
    ISBN-10: 0-13-158673-4
    1. History—Study and teaching (Middle school)   2. History—Study and teaching (Secondary)
I. Nelson, Lynn R.   II. Title.
    D16.2.D66 2009
    907.1′2—dc22

2007048962

Vice President and Executive Publisher: Jeffery W. Johnston
Publisher: Kevin M. Davis
Editor: Meredith D. Fossel
Editorial Assistant: Maren Vigilante
Senior Project Manager: Linda Hillis Bayma
Production Coordination: Michael Krapovicky, Pine Tree Composition, Inc.
Design Coordinator: Diane C. Lorenzo
Cover Designer: Aaron Dixon
Cover Image: Jupiter Images
Operations Specialist: Susan Hannahs
Director of Marketing: Quinn Perkson
Marketing Manager: Darcy Betts Prybella
Marketing Coordinator: Brian Mounts

This book was set in Book Antiqua by Laserwords, Pvt. Ltd., Chennai. It was printed and bound by
R.R. Donnelley & Sons Company. The cover was printed by R.R. Donnelley & Sons Company. The
photos on pages 179, 181 and 204 were supplied by the author.

Pearson Education Ltd.
Pearson Education Singapore Pte. Ltd.
Pearson Education Canada, Ltd.
Pearson Education—Japan

Pearson Education Australia Pty. Limited
Pearson Education North Asia Ltd.
Pearson Educación de Mexico, S.A. de C.V.
Pearson Education Malaysia Pte. Ltd.

Merrill
is an imprint of

10 9 8 7 6 5 4
ISBN-13: 978-0-13-158673-4
ISBN-10:   0-13-158673-4

Preface

At a recent social studies educators' conference, convened in 2003, we listened attentively to the varied attempts of social studies educators to answer this important question: What teaching strategies are consistent with an aim toward education for democracy? The social studies specialists came from all regions of the United States. We listened as they brainstormed to come up with a list of teaching strategies. These included mock trials, debate, Socratic dialog, simulated congressional hearings, role-playing, cooperative learning, moral dilemmas, deep concept exploration, problem solving, research in public policy, hearings, good lectures, docudramas, and community resources. All of these ideas represent very good teaching and useful teaching strategies. Note, however, that not one social studies expert mentioned the use of primary sources. Written history is based on primary sources such as official documents, letters, diaries, oral histories, speeches, newspaper articles, and other archival materials.

This book seeks to reinvigorate history as an integral part of liberal and civic education. As social studies evolved into a broad field of study, history, as a subject, lost its central role. The study of history loses its importance when students do not realize that significant knowledge of the past is based on the interpretation of factual data. Knowing about the past gives meaning to the present and may give hints as to what will happen in the future.

How Do We Effectively Teach History?

How can history be taught effectively? That is the question! Should we lecture? David M. Kennedy and Michael Whelan assure us that a good story is a powerful way to help students learn. Kennedy, a Stanford University history professor who has written a well-known AP U.S. history textbook, states, "There is something innate in the human mind that makes the narrative form an especially attractive medium in which to contain, transmit, and remember important information."[1] Whelan remarks, "If you are going to lecture, you had better make it memorable."[2]

How often should we lead classroom discussions? Discussions of content help students formulate their thinking about history. How can we ensure that all students have an opportunity to participate in an informed way during discussions? How can we generate informed discussions that avoid opining and "blather," which are often the pitfalls of discussions? How can we organize discussions so they result in historical understanding?

When and how do we introduce students to primary sources? Primary sources offer a rich contextual understanding of the past. How can we help students analyze primary sources and make connections to a larger narrative of the past? How do we connect our teaching with national and state standards? How should we evaluate students' knowledge and understanding of history?

This book responds to these questions as we explore the following key elements of history instruction:

- Student involvement in historical inquiry
- The careful integration of primary sources and narratives in the teaching of history
- Teaching toward chronological thinking and vital themes and narratives with historians' habits of mind
- The use of historical documents to develop in students a detective approach to solving historical problems
- The use of a systematic approach to improve students' historical thinking
- The use of deliberative discussions, in a controlled setting, to develop a durable framework of historical knowledge
- The use of practical means of evaluation to measure the level of students' learning

Teachers will be able to apply our ideas for selecting content, methods of instruction, and assessment of student learning. The methods we present in this book are a powerful means to develop students' understanding of history and their ability to use this knowledge in discussing issues past and present. These methods are not novel or magical, but they are useful and effective. This book emphasizes certain strategies that will help students know more about the past in ways that will help them in their lives today.

How Is This Book Organized?

This book comprises three parts. In Part I, we describe the theoretical background to teaching history. In Chapter 1, Teaching History, we propose the "history laboratory." We deal with the present world situation in teaching history. We suggest a theme of freedom and provide interrelated questions you can pose to organize your history course. What are the meanings of freedom in the United States and in the world? What are the political conditions and social conditions that make freedom possible in the United States and in the world? What are the boundaries of freedom in the United States and in the world and how have they been reduced as well as expanded? Moreover, why is history important for your students? Why is historical inquiry important?

In Chapter 2, The History of Teaching History, we describe the history of your profession. When, how, and why did history emerge as a subject for study in schools? We provide an overview of the circumstances that gave rise to the teaching of history in the early American experience, and we examine 20th-century contro-versies surrounding history and the social studies. Why have history and social studies become contested areas in the curriculum?

In Chapter 3, Historical Thinking, we establish an instructional and cognitive framework for your instructional strategies. What is historical thinking? Why is historical thinking important for all students? How is historical thinking unique and different from other forms of sophisticated thought?

In Part II, Planning and Assessment, we emphasize that teaching involves organizing your courses and creating ways to assess what your students learn. In Chapter 4, Organizing Your History Courses: Making Content Choices, we discuss chronological and thematic organization for teaching history. How is such organization helpful?

In Chapter 5, Lesson and Unit Planning, we offer suggestions for creating both lesson and unit plans in teaching history. How does long-range planning help students learn history? What are the common features of all lesson plans? How are unit plans developed?

In Chapter 6, Creating Historical Understanding and Communication Through Performance Assessment, we deal with the need to assess your students' knowl-edge, reasoning power, and effective use of communication in the setting of a his-tory classroom. How can assessment go beyond the typical multiple-choice test? How can you create an effective authoritative rubric to share with your students?

In Part III, Instruction, we focus on the use of primary sources, discussion, images, and writing in teaching history. In Chapter 7, Using Primary Sources: The First-, Second-, and Third-Order Approach, we discuss typologies of pri-mary sources, how to choose primary sources, and how to use an inquiry method in teaching history. Whereas Chapter 3 provides a theoretical grounding for the first-, second-, and third-order approach, Chapter 7 offers practical illus-trations for you to use in the classroom. How can primary sources become an in-tegral part of teaching and learning? How can primary sources be used effectively in teaching?

In Chapter 8, Considering and Doing Discussion in History Teaching, we focus on deliberative discussions and the use of first-, second-, and third-order documents. How are deliberative discussions distinguished from other types of classroom discussions? How does the approach we suggest give your teaching an intellectual direction?

In Chapter 9, Using Historical Images to Engage Your Students in the Past, we provide three teaching strategies to incorporate photographs and paintings in the teaching of history, among other strategies. How do visuals contribute to the teaching and learning of history? How can you involve students in actively ana-lyzing images (rather than depending on you to do it for them)?

In Chapter 10, Using Writing to Engage Your Students in the Past, we de-scribe effective writing assignments related to teaching history. What strategies can you use to encourage writing in the history classroom? How does writing im-prove knowledge and understanding of historical content?

Our conclusion points to the need for good history teaching in the 21st cen-tury. We summarize the importance of history as a subject in the curriculum, the use of primary sources, and the value of deliberative discussion for developing informed individuals who are lifelong learners. Above all, we hope that what follows will be useful as you begin your role as a scholar, teacher, and student of history and the social sciences.

What Are the Special Features?

Both the study of history and the teaching of history are multifaceted. Throughout this book we intersperse over 20 **Ideas for the History Classroom** to help both new and experienced history teachers engage students in inquiry and discussions. We also provide teachers of methods courses with chapter-ending activities under the heading **Translating History into Classroom Practice.** These activities can be readily used in a History Education, Social Science Education, or Social Studies Education Methods course.

We make no pretense of covering all the best practices of a classroom teacher and methods teacher. We do, however, hope that our book engages new and experienced teachers in thoughtful discourse regarding the teaching and learning of history.

Acknowledgments

In the first edition of this book, we began with a belief that "just telling stories" was not enough to teach history effectively. We still feel that way. Stories are important. They offer much more than history teachers who are servants of the textbook. Stories alone, though, are inadequate in history teaching.

The engine of our argument for the second edition of *Engagement in Teaching History*, much like the first, calls upon each history teacher to offer an intellectual direction for their students. We believe *history* is an action verb and that the history classroom is a "laboratory" where the teacher and students have an opportunity to co-investigate the past and "do history." The questions teachers and students ask about stories and primary sources can help us construct meaningful durable knowledge that sustains us in our lives as citizens.

Portions of this book were drawn from earlier publications. Fred had written with his colleague, Lawrence W. McBride, "Reinvigorating the Teaching of History through Alternative Assessment," *The History Teacher* 30, no. 2 (February 1997): 145–173. He had also written with Sarah Drake Brown "A Systematic Approach to Improve Students' Historical Thinking," *The History Teacher* 36, no. 4 (August 2003): 465–489. Fred and Lynn also had written a chapter, "Civic Intelligence and Liberal Intelligence in the History Education of Social Studies Teachers and Students." Their chapter appeared in John J. Patrick and Robert Leming's work, *Principles and Practices of Democracy in the Education of Social Studies Teachers* (2001), the first of several books to be derived from the R. Freeman Butts Institute on Civic Learning in Teacher Education.

While previous writings served as a foundation for writing this book, we want to thank several people. A number of teachers and preservice teachers helped us write this book. We have observed many outstanding classroom teachers in the United States, China, Russia, and the Baltic nations of Lithuania, Latvia, and Estonia. We have discussed with them their teaching practices, and we have shared ideas with them about teaching history and using primary sources. Their names are too numerous to mention here. The opportunities we had to meet with them will always be remembered.

We would like to thank in particular Sarah Drake Brown, an assistant professor of history at Ball State University. Sarah should really be named as a third author of this book. We have discussed ideas with her, Fred has written articles with her, and we have consulted her throughout the writing of this book as we thought about the multiple and varied best practices of teaching history. Sarah has been part of this book through all its stages. She is the daughter of one of us, friend and colleague to us both, and her help has gone beyond her many useful suggestions for improving the teaching of history.

We would like to thank the reviewers of our manuscript for their suggestions and insights: Ernest Barnett, Northern Kentucky University; Douglas Fisher, San Diego State University; Axel D. Ramirez, Utah Valley State College; Jennifer Groendal-Cobb, University of South Florida; Kent Freeland, Morehead State University; John K. Lee, Georgia State University; John H. Litcher, Wake Forest University; Thomas B. Goodkind, University of Connecticut; John J. Patrick, Indiana University; Linda D. Addo, North Carolina A&T State University; Stephen J. Thornton, Columbia University; Steven Thorpe, Southern Oregon University; Margaret Laughlin, University of Wisconsin–Green Bay; and Lynette K. Oshima, University of New Mexico.

Finally, we would like to thank the reviewers of the second edition for their thoughtful feedback: Dean Cristol, The Ohio State University; Janet Hecsh, California State University, Sacramento; Wilbur J. Johnson, Brown University; and Todd Kenreich, Towson University.

William Faulkner once observed that a book is never completed, but merely abandoned. We have had a difficult time abandoning this one, largely because it opens new avenues of inquiry for teachers of history. We hope this second edition continues to nudge history teachers and students to co-investigate the past and engage in deliberative discussions.

Frederick D. Drake   Lynn R. Nelson
Illinois State University   *Purdue University*

About the Authors

Dr. Frederick D. Drake is a Professor of History and Director of the History-Social Sciences Education Program at Illinois State University. He has taught for 38 years: 20 years teaching high school history and the social sciences and 18 years at the university level. He was named Illinois State University's Outstanding University Professor for 2003–2004.

Dr. Lynn R. Nelson is an Associate Professor of Curriculum and Instruction at Purdue University. He has taught 39 years: 12 years teaching high school and middle school social studies and 27 years at the university level.

Contents

Note: Every effort has been made to provide accurate and current Internet information in this book. However, the Internet and information posted on it are constantly
changing, so it is inevitable that some of the Internet addresses in this textbook will
change.

Part

I Theoretical Background

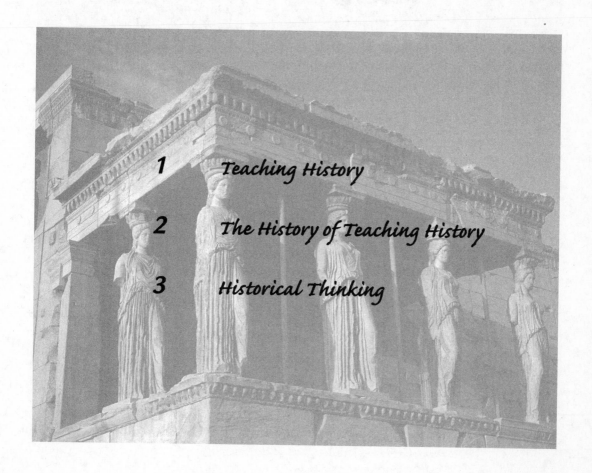

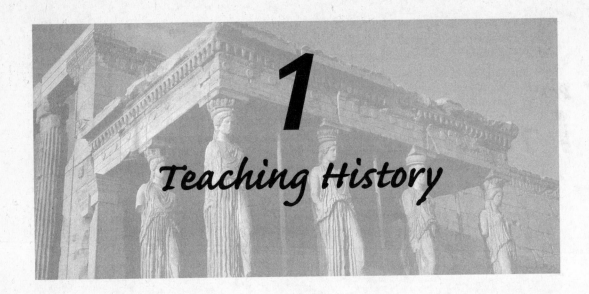

1
Teaching History

Vision without action is a daydream. Action without vision is a nightmare.

—Japanese Proverb

The trouble with our times is that the future is not what it used to be.

—Paul Valery

Because the Past is the Present and the Future too.

—Center for History and New Media: History News Network:
http://hnn.us/

*I*f you are beginning your teaching career in history or social studies, you are mired in myriad concerns. Along with facing a varied group of students, you are confronted with issues such as globalization, consumerism, multiculturalism, vocational education, democracy, urbanization, immigration, and economic problems both at home and throughout the world. And, we might add, student apathy. When you walk into the classroom as a history teacher, keep this in mind: History is important, and history teaching is getting better and better. History raises questions, but also provides answers. Effective history teaching, we hope, will make your students wiser. As the Roman statesman Seneca once remarked, "No one ever became wise by chance."

Focus Questions

1. What is a history "laboratory"?

2. What are the relationships of the past to the present?

3. What questions will you ask to foster historical inquiry?

4. What is historical thinking? What are the habits of mind of historians, history teachers, and students of history?

5. What are defining themes that you can use to organize historical content for your students?

6. What are your purposes in teaching history?

7. What are the relationships between historical understanding and civic knowledge and behavior?

The History Laboratory

Some sound advice for teaching history is "Just tell stories." History, after all, includes dramatic stories of people whose experiences can be drawn from all walks of life. These stories are often ones we share as human beings. Stories, when chosen carefully and told well, serve as a powerful attraction to the study of history in classrooms. As listeners, all of us—including our students—can relate to the past. The stories often need no "artificial" connection to the present.

Stories alone, though, will not suffice in history teaching. We need classrooms where active learning takes place, the "doing of history." *History* is an action verb. The history classroom is a "laboratory" where students and teachers ask questions together, discuss the past, and make meaning of the past, the present, and sometimes even the future. The stories draw our interest to the past and frame our knowledge; the questions we ask about stories and primary sources potentially help us construct meaningful, durable knowledge that sustains us in our lives as individuals and citizens.

In the history "laboratory," teacher and students co-investigate the past. As the teacher, you provide the intellectual direction for your students in the specific laboratory that examines the past and makes meaning of the present. History is unique to all other academic disciplines and school subjects. No other discipline emphasizes *time* as does history; no other school subject holds such a prominent place in the curriculum. History is the rare academic discipline that thrives on placing peoples' lives and experiences in the context of their own time.

You should introduce your students to five key terms in your history laboratory:

- Primary sources
- Secondary sources
- Historiography
- Hermeneutics
- Heuristics

All five terms have important bearing in the history laboratory and your effectiveness as a history teacher. Throughout the school year, you and your students should unashamedly use these words in your discussions. You need not mystify your students with these words; simply make them part of their everyday vocabulary.

Primary sources, secondary sources, historiography, hermeneutics, and heuristics are to the history teacher's laboratory what nucleus, neutrons, protons, isotopes, and quarks are to the physics teacher's laboratory. They frame the very basis of helping your students understand what history is as an academic discipline and how it contributes to the durable knowledge they have as citizens. By introducing your students to these five terms you set a high bar for your students, yet one that can be achieved. Your students will come to understand that while knowing key dates, names, and places are important, these are not the culmination of historical understanding. Your students will come to realize that history is constructed and when constructed meaningfully it provides a foundation of enduring knowledge and skills that will sustain them long after they have left your classroom.

When you think of your classroom as a history laboratory you open up opportunities for your students in urban, suburban, and rural settings to know who they and others are in place and time. Your responsibility is to tap into their curiosity and to help them *think historically*. It isn't always easy; indeed, it can be frustrating; but it is achievable and important.

In the history laboratory, you and your students co-investigate historical issues and you accentuate the importance of determining the credibility of sources, improving students' historical knowledge and understanding, and improving students' historical thinking. We suggest you organize your history laboratory with historical themes, history's habits of mind (informed ways of thinking), and with some sound teaching strategies that actively engage your students to become historical beings[1], whose lives are contextualized in the stream of time, and help them become effective historical citizens.[2]

The history laboratory shares similarities with science laboratories. Science demands rigor; so too does careful historical investigation. The lively historical mind is open to myriad ideas and ultimately examines events in historical context and establishes interpretations based on evidence. In what other ways is the history laboratory similar to science laboratories?

There is a distinct difference between history and scientific laboratories. Often, the sciences seek replication by maintaining exact conditions and circumstances. In the history laboratory, replication is neither achievable nor the point. Each time period has its own set of circumstances. While an exact repeat of everything in the past can never be attained, we can glean from each period important ideas, decisions, and experiences that contribute to our understanding of human beings, civilizations, nations, and the world of ideas. Even in this era of standardized expectations, you as the teacher establish the intellectual direction for your students as they become historical citizens.

The Present and the Past

Three recent events—the terrorist acts of September 11, 2001, legislative acts to create a cabinet-level U.S. Department of Homeland Security, and the decision to go to war with Iraq in 2003 and talk in 2007 of potential war with Iran—remind us of the importance of history and especially the study of U.S. history from a local, national, and international perspective.

The September 11 attacks involving planes crashing into the north and south towers of the World Trade Center, the Pentagon in Washington, D.C., and a field in western Pennsylvania illustrate the need for historical understanding and discussion among citizens. These events served as a turning point in history for people both in the United States and throughout the global community. To make sense of these attacks and to respond appropriately, citizens must become engaged. The historically literate individual and engaged citizen takes responsibility for involvement in the public sphere. This involvement may be played out in local, state, national, or international arenas. In effect, you should ask yourself these very important questions: What do your students already know about these acts of terrorism? What would your students need to know to organize and make sense of these attacks on the United States? What knowledge is required to participate as effective citizens in our republic? How do we organize historical knowledge so it is memorable?

Students need historical guidance to understand the September 11 events and the war with Iraq. They should be aware of the cultural differences between Muslim countries and Western democracies (including Islamic culture, law, and the challenges of modernity within Arab-Islamic societies). They should know something about the founding of Israel and the many Middle Eastern conflicts that continuously have taken place.[3]

As a result of terrorism, the administration of George W. Bush created, with congressional approval, the Department of Homeland Security; touted as the most important change in the government of the United States in half a century. The newly created cabinet-level position and laws that have accompanied its creation have led to controversy regarding the values of liberty, order, and justice. Will Americans trust their government to provide security and at the same time protect individual liberties? Should we give up some liberties for security reasons? How much? These are lively topics for discussion, using history as a guide.

Americans have long believed that the highest purpose of government is to protect the rights of the people to whom it is responsible. At times, no doubt, rights have been marginalized, revived, or even denied by governments. History can enlighten students on these issues. The Alien and Sedition Acts of 1798 abridged certain liberties. The suspension of the writ of habeas corpus was invoked in both the War of 1812 and the Civil War. Likewise, the Espionage Act of 1917 and the Sedition Act of 1918 marginalized rights during World War I. The Smith Act of 1940 (which has never been repealed) banned sedition on the eve of the American entrance into World War II and was used to crack down on American communists in the late 1940s and 1950s. After President Roosevelt issued Executive Order 9066 in 1942, the U.S. Supreme Court upheld the incarceration of Japanese Americans. These examples are just a few that you can draw on in classroom discussions related to liberty and security.

Each of the previous historical events occurred in the context of its own time. As a teacher, you are responsible for enlarging your students' understanding of the uniqueness of the past. How will you do that? In part, that is the purpose of this book.

Our history is replete with instances of balancing the values of liberty and order. Over 200 years ago, the architect of the Bill of Rights, James Madison, wrote that in "charters of liberty" as the U.S. Constitution, "every word . . . decides a question between power [order] and liberty."[4] Madison's 1792 observation raises a question for us as a nation at this time when most of the American public perceives a threat to our national security: What have been and what are the fundamental relations between collective national security and individual liberty?

Moreover, how do constitutional powers play out in wartime? In 1787, the founding fathers anxiously discussed powers, competence, ambitions, and avarice of elected leaders in the legislative and executive branches. James Madison, whose forte was creating constitutional structures, had played a leading role in the discussion of where the greatest powers must reside. Ten years after the Constitution had been ratified, Madison wrote a letter to his friend and political ally Thomas Jefferson about war powers and authority. He commented, "The Constitution supposes, what the History of all Governments demonstrates, that the Executive is the branch of power most interested in war, & most prone to it. It has accordingly with studied care, vested the question of war in the Legislature."[5] How will you engage your students in a thoughtful discussion of Madison's observation?

The war with Iraq also has historical overtones. In the 2002 State of the Union message, President Bush referred to an "axis of evil"—namely, the nations of Iraq, Iran, and North Korea. His use of the term *axis* referred to the Axis powers of Germany, Italy, and Japan during World War II.

The war with Iraq and its resulting occupation yielded primary sources for use in the classroom such as eyewitness reports of battle, journalists' on-the-scene reporting, and live television. Way back in 431 BCE, Thucydides, an exiled Athenian general, based his *History of the Peloponnesian War* on his own observations of Athenians and Spartans alike. Many have written admirably of Thucydides as the greatest historian who ever lived. Thucydides recognized that "different eyewitnesses give different accounts of the same events, speaking out of partiality for one side or the other or else from imperfect memories." Thucydides subsequently became known as the father of history.

The treatment of civilian populations and the capture of military personnel during the Iraq war relate directly to the 1949 diplomatic conferences held in Geneva, Switzerland. The Geneva Convention (a series of conventions that originated in 1867 and was subsequently updated) set standards for the treatment of both civilian populations and prisoners of war. How did the U.S.-led coalition treat the civilian population during this war? How did the Iraqi and coalition forces treat military captives? How have insurgents treated the indigenous population and coalition forces? How did coalition forces and the United Nations address the oil-for-food controversies and the treatment of archives of the cradle of civilization? Your students may not even be aware of the constraints on warring nations imposed by the Geneva Convention. They should be.

Diplomatic historian Robert Divine raised a taunting question about war. In his recent book, aptly titled *Perpetual War for Perpetual Peace*, Divine asserted "that war, rather than being an exceptional event, is in fact the norm in international affairs."[6] How will your students tackle this assertion using evidence from history?[7] Your students should also know that following the collapse of the Soviet Union in 1991, the United States had a preponderance of power. When the U.S. invaded Iraq in 2003, it claimed that it could act alone, threatening to do so when Germany, Russia, and France publicly opposed preemptive strike action. The United States enlisted several nations, including its ally Britain, in a "coalition of the willing." By 2007, the United States had deposed and captured Iraqi dictator Saddam Hussein, proposed to establish a stable democratic government, yet failed to restore order in Iraq. The Bush administration threatened that the United States might conduct strikes against Iran in part because of claims Iran was helping Iraqi insurgents and Al-Qaeda and because Iran sought nuclear power that could be transferred into weaponry. Both Iran and Russia are emerging from the war in Iraq with more influence, and China's burgeoning economy has become one of the world's fastest growing economies.

To those advocating U.S. foreign policy, the United States has had an international obligation to use its power to its advantage and to promote a stable economy and republican governments based on the premise that democracies do not fight democracies. The United States sent its troops to Iraq to establish democracy and halt threats of potential Islamic terrorism. The United States, this position maintains, must remain steadfast and vigilant against Iran's potential growth as a nuclear power that could exacerbate conflicts in the region.

To those in opposition of U.S. policy, destabilization in the Middle East rests squarely on the shoulders of the United States, whose proclivity to intervene in the affairs of foreign nations has dominated American foreign policy in the 20th century. The critics charge that U.S. compulsive aggression surfaced in the early 20th century and became much more pronounced after World War II, when the United States emerged as clearly the world's most powerful military and economic force. This tendency to intervene has made the world much less safe. How does war eclipse other important international and domestic issues?

When examining U.S. foreign policy, it is tempting to frame discussions around ideas of who is "good" and who is "bad." What about individuals who believe that democracies are less likely to fight other democracies and therefore support a democratic Middle East, and yet are uncomfortable with U.S. action in the region? What about those who believe Saddam Hussein provided a restraint to Iran and that balance of power should have been the guiding force even if it meant the Iraqi people suffered under his leadership? U.S. foreign policy and international relations are far more nuanced than "good" vs. "evil." Your teaching must resist the temptation to reduce a discussion of international relations to filling out a "T-chart." How will you help your students understand historical and contemporary complexities and nuances?

Your students enter your classroom with some ideas about democracy as garnered from other teachers, their parents and relatives, their friends, and the popular media. Most students, while possessing some knowledge, believe democracy has always been present in the United States and that it was inevitable. How will you help your students understand that democracy was *not* inevitable in the United States and elsewhere? It is paramount for you to help your students avoid the ill-informed trappings of inevitability. For example, when the Constitution was written in 1787, there were no *prima facie* reasons to have ordinary people choose a leader. The idea that common people (especially those without property) should vote was as strange to the founding fathers as believing today that ordinary people should perform brain surgery.

Democracy has spread from a few nations in the early 19th century to hundreds today. Democracy, though contagious, is not irresistible. When Alexis de Tocqueville traveled the United States in the 1830s, democracy was new and not only in the United States. How did democracy spread in the United States? What is the relationship between republican government and a capitalist economic system? Why did the belief in democracy take hold and spread? How was the Civil War in the United States a war over slavery *and* preserving the Union, and what relationship does it have to democracy? A traditional interpretation of the Civil War is that the war was a "vindication" of democracy. A far different interpretation is it was a "collapse" of democracy. How will your students react to a discussion of democracy as it relates to capitalism? To the Civil War? We suggest you and your students discuss these historical questions in the context of the times in which people lived and acted.

How will you and your students address the issues comprising democracy as a form of government? Winston Churchill, as Leader of the Opposition in Parliament after World War II, responded to Clement Attlee and his Labour Government in 1947 with these often quoted words:

> Many forms of Government have been tried, and will be tried in this world of sin and woe. No one pretends that democracy is perfect or all-wise. Indeed it has been said that democracy is the worst form of Government except all those other forms that have been tried from time to time.

How will your students wrestle with Churchill's comment? Why does understanding the time period and the political situation in Britain give us a more informed understanding of Churchill's quote about democracy as a form of government? How have current commentators called upon Churchill's quote to vindicate their own point of view?

Clearly, you have many opportunities to discuss the connection of the past and the present with your students. Throughout this book we suggest you emphasize that history is an action verb, not simply a noun. Your history classroom should be more akin to a "laboratory" in which questions are asked, evidence is examined, and discussions and hypotheses occur. Some teachers have content strengths in diplomatic, constitutional, economic, intellectual, cultural, or political history. Others have content strength in social history; that is, they are concerned with the ground-level experiences of ordinary people. Connect political and social history in your teaching. In your history laboratory, emphasize to students primary sources, secondary sources, historiography, hermeneutics or interpretations, and heuristics (all five are described later in this book). The five aspects are essential to students' development in historical knowledge and thinking. They are the attributes of the actively engaged history laboratory in which teacher and students co-investigate the past. As an adult and educated teacher, your responsibility is to guide your students intellectually, not leave them to educating themselves. John Dewey's valuable book, *Experience and Education*, pointed out how foolish is the teacher who misunderstands the conditions that enhance independent thinking.[8] The teacher sets the intellectual tone in the history laboratory, a powerful and attainable responsibility.

Organizing History Around Questions

Present world conditions offer an excellent opportunity to organize a lesson plan(s) that revolves around these three interrelated questions: What are the meanings of freedom in the United States and in the world? What are the political conditions and social conditions that make freedom possible in the United States and in the world? What are the boundaries of freedom in the United States and in the world, and how have they been reduced as well as expanded?[9] These questions allow you to connect U.S. history to world history.

What about globalism? Are we moving toward a global economy—a global government? Are we a world with deep cultural divides, as Samuel Huntington argues, that should be cautious about interfering in one another's business? Or are we a world in the process of globalization that compels us to be interdependent, and will thrive only if shared, universal values are enforced by an international community? Huntington's admonitions can stir debate when history is at the forefront of the discussion. What does history say about it? Recent French and German opposition to the war with Iraq has caused concern. Should one question the role of international organizations created in the 1940s—for example, the United Nations (1945) and the North Atlantic Treaty Organization (1949), the International Monetary Fund (originating at the Bretton Woods Conference in 1944), and the World Bank (also the result of the Bretton Woods Conference)? Does a high-profile international forum such as the G-8 mean that global issues can be decided without the administrative structure of the United Nations or World Bank? What happens if there is a transatlantic divide as suggested by such intellectuals as Robert Kagan? Kagan asserted in 2003: "It is time to stop pretending that Europeans and Americans share a common view of the world, or even that they occupy the same world. . . . Europe is turning away from power . . . into a self-contained world of laws and rules and transnational negotiation and cooperation. . . ."[10] Kagan's quote can stir up an exciting discussion or be the subject of a debate with historical facts as the basis of argument. And discussion can be further stirred with a question on the viability of the United Nations' participation in the reconstruction of Iraq and potential sanctions and military action aimed toward Iran.

Ideas for the History Classroom

Potential Organizing Questions for Your History Class

1. What are the meanings of freedom in the United States and in the world?
2. What are the political conditions and social conditions that make freedom possible in the United States and in the world?
3. What are the boundaries of freedom in the United States and in the world, and how have they been reduced as well as expanded?

Do not underestimate the importance you have as a history teacher. You can ensure that *all* your students have opportunities to read primary sources and narrative accounts. Many primary sources and narratives are available through the Internet, in public and school libraries, and in historical museums. How will students organize the information they find? Your role—to help students organize information and construct this knowledge around larger themes—is an important responsibility. In this book we suggest several themes to help you organize content for your students. Your responsibility is to engage your students in historical and contemporary issues with careful, thoughtful consideration. Themes provide a powerful teaching strategy. Teaching to larger ideas helps your students make the information they find meaningful and use this information to organize subsequent historical learning.

Ideas for the History Classroom

Historians' Questions and History Teaching

To consider:

1. How are the questions of historians and teachers similar? How do they differ?
2. What questions would you ask to cause your students to inquire about the past? In world history? In U.S. history?

> A moment's reflection should suffice to establish the simple proposition that every historian, willy-nilly, must begin his research with a question.
>
> —David Hackett Fischer, *Historians' Fallacies: Toward a Logic of Historical Thought* (New York: Harper & Row, 1970), 3–4.

> Without questions of some sort, a historian is condemned to wander aimlessly through dark corridors of learning. Specific forms of question-framing depend in a considerable degree upon the kinds of answers which are sought. These elemental aspects of questioning are common to all historical inquiry, and indeed to empirical investigation in every field.
>
> —David Hackett Fischer, *Historians' Fallacies: Toward a Logic of Historical Thought* (New York: Harper & Row, 1970), 3–4.

> Many educators no longer were content at having pupils learn history just by reading history texts. Historians analyzed numerous types of documents. To learn the historical approach, pupils also should function in a manner resembling that of the historian [to ask questions]. Such functioning would enable pupils to gain an increased understanding of relationships among historical data. It could also develop more positive student attitudes toward the discipline.
>
> —Francis P. Hunkins, *Questioning Strategies and Techniques* (Boston: Allyn and Bacon, 1972), 2.

> Questions [the teachers asks] do not exist in isolation. They exist within a scheme which is either planned or assumed.
>
> —Francis P. Hunkins, *Questioning Strategies and Techniques* (Boston: Allyn and Bacon, 1972), 78.

Ideas for the History Classroom

Ten Persistent Questions Drawn from Western Historiography

1. How and why do societies change?
2. When societies compete with one another, what makes for success or failure?
3. How does a society cohere, and how do some groups within it gain and retain authority over others?
4. At what point, and why, does political and/or social conflict erupt, and how is it resolved?
5. What are the causes and consequences of economic success?
6. Why does a distinct outlook or "culture" arise in a society, and why does it change?
7. How are religious beliefs related to political, social, intellectual, and economic developments?
8. Are individuals as important as underlying structures in bringing about change?
9. By what arguments or presentations of evidence does a historian most effectively explain the events of the past?
10. Are there general lessons to be learned from history?

Source: Adapted from Theodore K. Rabb, "Patterns and Themes for the History of Western Civilization," *History Matters* 13, no. 4 (December 2000): 1, 6–7.

Primary Sources and Interpretive Narrative Sources

Your students' curiosity about the people and policy makers in the United States and in the larger global community provides opportunities for you as a history and social science teacher. The questions you and your students raise regarding national power (at home and abroad) and its worthiness, its effect, and its moral conduct provide opportunities to examine primary sources, to create historical narratives, and to discuss the sources and narratives meaningfully. In this book we emphasize the blending of primary sources and narratives in teaching history.

About 20 years ago, Lee S. Shulman proposed a particular category of teacher knowledge that he said should be at the top of the list of teacher knowledge taxonomy. *Pedagogical content knowledge,* he said, is critical for all teachers, and this critical knowledge is especially appropriate for history and social studies teachers. The current President of the Carnegie Foundation for the Advancement of Teaching wrote:

> Saying that a teacher must first comprehend both content and purposes, however, does not particularly distinguish a teacher from non-teaching peers. We expect a math major to understand mathematics or a history specialist to comprehend history. But the key to distinguishing the knowledge base of teaching lies at the intersection of content and pedagogy, in the capacity of a teacher to transform the content knowledge he or she possesses

into forms that are pedagogically powerful and yet adaptive to the variations in ability and background presented by the students. . . .[P]edagogi-
cal content knowledge is of special interest because it identifies the
distinctive bodies of knowledge for teaching. It represents the blending of
content and pedagogy into an understanding of how particular topics,
problems, or issues are organized, represented, and adapted to the diverse
interests and abilities of learners, and presented for instruction. Pedagogical content knowledge is the category most likely to distinguish the understanding of the content specialist from that of the pedagogue.[11]

History teachers should know about the discipline of history and how to engage
their students in the "doing of history."

We advocate the use of multiple teaching strategies. Current literature on best
teaching practices advances the value that both young children and older students
should be engaged in "doing history." This book provides beginning and experienced history teachers, as well as history teaching methods professors, with a helpful strategy that aims to improve students' historical understanding and historical
thinking. We introduce a systematic approach that prescribes best practices to help
students analyze primary sources and think historically.

In a history classroom all discussion must be based on historical facts—the
more primary, the better. We have devised an approach to evaluate the degree of
importance of primary sources. We label them **first-order, second-order,** and **third-
order documents.** The first-, second-, and third-order approach engages students
in "doing history" and is one strategy among many to stir your students' historical thinking. This approach will be described more fully in Chapter 7 of this book.

Importance of Historical Thinking

Education historian Larry Cuban noted the importance of historical thinking with
this comment: "[C]itizenship is best cultivated when students learn the critical skills
of historical investigation and draw their own conclusions supported by evidence
drawn from primary sources."[12]

There are many reasons to study history. In the opening pages of the *National
Standards for History,* the statement "knowledge of history is the precondition of
political intelligence" appears boldly. History, the authors of the *Standards* state,
helps society share "a common memory of where it has been, of what its core values are, or of what decisions of the past account for present circumstances." Moreover, the authors of the *Standards* assert that history helps us engage in a "sensible
inquiry into political, social, or moral issues in society." In sections for both grades
K–4 and grades 5–12, the authors of the *Standards* assert that knowledge of history
and the inquiry it incites provides the foundation for "the informed, discriminating
citizenship essential to effective participation in the democratic processes of governance and the fulfillment for all our citizens of the nations' democratic ideals."[13]

Let's explore the lively nature of history. History is a systematic way of thinking that organizes knowledge in a way that is different from other disciplines. Your
students will enter your classroom with a varied body of historical knowledge and

skills. Many teachers used to believe that students' minds were blank slates and that their job as teachers was to fill them with knowledge. This was never true. Kids gain views from the popular media, parents and relatives, and their peers. With your assistance, students can gain skills in historical reasoning.

The former Bradley Commission (now the National Council for History Education, or NCHE), in its description of 13 "habits of mind" of historians, provided a useful explanation of historical reasoning.[14] These habits of mind are presented in Figure 1.1.

Most historians try to avoid present-mindedness (technically called "presentism"), that is, the use of our current values, beliefs, and knowledge to judge people who lived in the past. Historical thinkers try to empathize, to truly understand people and events within the framework of their time. We can make judgments about the past, but we must keep in mind that previous eras had different morals and mores. Although we cannot be totally objective, we should at least beware of our subjectivity.

The National Council for History Education identified what it calls six "vital themes and narratives" to help teachers organize the knowledge domain of a history curriculum.[15] These themes and narratives are presented in Figure 1.2.

The six vital themes and narratives set the context for both explaining historical processes and events and understanding why they matter. These themes and narratives serve as a schematic framework that students can use to organize historical knowledge—durable knowledge—that they can draw on in the future.

The National Assessment of Educational Progress (NAEP) in U.S. History prescribes four themes to help organize the content of U.S. history.[16] See Figure 1.3 for these themes that, like the NCHE themes, cut across periods of history. The National Council for the Social Studies has 10 themes, sometimes called thematic strands, as presented in Figure 1.4.

The study of history should encompass more than the acquisition of discrete pieces of historical information. Although mastering the contours of a given narrative and knowing about significant individuals and events are important, it is essential that you and your students also know about the universal themes and ideas that cut across the human experience. These themes and ideas serve as screens that help students differentiate between what is important and what is insignificant in the historical record. Additionally, these themes provide students with patterned historical understandings that are memorable.

We advocate either the use of the six NCHE vital themes and narratives or the four NAEP themes. What qualities do the NCHE and NAEP themes share? How do they differ?

As a teacher of history and the social sciences, you should first introduce your students to history's habits of mind and themes. Second, you should post the habits of mind and themes in your classroom and refer to them as you encounter new historical topics. Third, you should use themes and habits of mind to organize your teaching and assessment of student learning. You will need to discuss with your students the importance of habits of mind and themes.

To help you and your students begin the school year, you should examine and restate these habits of mind and themes. Let your students translate these ideas into their own words. They could, for example, create a PowerPoint presentation and use it as an analytical framework to discuss historical events.

FIGURE 1.1   History's Habits of Mind.

The perspectives and modes of thoughtful judgment derived from the study of history are many, and they ought to be its principal aim. Courses in history, geography, and government should be designed to take students well beyond formal skills of critical thinking, to help them through their own active learning to do the following:

- Understand the significance of the past to their own lives, both private and public, and to their society

- Distinguish between the important and the inconsequential, to develop the "discriminating memory" needed for a discerning judgment in public and personal life

- Perceive past events and issues as they were experienced by people at the time, to develop historical empathy as opposed to present-mindedness

- Acquire a comprehension of diverse cultures and shared humanity

- Understand how things happen and how things change, how human intentions matter, but also how their consequences are shaped by the means of carrying them out, in a tangle of purpose and process

- Comprehend the interplay of change and continuity, and avoid assuming that either is somehow more natural, or more to be expected, than the other

- Prepare to live with uncertainties and exasperating, even perilous, unfinished business, realizing that not all problems have solutions

- Grasp the complexity of historical causation, respect particularity, and avoid excessively abstract generalizations

- Appreciate the often tentative nature of judgments about the past, and thereby avoid the temptation to seize on particular "lessons" of history as cures for present ills

- Recognize the importance of individuals who have made a difference in history, and the significance of personal character for both good and ill

- Appreciate the force of the nonrational, the irrational, and the accidental, in history and human affairs

- Understand the relationship between geography and history as a matrix of time and place, and as a context for events

- Read widely and critically to recognize the difference between fact and conjecture, between evidence and assertion, and thereby to frame useful questions

Nurturing such habits of thought, narrative history illuminates vital themes and significant questions, including but reaching beyond the acquisition of useful facts. Students should not be left in doubt about the reasons for remembering certain things, for getting facts straight, and for gathering and assessing evidence. What of it? is a worthy question, and it requires an answer.

Source: From National Council for History Education, *Building a History Curriculum: Guidelines for Teaching History in Schools* (Washington, D.C.: Educational Excellence Network, 1988), 9. Reprinted with permission.

FIGURE 1.2 Vital Themes and Narratives.

In the search for historical understanding of ourselves and others, certain themes emerge as vital, whether the subject be world history, the history of Western civilization, or the history of the United States.

To comprehend the forces of change and continuity that have shaped—and will continue to shape—human life, teachers and students of history must have the opportunity to pursue many or most of the following matters:

Civilization, Cultural Diffusion, and Innovation

The evolution of human skills and the means of exerting power over nature and people. The rise, interaction, and decline of successive centers of such skills and power. The cultural flowering of major civilizations in the arts, literature, and thought. The role of social, religious, and political patronage of the arts and learning. The importance of the city in different eras and places.

Human Interaction with the Environment

The relationships among geography, technology, and culture, and their effects on economic, social, and political developments. The choices made possible by climate, resources, and location, and the effect of culture and human values on such choices. The gains and losses of technological change. The central role of agriculture. The effect of disease, and disease-fighting, on plants, animals, and human beings.

Values, Beliefs, Political Ideas, and Institutions

The origins and spread of influential religions and ideologies. The evolution of political and social institutions at various stages of industrial and commercial development. The interplay among ideas, material conditions, moral values, and leadership, especially in the evolution of democratic societies. The tensions between the aspirations for freedom and security, for liberty and equality, and for distinction and commonality in human affairs.

Conflict and Cooperation

The many and various causes of war, and of approaches to peace-making and war prevention. Relations between domestic affairs and dealing with the outside world. Contrasts between international conflict and cooperation, between isolation and interdependence. The consequences of war and peace for societies and their cultures.

Comparative History of Major Developments

The characteristics of revolutionary, reactionary, and reform periods across time and place. Imperialism, ancient and modern. Comparative instances of slavery and emancipation, feudalism and centralization, human successes and failures, or wisdom and folly. Comparative elites and aristocracies; the role of family, wealth, and merit.

Patterns of Social and Political Interaction

The changing patterns of class, ethnic, racial, and gender structure and relations. Immigration, migration, and social mobility. The effects of schooling. The new prominence of women, minorities, and the common people in the study of history, and their relationship to political power and influential elites. The characteristics of multicultural societies; forces for unity and disunity.

Source: From National Council for History Education, *Building a History Curriculum: Guidelines for Teaching History in Schools* (Washington, D.C.: Educational Excellence Network, 1988), 10–11. Reprinted with permission.

FIGURE 1.3   NAEP History Themes

Theme 1—Change and Continuity in American Democracy: Ideas, Institutions, Events, Key Figures, and Controversies

Theme 2—The Gathering and Interactions of Peoples, Cultures, and Ideas

Theme 3—Economic and Technological Changes and Their Relations to Society, Ideas, and the Environment

Theme 4—The Changing Role of America in the World

FIGURE 1.4   Ten Social Studies Themes

Many social studies educators choose to organize their teaching according to the standards of the National Council for the Social Studies. NCSS offers 10 themes:

1. Culture
2. Time, continuity, and change
3. People, places, and environments
4. Individual development and identity
5. Individuals, groups, and institutions
6. Power, authority, and governance
7. Production, distribution, and consumption
8. Science, technology, and society
9. Global connections
10. Civic ideals and practices

The second theme—time, continuity, and change—mentions history.

Fourth, you should introduce your students to the word *historiography.* This word is not frightening. Encourage your students to pronounce the word and use it in their everyday discussions in your class. All grade levels of students should understand that each new generation writes a history of the past. Because new questions are asked and because newly uncovered primary sources are examined, interpretations of the past can and do change. That is, historians give new meaning to the past.

Historiography—the study of historical writing—should be part of your students' everyday vocabulary. Let's take the origins of the Cold War as an example. Historians are able to look afresh at the origins of the Cold War, aided by the new evidence that has emerged from Soviet archives. Interpretive accounts of the major diplomatic, political, and strategic issues are being given new meaning with regard to our understanding of Joseph Stalin's beliefs and decisions.

How can you help your students understand what historians mean by historiography? One way is to locate images of an individual or an event as portrayed during different decades. Show the images to your students and let them describe how the image of the person changes from one time period to another. For example, the media's characterization of Abraham Lincoln changed from his own time as president in the 1860s, 1930s, the 1960s, and the present. The Brady Lincoln photograph casts a different image of Lincoln than images published at other times in our history. Joseph Stalin's images changed dramatically throughout the 20th century: from photos of the leader of the Bolshevik Revolution with Lenin, Russian dictator signing the Nazi-Soviet Pact, member of the Grand Alliance, and Cold War enemy. The contemporary media's portrayal of social activist Angela Davis, likewise, has changed: from radical leader on the FBI's 10 most wanted list in the 1960s to intellectual and professor of issues of social justice today. As your students analyze these various portrayals in photographs, they come to understand how historiography—the history of the writing of history—is part of your history classroom.

In the section that follows we describe why history is a vitally important component of a liberal and civic education.

History as an Essential School Subject

We view history as one of the most important disciplines in academia. "Historical knowledge," historian William Hardy McNeill wrote, "is no more and no less than carefully and critically constructed collective memory. As such, it can make us both wiser in our public choices and more richly human in our private lives."[17]

History is important because it provides a powerful way to find out who and where we are in the human experience and in human affairs. History involves people, space, and time, and as human beings we are curious about where we have come from, where we are currently, and where we are going.

History gives us special forms of thinking, or habits of mind, about human affairs. It offers a method of inquiry about others, and in the process we find out more about ourselves. Carl Becker, a former president of the American Historical Association, suggested that history's value is less scientific than moral by "liberalizing the mind, by deepening the sympathies, by fortifying the will." History, he continued, "enables us to control, not society, but ourselves—a much more important thing." History "prepares us more humanely in the present, and to meet, rather than to foretell, the future."[18] History provides the context for the student to define and give direction for his or her life.

History teaching is both a science and an art. History involves us in the science of asking informed, structured questions about the past. History also involves us in the art of explaining how elements of the past are alive today while understanding the uniqueness of historical periods of time.

William McNeill, a world historian, made a persuasive argument about why we study and teach history. History, he stated, "got into the classroom to make nations out of peasants, out of localities, out of the human raw material that existed in the countries of Europe and in the not so very old United States as well."[19] McNeill reminded us that history is about identity formation. Through the study of history, we identify national perspectives and understand what it means to be human and where we are as people in space and time. History helps us to identify what we share with other human beings and how we are distinct from everyone else. It helps us understand our rights as persons and it helps us reason together in matters concerning the public good.

History provides a "furniture of the mind" so we can participate intelligently in political life. It also provides personal satisfaction as an individual develops a broader perspective on changes in society over time.[20] History offers students a laboratory of human experiences,[21] a place where the individual measures perceptions of the world against the background of prior ideas and events. Figure 1.5

FIGURE 1.5   Why We Study History.

A. *History is a method of inquiry. It is a systematic way of thinking about the past.*
B. *The study of history has an aim:*
  1. Studying history provides the perspective a student needs to "know thyself." Liberal intelligence, which is organized knowledge, draws on history and other disciplines. History helps each individual satisfy the yearning to make sense of the world.
  2. Studying history helps students to develop a sense of shared humanity and to understand "otherness" by learning how they resemble and differ from others over time and space.
  3. Studying history provides a powerful way to explore democracy and develop civic intelligence.
  4. Studying history helps students to question stereotypes and generalizations and to discern the differences between fact and conjecture.
C. *The study of history has a purpose:*
  1. Studying history provides a foundation for civic intelligence.
  2. Studying history helps students to grasp the complexity of historical cause, and to distrust the simple answer and dismissive explanation.
  3. Studying history helps students to avoid false analogy, to recognize the abuse of historical "lessons," and to weigh the consequences of such abuse.
  4. Studying history helps students to consider that ignorance of the past may make us prisoners of it, and, at the same time, realize that not all problems have solutions.
  5. Studying history helps students to be prepared for the irrational and the accidental in human affairs.
  6. Studying history helps students to grasp the power of ideas and human character.
  7. Studying history provides the knowledge that students need to reflect critically on the past and to understand how it has affected the present.
  8. Studying history establishes the context of people, space, and time that is the foundation of all social sciences and humanities courses.
D. *History has lifelong application:*
  1. Studying history prepares people to enjoy the world around them. History reflects the human adventure in all its triumphs and tragedies.
  2. Studying history prepares students for civic life.
  3. Studying history prepares students for professions and other pursuits that require a refined critical apparatus.

Source: Based, in part, on Paul Gagnon, "Why Study History?" *The Atlantic Monthly,* November 1988; the Bradley Commission on History in the Schools, *Building a History Curriculum: Guidelines for Teaching History in Schools,* 1988; Lawrence W. McBride, "Could This be the End of History?" *Social Education,* October 1992; Peter N. Stearns, "Why Study History?," American Historical Association, http://www.historians.org/PUBS/Free/WhyStudyHistory.htm; and Lynn R. Nelson and Frederick D. Drake, "Civic Education: The Role of History and the Social Sciences in a Civil Society," *The Journal of the International Society for History Didactics, Information Mitteilungen Communications* 20, no. 1, 1999.

provides some reasons for studying history. As you consider the principles that comprise Figure 1.5, which strikes you as being most important for the organization of your course? You may also use Figure 1.5 as a handout to stimulate a discussion among your students regarding the importance of history.

Understanding the Meanings of History

To some, history is defined as the total of all that has actually happened in the past. The French refer to this total history as *l'Histoire.* On the other hand, history is perhaps more modestly and more accurately defined as an interpretive and partial account of some portion of past reality. The French refer to this interpretive history as *l'histoire* in lowercase to indicate that it is partial and interpretive. (See Figure 1.6 for several definitions of history. You may use these definitions as points of departure in your discussions of history with your students.)

Over 100 years ago, the German historian Leopold von Ranke said the historian's task was to reconstruct a past event "wie es eigentlich gewesen"—"as it really was" or "as it actually was" or "as it essentially was." Indeed, most people accepted this "scientific" method and the historian's claim to writing "objective history." They claimed they were writing history "as it actually was." Civilization, according to scientific historians, could produce, say, a history of the Franco-Prussian War that would be complete and unquestionable.

Peter Novick's work, *That Noble Dream: The "Objectivity Question" and the American Historical Profession,*[22] informs us about the very nature of history and provides a parallel for the historian and history teacher. Novick pointed out that when we write and teach history, we do so as it *essentially* was rather than as it *actually* was.

Teachers who strive to teach history as it *actually* was confuse chronology and antiquarianism with history. Chronology, although important to history, is a part, not the whole of the discipline. A grasp of chronological thinking requires one to understand change over time, with relationships derived from a baseline of phenomena. Students must have a "baseline against which to measure change."[23] The National Center for History in the Schools describes chronological thinking as an important dimension of historical thinking:

> Chronological thinking is at the heart of historical reasoning. Without a strong sense of chronology—of when events occurred and in what temporal order—it is impossible for students to examine relationships among those events or to explain historical causality. Chronology provides the mental scaffolding for organizing historical thought."[24]

Too often, students and the public believe that chronological thinking constitutes chronological order, which implies linearity and brute memorization. Expertise about the past may offer some satisfaction, but it is not the same as interpreting the importance of past events. The teacher must identify key turning points to do justice to the past and to engage students in the study of history. And to identify key turning points, the teacher must establish a baseline.

FIGURE 1.6   What Is History?

History, by apprizing them of the past, will enable them to judge of the future; it will avail them of the experience of other times and other nations; it will qualify them as judges of the actions and designs of men; it will enable them to know ambition under every disguise it may assume; and knowing it, to defeat its views.

—Thomas Jefferson, *Notes on the State of Virginia*, 1782

In history, as in all serious matters, no achievement is final. . . . Every new generation must rewrite history in its own way; every new historian, not content with giving new answers to old questions, must revise the questions themselves. . . . Historical thought is a river into which none can step twice.

—R. G. Collingwood, *The Idea of History*

History is "the stuff of daily struggle."

—Lillian Schlissel, *Women's Diaries*

History is the memory of things said and done.

—Carl Becker, *Everyman His Own Historian*

History is simply social development along the lines of weakest resistance and that in most cases the line of weakest resistance is found as unconsciously by society as by water.

—Henry Adams in *Henry Adams and His Friends*

The historian . . . consciously or unconsciously performs an act of faith, as to order and movement, for certainty . . . is denied to him. . . . [I]n writing he acts and in acting he makes choices, large or small, timid or bold, with respect to some conception of the nature of things. . . . His faith is at bottom a conviction that something true can be known about the movement of history and his conviction is a subjective decision, not a purely objective discovery.

—Charles Beard, "Written History"

The inquiry of the historian, to be sure, is always, in intent, instrumental to the present . . . satisfaction of having a verified probable answer to his *historical* question; and the knowledge of the answer, if attained, will presumably continue to afford some sort of satisfaction. But the answer need not, in any other sense, be assumed to be contributory to the solution of a problem which is not about the past.

—Arthur O. Lovejoy, "Present Standpoints and Past History"

[Historians] must accomplish these manipulations in such a way as at least to approach the standards for verification that exist within the social, physical, and biological sciences. Artists don't normally expect to have their sources checked. Historians do. That fact suspends us somewhere in between the arts and the sciences: we feel free to rise above the constraints of time and space, to use our imagination. . . . But we have to do this in such a way as to convince our students, our colleagues, and anyone else who reads our work that these departures from the dimensions in which we usually live our lives do indeed give us reliable information about how people in the past lived theirs. This isn't an easy task.

—John Lewis Gaddis, *The Landscape of History*

Imagination and accuracy are the fundamental attributes of the historian and teacher-as-scholar, but neither of these attributes can command a monopoly of attention. In *That Noble Dream*, Peter Novick noted that historians can hope for nothing more than plausibility. Historians and history teachers must recognize their own limitations, biases, and access to incomplete sources and information. Plausibility is not achieved through the arbitrary invention of historical accounts, which would constitute the work of a polemicist. Plausibility requires rational strategies of determining what is worthy of belief. E.H. Carr, in his monumental work *What Is History?* argued there is an interaction between the historian and his or her facts. Thus, there is a never-ending dialogue between the present and the past in search for a plausible truth. As Georg Iggers wrote in *Historiography in the Twentieth Century: From Scientific Objectivity to the Postmodern Challenge*, "[T]he historical account relates to a historical reality, no matter how complex and indirect the process is by which the historian approximates this reality."[25]

Often, history is differentiated from literature because history is regarded as the "truthful" description of past events. Historians *do* seek the truth, but they also recognize the impossibility of truthfully describing all events that occurred in a particular historical period. Historians, unlike writers of literature, must verify their sources.[26]

An analogy may help explain the difficult struggle we encounter in the search for truth. If a geologist were asked to describe the Grand Canyon to a colleague, she would not give a "truthful" description. She would interpret this geological feature from her point of expertise. If she were a historical geologist, she would describe the evolution of the contemporary landscape as the result of the actions of the Colorado River over eons of time. If she were a physical geologist, she would describe the various rock strata and layers. And if she were an ecologist, she would describe the various biotic communities and microclimates throughout the canyon. A "complete" description, therefore, much less an interpretation of the whole truth, of this one geological feature is virtually impossible. It would certainly extend to multiple volumes of texts, an unwieldy narrative.

If this is true of one geological feature, then we can imagine the impossible task facing the historian who attempts to describe and interpret the landscape of history. History entails a good narrative, or account, of some *portion* of past reality. It necessarily excludes elements that are not vital to the story. The intriguing story enables the reader to make sense out of information and to recall it years later. Yet, history is also open-ended to a degree, offering the reader opportunities to make guesses, jump ahead, and hypothesize about where the author and the story are going.

History involves an investigation of documents that provide insights into people, places, and events in the past. Such primary sources as letters, diaries, speeches, paintings, photographs, and artifacts of daily life are examples of "the ore from which history is made."[27] Without primary sources and the stories that are told about them, history cannot exist. Historians and history teachers *blend* primary sources and historical narratives to create cogent frameworks of historical understanding. It is incumbent upon you as a history teacher to introduce and discuss primary sources with your students.

Historians primarily question their sources when they are "doing" history. Similarly, teachers encourage their students to interrogate sources as they are learning history. The "doing of history"—or better yet, the "doing of teaching history"—occurs as history teachers induce their students to reconsider and recast the historical understandings that they bring to the class.[28] The methods we introduce in later chapters share the common characteristic of prompting students to become engaged in the study of history on a more mature level rather than just to absorb facts from a textbook.

History teachers, by selecting primary and secondary sources and organizing their teaching around particular themes, promote real understanding of the past.

Teachers who embrace the art of teaching history create opportunities for themselves and their students to share the excitement of historical understanding. At the same time they provide an avenue for individuals who object to the ideas and interpretations that they and their students are developing.

Picture yourself at the center of a variety of teaching resources. Surrounding you are core documents, a number of narratives, a variety of teaching and assessment strategies, and students with varying abilities and dispositions. Each of these resources requires you to make thoughtful decisions as you combine these elements into effective instruction.

The Relationship Between History and Civic Education

Historical study provides students with opportunities to see themselves in a political and social context with obligations to others. To possess civic competence, they need to be informed. Good citizenship means being able to interpret evidence amid political circumstances and understand the role factual information plays in the formation of public policy. At one pole is the individual who is apathetic or simply repeats the ideas of peers. At the other pole is the individual who does not parrot others but speaks from an uninformed perspective. Informed, critical citizenship, like the study of history, involves the interpretation of circumstances, both past and present.

Historical study is a necessary component of both the liberal intelligence and the civic intelligence necessary to understand that political positions on issues are subjects of deliberation and debate.

A word about liberal intelligence. Liberal intelligence is organized knowledge that draws upon history and other disciplines. Liberal intelligence appreciates the uniqueness of the past. A student who reads about and discusses the ideas and life of W.E.B. Du Bois, the entrepreneur Madame Walker in Indianapolis, and countless African Americans throughout the United States in the years following the Civil War appreciates the uniqueness of the historical circumstances that defined their lives and contributed to their ideas in the latter part of the 19th century and first half of the 20th century. Du Bois' ideas were forged in his upbringing in Boston, as a witness to the aftermath of Reconstruction and *Plessy* v. *Ferguson* (1896), and his experiences in German seminars as a scholarship student during the 1890s.[29] Students of history appreciate the tentative nature of judgments when examining Du Bois' thoughts and reactions to these ideas in African American and white communities. Historians and their students perceive past events and issues as Du Bois and others experienced them at the time, and develop historical empathy as opposed to present-mindedness.

Such examples of historians' habits of the mind are the intellectual property of liberally educated individuals. These important ways of thinking serve as a foundation for liberally educated individuals to distinguish Du Bois, Walker, and other African Americans and their circumstances from the circumstances of the Reverend Dr. Martin Luther King, Jr., Rosa Parks, and civil rights activists of the mid-20th century. The Reverend King's public life was informed by the opportunities for black Americans to promote racial equality that were afforded by the scenes of racial segregation as framed within the Cold War struggle between the United States and the then Soviet Union. Also contributing to Dr. King's understanding of the condition of African Americans were such Supreme Court decisions as *Sipuel v. University of Oklahoma* (1948), *McLaurin v. Oklahoma State Regents* (1950), *Sweatt v. Painter* (1950), *Brown v. Board of Education of Topeka, Kansas* (1954), and *Bolling v. Sharpe* (1954) and the legal leadership of African American lawyers Charles Houston and Thurgood Marshall.

Liberal intelligence requires the cautioned use of historical knowledge. The liberally educated individual draws examples from various historical periods often far removed in time and even geographic distance to support ideas and arguments. However, the examples drawn upon in conversation are fragile exports. The ideas exported out of their time periods may be damaged and changed when brutally joined to what appear to be similar ideas and examples drawn from a different time period. Historical knowledge travels best when packaged in detailed understanding that includes a realization of each historical period's unique qualities. Liberal intelligence takes satisfaction in knowledge regarding the past and informs individual judgment regarding the meaning of past events; it pursues a natural curiosity to understand an idea or event for its own sake. Liberal intelligence balances two opposing forces—antiquarianism, the love of knowledge for its own sake unique to the past, and presentism, the rush to use ideas across time and place. This form of intelligence is the product of an intellectual foundation nurtured by the study of history and other disciplines. Liberal intelligence is both a pre-requisite and a co-requisite to the development of civic intelligence.

Civic intelligence draws upon historical knowledge as a foundation for democratic deliberations. Americans must be cognizant of the key principles that historically have been fundamental to civic life. As students deliberate the meaning of these principles in contemporary society, they must understand that accurate construction of past events is more important than making convincing arguments. Evidence that counters their existing position on issues should result in a refining of their position, not a discarding of evidence. Deliberation is the purpose of the inquiry of citizens. Democratic citizenship requires intellectual honesty in the use of information, not the use of biased information to win points in a debate. The purpose of studying history and placing deliberations in a historical context is to help students engage in historical thought processes rather than prepare them for the mere regurgitation of facts.

David Mathews reminds us that civic intelligence is not a singular intellectual entity; rather, it comprises no less than four distinct levels of intellectual construction (see Figure 1.7).[30] The first and most basic level is to amass facts and gather information. Mathews cautions, however, that unorganized information is not very useful by itself.

A second level of organizing civic intelligence is the ability to sort and categorize information. This intelligence is a process of the creation of theories. By joining facts into larger structures the individual sees parts in relationship to wholes. A third level of intelligence is the ability to invent, to innovate, or to imagine. This level of civic intelligence joins theories to empirical realities. This third level of civic intelligence calls upon the creative and imaginative capacities of a liberally educated person.

FIGURE 1.7   David Mathews' Taxonomies of Civic Intelligences

1. Amass facts and gather information.
2. Assign meaning to facts by theorizing.
3. Invent, innovate, and create.
4. Think together.

Levels 1, 2, and 3 are private; level 4 is a public act.

Mathews notes that these three levels of civic intelligence are privatized. An individual can collect and gather facts; an individual can theorize; and an individual can invent and create. The fourth level of civic intelligence is deliberation, in which the highest good is the creation of "good public philosophies" and "good public practices." Mathews notes that public thinking together is essential to a republic. It is necessary if public policy issues are going to be carefully and thoughtfully addressed in cities, states, and the nation.

Citizenship has a moral agency in which the common good shares a stage with individualism. History plays a most significant role because of its power to create images and models of the actions taken by individuals and collectives to grapple with issues in the past. History offers a laboratory of human experiences, a place where the individual measures perceptions of the world against the background of prior ideas and events. Civic intelligence can draw upon history as a foundation of our common interests.

Liberal and civic intelligences are overlapping constructs that share many of the same characteristics.[31] They are grounded in the use of rational thinking, in the collection of evidence to support assertions, and they are based upon the principles of honesty in the analysis of evidence that runs counter to the individual's preferred ideas. The historian who uncovers or is presented with ideas that challenge or modify his scholarly positions is bound by the canons of his craft to reflect and recant his positions if warranted. Participants in political deliberation continuously reflect upon the tenability of their positions on issues in light of the evidence and arguments presented by others during discourse.

Discussions have long served as the preferred primary method of history and social science instruction in schools.

In later chapters we will give more consideration to the importance of **deliberative discussions** in developing both liberal and civic knowledge. Briefly, let's explore the significance of deliberative discussions.

Deliberative Discussions

In addition to using primary sources, good teaching of history requires deliberative discussions. By *deliberative discussion*, we do not mean sharing uninformed opinions. Deliberative discussion is a focused and organized method for establishing the credibility of historical evidence and logically interpreting that evidence to develop historical understanding in students. Deliberation involves interactions among teachers and students as they carefully examine historical sources to extract their meaning. Students draw on their own deliberations as they explain their ideas to one another. The two products of deliberation are the knowledge of a particular event or idea and the reconstruction of that knowledge within a larger narrative framework. Both primary and interpretive narrative sources are complementary. Neither acquiring knowledge nor reasoning occurs in a vacuum. Your responsibility as a teacher is to cultivate in your students both knowledge and intellectual vigor.

SUMMARY

In summary, your responsibilities as a teacher are sixfold:

First, think of your classroom as a history laboratory in which, under your direction, you and your students co-investigate the past.

Second, teach history simultaneously from a local, national, and international perspective.

Third, blend political and social history in your teaching.

Fourth, discuss the boundaries of freedom in the United States and the world. Children grow up taking freedom for granted. They don't know how it was gained or that it is vulnerable. Help them understand the political and social conditions that expanded opportunities for freedom. What freedoms exist in the United States and the world, and how have they been limited and expanded? Guide your students into thinking about these questions in the context of historical settings.

Fifth, to achieve the previous goals, foster historical thinking. Introduce your students to primary sources and historiography and the first-, second-, and third-order approach (as described later in Chapter 7).

Sixth, make use of deliberative discussions in your teaching.

These six suggestions, in concert with other teaching methods you are already using, will breathe life into your active history and social science classroom.

As mentioned earlier, one of your tasks is to help your students become wiser. In many ways their wisdom depends on your being a "wise practitioner."[32] You must possess more than just knowledge of your subject. History is not inert, motionless. Nor is teaching. You cannot be one-dimensional in your methodology. By drawing from a wide range of content and best practices in pedagogy, you will move toward becoming a "wise practitioner."

A reliable web site dedicated to history and history teaching uses this caption to illustrate the importance of history: "Because the Past is the Present and the Future too."[33] History helps us know who we are in space and time. We stated at the outset that history teaching is getting better and better. This is good news. History is alive and well!

TRANSLATING HISTORY INTO CLASSROOM PRACTICE

Activity 1.1   Creating an Image of History

Draw a picture of history on a blank piece of paper. Then put yourself in the picture. Now consider these questions: What scene does your picture depict? Does your picture illustrate a great event with great people? Does it include the mundane events that define the lives of most individuals? Are there symbols in your picture that illustrate nationalism? Does your drawing relate to local, state, national, or international issues? How far back in time is your picture? Where are you and others in your picture? Are you on the fringe? Are you at the center? Are you acting on your own behalf, or are others acting on you? Share your picture with two or three other students in your class. Each of you should describe your drawing and how it relates to one of history's 13 habits of mind. The former Bradley Commission (now the National Council for History Education), in its description of the 13 habits of mind, provides a useful explanation of historical reasoning. What vital theme and narrative (also from the National Council for History Education) organizes the content of your picture?

Activity 1.2   Examples of Fourth Graders' Images of History

A fourth-grade teacher asked her students on the second day of the school year if they had ever heard the word *history*. Then she asked them to draw a picture of history. Finally, she had her students explain their pictures.

Here are seven examples (Figures 1–7) of how fourth-grade students in her class viewed history at the start of the school year. The teacher labeled each picture with the explanation her students gave. (Note that a little girl who came from Kosovo 5 years ago drew Figure 2.)

- How do the pictures relate to the students' lives?
- What do the students' pictures reveal about meaningful ideas and events?
- What perceptions and misperceptions are revealed in these pictures?
- What do the pictures tell us about the students' understanding of history and time?
- What interesting themes are revealed in these pictures?
- How will your students draw a picture of history?

FIGURE 1   Statue of Liberty with World Trade Center in the background.

FIGURE 2   People living in houses—community.

FIGURE 3   Man and fighting dinosaurs.

FIGURE 4   Man and environment.

FIGURE 5   Martin Luther King giving his speech.

FIGURE 6   Benjamin Franklin and electricity.

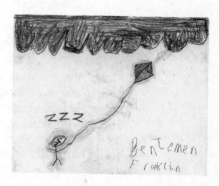

FIGURE 7   Hank Aaron breaking Babe Ruth's record.

Activity 1.3   Procedures for Creating an Image of History (for Middle and High School Students)

I. Students draw a picture of history.
    A. Ask your students to draw a picture of history.
    B. Ask your students to put themselves in the picture.
    C. Ask your students to give their picture a theme or title.

II. Students share their pictures with two or three other classmates.
    A. In these small groups, students explain their picture to each other.
    B. Students discuss their pictures.

III. Large-group discussion questions:
   A. What ideas, events, places, and people are represented in the picture?
   B. How does the picture illustrate people's lives?
   C. How does the picture illustrate local, regional, national, or international issues?
   D. How far back in time is the picture?
   E. Are students at the center or on the fringes of the picture?
   F. What elements of the picture did students want to include but decided to omit?
   G. How do students' pictures represent their experiences as students of history?
   H. How do students' pictures represent history's habits of mind?
   I. How do students' pictures represent history's vital themes and narratives?

Activity 1.4   Teaching Historiography Through Photographs

Introduce historiography to your students through photographs. Find two to four photographs of an individual to illustrate how the media's interpretations (giving meaning) change from one time period to another. Examples of individuals whose portrayal has changed include:

1. Thomas Jefferson
2. Abraham Lincoln
3. Helen Keller
4. Booker T. Washington
5. W.E.B. Du Bois
6. Jack Johnson
7. Eugene V. Debs
8. Woodrow Wilson
9. Franklin D. Roosevelt
10. Joseph Stalin
11. Eleanor Roosevelt
12. Harry Truman
13. Mahatma Gandhi
14. Mao Tse Tung/Mao Zedong
15. Joseph McCarthy
16. Dwight Eisenhower
17. Betty Friedan
18. Fidel Castro
19. John F. Kennedy
20. Marilyn Monroe

21. Cassius Clay/Mohammed Ali
22. Lew Alcindor/Kareem Abdul Jabbar
23. Cesar Chavez
24. Henry Kissinger
25. Angela Davis

REIEWING THE CHAPTER

1. How can we teach wisdom?
2. What is the difference between wisdom and knowledge?
3. How do historiography and primary sources contribute to both wisdom and knowledge?
4. Democratic political theory and constructivist learning theory argue that students are far more active and responsible for constructing their understanding of the past. Students actively engage in analysis of documents, interact in discussions, interpret documentary evidence of past events, and create their framework of understanding events and issues in the past and present.

   Consumers of history, like consumers of fast food, wait for the teacher to provide their historical understanding. They have expectations of the teacher and they expect those expectations to be met in the content and the teaching strategies they encounter. They sit passively at their desks, perhaps taking notes, in anticipation that their beliefs will be affirmed. Often they wait for the answers to be given, and they accept the interpretations of individuals in authority. They don't seek documentary evidence to support or challenge the authorities. A common response of consumer students is "Just give me the facts and tell me what I have to remember for the test."

   ■ When you were in high school, were you a student of history or a consumer? Were most of your friends and classmates students of history or consumers of history? Did you have a teacher (or teachers) who compelled you to be a student of history? What did your teacher do to counter consumerism in the classroom?

   ■ What are the consequences for you as a teacher when a number of your students view themselves primarily as consumers of history? What actions can you take to convince them that they are responsible, in part, for the creation of their own historical understanding?

5. In your career you might teach in urban, suburban, and rural schools. How might the historical content be similar in urban, suburban, and rural schools? How might it vary? How are the teaching methods similar and how might they vary?

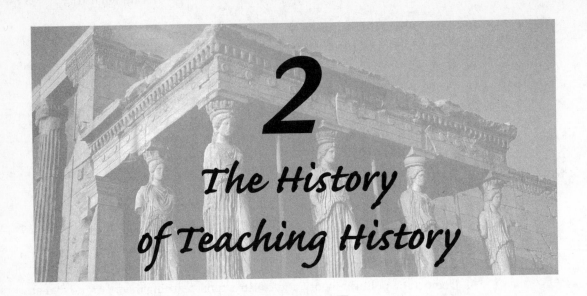

2
The History
of Teaching History

The educated differ from the uneducated as much as the living from the dead.

— Aristotle

I know no safe depository of the ultimate powers of the society but the people themselves; and if we think them not enlightened enough to exercise their control with a wholesome discretion, the remedy is not to take it from them but to inform their discretion by education. This is the true corrective of abuses of constitutional power.

— Thomas Jefferson

There are two educations. One should teach us how to make a living and the other how to live.

— James Truslow Adams

Teaching is not a lost art, but the regard for it is a lost tradition.

— Jacques Barzun

*I*n the 1790s Benjamin Rush considered the relationship between education and the continuation of the republic. The physician and revolutionary political leader wrote: "From the observations that have been made it is plain, that I consider it is possible to convert men into republican machines. This must be done, if we expect them to perform their parts properly, in the great machine of the government of the state."[1]

Rush's sentiments of connecting the well-being of the republic and the education of youth are timeless. The 1983 report, *A Nation at Risk,* warned Americans that their schools were failing and that the United States' place of eminence among the world's nations would be threatened unless we made drastic improvements in our educational system. Out of this and subsequent reports and treatises of the 1980s a cry for standards and a "back to the basics" movement emerged. As part of the call for "basic" studies, many Americans, including history teachers, looked back in time for a golden age of education.

Focus Questions

1. How far back in time would you look for the golden age of history education? Fifty years? One hundred years?

2. When and why did primary sources first become part of teaching and learning in textbooks and in schools?

3. How, when, and why did history emerge as a subject?

4. How will you combine mimetic and transformative teaching traditions in your history classroom?

5. How have debates surrounding the purposes of public education affected the teaching of history?

6. In what ways and for what purposes has history been used—and misused—as part of the curriculum in the United States and other nations?

Searching for the Golden Age of History Education

History as a separate school subject in U.S. education is a relatively recent addition. Some educators and citizens today debate history's merits as a required, rather than optional, subject that prepares students for life as part of a liberal education. Other members of the community question the necessity of studying a discipline that does not train individuals for the high-tech job markets of the future. Such debates as these concerning history did not exist when early Americans first began educating their children.

Contrary to some popular myths that exist today, history was not an important subject in schools—elementary through college—during the first 8 decades of the 19th century. Although citizenship education has long been a staple of the public school curriculum, history as a subject entered the school curriculum only in the last 2 decades of the 19th century.

History, Primary Sources, and Literature

History as a subject made its first appearance in the schools as a reaction to the English textbooks that had been used during the colonial period. In the years immediately following the American Revolution, such founders of the new national government as George Washington, Thomas Jefferson, and James Madison considered schooling to be a means to maintain republican virtues and leadership in the general population. Republicanism stressed the development of virtuous citizens whose personal rights were defined with reference to the public good. The virtuous citizen elevated the public good above personal interest or advancement. Leaders such as Samuel Harrison Smith, a newspaper editor, focused on the perpetuation of individual liberty through republican government and education.[2] Benjamin Rush, a physician, took a firmer stance. He outspokenly advocated civic conformity by developing citizens into "republican machines" through education.[3] Rush's point of view raised a question regarding the use of education to deliberately create patriotism. Is the education of a citizen a rational process, as advocated by Smith? Or is the creation of a citizen an emotional one, as advocated by Rush? The question is still debated.

Noah Webster expressed grave concern over the content of the colonial schoolbooks, published in England, that had been used in schools prior to the revolution. Consequently, new American textbooks emphasized loyalty to the United States by combining short histories, biographies, and stories that sought to promote the development of good character through the literature students read in their classrooms. Stories concerning American heroes such as Washington and Jefferson were used to promote virtues in young readers. Such values as courage, self-sacrifice, hard work, and prudence were all touted by example in the lives of patriotic individuals who served their communities and the republic. The stories of Mason Locke "Parson" Weems taught children mythic history and sacrificed truth for a more important goal: providing worthy characters for children to emulate.

Noah Webster integrated primary sources in his works of history for educational purposes. For instance, his 1787 reader included an important document, the Declaration of Independence, for all students to read. Weems' widely read textbook *The Life of George Washington* dedicated an entire chapter to another essential document, George Washington's farewell address.[4]

Nearly 100 years later, leading professional historians urged the incorporation of primary sources into the repertoire of teaching strategies. In 1897, for example, historian Albert Bushnell Hart urged history teachers to use primary sources, particularly original sources, in their classrooms. An important 1897 committee known as the Committee of Seven discussed and advocated the use of primary sources in history education.

In the years before and after both World War I and World War II, journals for teachers suggested the use of original materials in classroom instruction. During the 1960s federally funded projects such as the Amherst History Project reinforced the idea of using primary sources. In the 1980s and 1990s the use of primary sources was encouraged to serve as an instructional foundation to reinvigorate the teaching of history.

History in the Common School

History education, as we tend to think of it today, did not exist in the early 19th century. The few stories that were told in textbooks were carefully chosen to emphasize ethical messages and were intermingled with fictional tales. Historical accuracy was sacrificed for the purpose of character education. Students between the ages of 8 and 16 spent several years in elementary, or common, schools. Their teachers were women whose primary responsibility was character education through the use of textbooks on morality.

Not all students attended common schools. Some attended private academies, where they were more likely to receive classical history as part of their instruction in the Greek and Latin languages. Classical history stressed ancient Greek and Roman history. World history or general history of the ancients took precedence over any reference to a history that focused on the more recent American experience. Prior to the establishment of public high schools in the 1880s, private academies prepared students to meet the specific admissions requirements of colleges.

U.S. History Rivals World and General History

Not until the decade of the 1890s, with the establishment of widespread secondary education in public high schools, did U.S. history courses begin to rival world or general history courses in terms of student enrollment. The teaching of U.S. history was complicated further because controversy over the issue of states' rights and federalism precluded a standard textbook on U.S. history. Well into the 20th century, publishers issued different versions of U.S. history texts for northern and southern markets. In the last decade of the 19th century, history remained a fairly unimportant study in schools.[5]

In the late 1800s, changes in U.S. society stimulated interest in higher education, which for most students meant the attendance and possible completion of high school. In 1890 only a small percentage of American youth attended high schools. Those who did encountered a variety of offerings in general history, including courses that combined world and U.S. history. Some schools offered a European history course stressing ancient Greece and Rome.

Mimetic and Transformative Traditions of Teaching

Two teaching outlooks, the mimetic and transformative, have long coexisted in U.S. society. These perspectives possess contrasting purposes for teaching. Each is characterized by content organization and methodology. Lectures, recitations, and worksheets are the core of the mimetic tradition of teaching. On the other hand, discussions, research assignments, and interpretation through role-playing represent teaching methods associated with the transformative tradition.

Mimetic teachers view themselves as responsible for the transmission of the existing culture across generations. These teachers are confident that they have the procedural and factual knowledge to pass on to their students. The word *mimetic* has as its root two Greek words, *mimesis* and *episteme*. *Mimesis* is a Greek word meaning to "mime" or to "mimic" or to "imitate," which suggests that a procedure should be followed. *Episteme* emphasizes knowledge. Thus, the mimetic tradition conceptualizes teaching as transmitting an identifiable body of knowledge from the teacher to the students. This knowledge is "added on" to what a student already knows.

Transformative teachers view their purpose as creating a "qualitative change" within students. This qualitative change requires students to be engaged actively with the materials of learning. This means students are engaged actively in analyzing primary sources, reading narratives, and synthesizing information. In effect, students are making understandable meaning of the past as opposed to accepting a set interpretation of the past. Transformative teachers strive to develop in students the knowledge and skills that change them in essential ways. Most teachers combine elements of both the mimetic and transformative teaching traditions.[6] Which tradition do you espouse? How did one of these traditions dominate your experiences as a middle and high school student?

Interest Groups Vie to Control the Schools' Curricula

William Torrey Harris paved the way for liberal education to serve as a foundation for the curriculum in elementary and secondary schools. Harris was a St. Louis educator and U.S. Commissioner of Education from 1889 to 1906. He held a deep commitment to five academic subjects, or "windows of the soul": grammar, literature and art, mathematics, geography, and history. History, one of the "windows," described individuals working in concert. Harris believed that history, as an academic subject, could show students how individuals established institutions that forwarded the purpose of civilization. The schools, by imparting knowledge, provided students with the means to individual improvement throughout their lives and a mechanism to establish a common culture. Schools provided each generation with knowledge and the collective wisdom of the past through academic disciplines. Knowledge, including historical knowledge, served as a foundation for individual and social progress.

William Torrey Harris was a humanist. His liberal curricular vision emphasized the education of individuals in the liberal arts. Academic disciplines such as history played a prominent role in helping individuals to understand the world. This view of liberal education should not be confused with liberal political ideals. Liberal education is the education of individuals who may use that knowledge to understand, appreciate, and participate in society. Their knowledge and actions can be used for conservative or liberal political purposes.

The purposes and practices of liberal education, which emphasized education to promote individualism, were challenged by the early Progressives. Starting in the early 1900s, Progressives stressed the importance of the group. Their perspective focused on the changing nature of U.S. society and the problems of youth in America's new industrial order. Clearly, the rise of the Progressives marked a turning point in the focus of education.

Progressive educators' challenge of traditional liberal education resulted in a shift in the goals for schooling. Changes in immigration, urbanization, and industrialization worried Progressives, who proposed a variety of sometimes contradictory educational programs. History teachers were caught in the rivalries among competing branches of Progressive education.

All variants of Progressive education focused on what was perceived as the changing nature of U.S. society in the last decade of the 19th century and the first decades of the 20th. Such Progressive curricular interest groups as child-centered educators, social efficiency educators, vocationalists, social meliorists, and social reconstructionists contested the purposes and practices of education.[7] (See Figure 2.1.) All Progressive educators emphasized the worth of group activities. For child-centered educators, the emphasis on groups meant nurturing children to fit in and work and play with their peers in a school environment. For social efficiency educators, the main purpose of schools was to sort out students by intelligence and other characteristics such as race. Social efficiency educators tested individual students so they could be efficiently tracked into their "proper vocational" niches. For social meliorists, the purpose of schools was to involve students in "group" investigations to discover the nature of the physical and cultural world. Groups would make decisions based on rational and interdisciplinary inquiry. Social studies, which was created shortly before the United States' entrance into World War I, is an example of a social meliorist, citizenship program.

The most radical of the Progressive interest groups was that of the social reconstructionists. For social reconstructionists, the purpose of school was to discover and rectify inequalities and injustices in U.S. society. Their curriculum required group participation. Social reconstructionists held a radical agenda of

FIGURE 2.1	Interest Groups Struggling to Control the Curriculum in the 20th Century	
Interest Group	**Leader**	**View of History as a School Subject**
1. Humanist, liberal	William Torrey Harris	Show students how individuals established institutions that forwarded the purpose of civilization. Knowledge, including historical knowledge, served as a foundation for individual and social progress.
2. Child-centered	G. Stanley Hall	Diminished the importance of such academic subjects as history. Emphasis was on the interests of the child.
3. Social efficiency	David Snedden	History was important only if it contributed to students' life in the present and their "social destiny." History might have a place in the curriculum if it infused students with the ideals of right social action or trained students for citizenship.
4. Social meliorists	Lester Frank Ward	School is the place that can provide social change. Historical study contributes to a reduction of social ills.
5. Social reconstructionists	George S. Counts	History is a tool that provides evidence of past inequalities.

reform. They were strong on indoctrination to reorient the thinking of young students along socialist principles.

All of these more activist and group-oriented interest groups challenged the older liberal, humanist view of education articulated by William Torrey Harris. Although all Progressives agreed that U.S. society was experiencing radical societal change, individuals in the various Progressive camps varied widely in their prescriptions for needed educational reforms. For example, the ideas of G. Stanley Hall influenced theorists and practitioners to adapt curricula and instruction to the needs and interests of students at their various stages of development. Child-centered educators, led by Hall, diminished the importance of such academic subjects as history.

By contrast, such social efficiency educators as David Snedden argued that modern industrial America required vocational education that involved students in manual training to prepare them for specific jobs. Social efficiency advocates measured the worth of school subjects primarily by how they contributed to the development of vocational skills. David Snedden, an outspoken leader of this interest group, argued that school subjects should prepare students for their vocational destinies. IQ tests, interest inventories, and surveys of workplace changes assessed capabilities. Snedden viewed students as human capital to be molded and "fitted" into their "proper place in society."

According to Snedden and other like-minded social efficiency educators, the subject of history was important only if it could help students get jobs. At best, history might find a place in the curriculum to infuse students with "ideals of right social action" or "train" students for citizenship. This to Snedden amounted to "submission to established political order [and] cooperative maintenance of the same."[8] Unlike William Torrey Harris, who thought all students should take courses in history, Snedden dismissed history and academic subjects as simply putting knowledge in "cold storage" for future use. In effect, Snedden dismissed the cultivation of creative intelligence and durable knowledge.

Snedden even preferred a differentiated curriculum that, when pushed to the extreme, advocated the establishment of separate high schools—college preparatory high schools and vocational schools for students bound for the blue-collar job market. Snedden and his disciples admired the efficiency ideas of Frederick Winslow Taylor, a practitioner of scientific management. Snedden considered the school to be a "factory system" run efficiently by educational experts. His contemporary, Franklin Bobbitt, marveled at the school system in Gary, Indiana. Bobbitt explained that Gary superintendent Willard Wirt had created a system in which "the educational engineer . . . operat[ed] his plant during school hours at 100 percent efficiency."[9] Social efficiency, as the paramount value, came to dominate U.S. education more than any other theoretical perspective in the 20th century.

Although the followers of Hall and Snedden vied with one another on various issues, they agreed on the relative unimportance of history as a school subject.[10] Each camp posed challenges to liberal and civic education, and the programs that these groups developed diminished the importance of both civic and liberal education in the 20th century.

Perhaps the least radical challenges to liberal education came from the followers of John Dewey and Lester Frank Ward. Social meliorists embraced the civic purpose of education while calling for a new curriculum and teaching methods organized around decision making and scientific inquiry. These individuals broadly organized around the principle of reflective thought. Dewey, Ward, and their followers shared an unshakable faith in the ability of education to redress social ills and advance social justice.

Social reconstructionists emphasized the power of education and the teacher to create a better social order. George S. Counts became the leader of this group when his speeches were compiled into the book *Dare the School Build a New Social Order*, at the height of the Depression in 1932. His ideas challenged teachers to be at the forefront of a reform of U.S. society. He confronted the prevailing notion of many

Progressive educators that reflective thinking should be the centerpiece of education. Instead, he argued that students should be told that U.S. society must be changed for the better. Although he continued the early American tradition of using the method of indoctrination (or inculcation), his purposes were new. Rather than using indoctrination to support and perpetuate the existing social order, he advocated the use of this method of instruction to criticize and transform the U.S. social order of the 1930s. Instead of behaving like "bab[ies] shaking a rattle" who are "utterly content with action, provided it is sufficiently vigorous and noisy,"[11] Counts demanded that teachers act as critical intellectuals. History would serve Counts' purpose if it could provide students with evidence regarding the failures and successes of U.S. society. This evidence could be used to formulate programs to "improve the social order."

Today critical theorists share many of the concerns voiced by social reconstructionists in the 1930s. Issues of inequality based upon race, ethnicity, and unequal access to resources serve as issues for historical inquiry and instruction. Critical theorists view education as a mechanism for social criticism, social reform, and active participation in society. Critical theorists often face three questions: Which social programs do critical theorists advocate in their reforms? What proposals do they have as an alternative to the existing social fabric? How appropriate, or ethical, is it to use the history curriculum as a means to recruit students into programs of social reform? How do students use historical knowledge to gain control of their own lives?

Divisions among educators at the turn of the 20th century contributed to familial and foreign battles that are fought by history and social studies educators today. Familial disagreements occur between history and social studies advocates. Should history be the integrative discipline or should contemporary issues organize the curriculum? On one hand, the familial divisions that separate history and the social studies emanate from the belief that decision making and a focus on contemporary social problems should be central in both. The foreign battles are fought with educators who discount history and the social studies, thereby demeaning history and the social sciences as having little importance in the curriculum.[12]

History as a Core Discipline

As discussed previously, history long held a tenuous position in the U.S. curriculum. History was first introduced as a profession at Johns Hopkins University in 1872. Shortly thereafter, in 1884, the American Historical Association was founded. The seminars of the German Leopold von Ranke influenced Americans. Von Ranke admired Thucydides, who was the subject of his dissertation. Von Ranke's purpose was to write a history that was a reliable reconstruction of the past with literary grace. He believed that the historian's task was to reveal the past *wie es eigentlich gewesen* ("as it truly or *essentially* happened").[13]

But how would history be taught? Advocates of history worked to establish the discipline's place in the secondary and elementary curriculum in the last decade of the 19th century. Among its many recommendations, the 1893 Committee of Ten proposed the 10 methods listed in the Ideas for the History Classroom feature. The methods are surprisingly similar to recent proposals for improved curricula.

In 1899 the American Historical Association joined in the call ｝ as a core discipline in secondary schools when it released the Commi｡ report recommendations to the public. The committee's report, which focus specifically on history, strongly recommended that students read primary sourc｡ which they referred to as "collateral readings."

Turn-of-the-century educator Fred Morrow Fling followed this advice when he advocated the source method. Teachers were encouraged to look to the primary sources. Fling's call for the use of primary sources was echoed in the 1960s as history educators created Jackdaws kits, a compilation of primary source materials on a particular topic.

What Fling's teaching method and Jackdaws kits neglected, however, was the connection between primary sources and the development of larger historical narratives. Fred Morrow Fling's source method emphasized only the use of primary sources. The result was that students had little grasp of the larger historical picture. Fling's method created only a partial understanding in his students of the nature of historical research. He ignored the requirement that sources be integrated into meaningful narratives. The lesson to be learned from Fred Morrow Fling's approach is that students need both primary and secondary sources when they study the past. The committee of seven recognized this important idea in 1899.

Ideas for the History Classroom

Effective Methods of Teaching History

If you were to write a list of suggested ways to teach history, would the following strategies be on your list?

1. Classroom discussion
2. Interpretation of history rather than rote memorization
3. Student oral and written reports
4. Debates
5. Involvement in the local community
6. Visits to historic places and museums
7. Integration of history, civics, and geography
8. Use of such primary sources as letters, diaries, maps, photographs, art, and artifacts illustrating daily life
9. Use of historical fiction
10. Use of visual aids

What else would you add to this list first recommended in 1893? How are these methods unique to history? How do teachers of other subjects incorporate these methods into their teaching? How are historical inquiry methods, such as the use of primary sources, incorporated into your history or social studies teaching methods course?

History and the Creation of Social Studies

In the early 20th century, history was a relatively new and important school subject and academic discipline in a liberal education. Henry Johnson, historian and teacher educator at Columbia University, cautioned against what he thought were disturbing trends in education. In 1916, for example, Henry Johnson took a jaundiced view of the newly created social studies. The social studies emphasized contemporary social concerns and the preparation of students to assume their roles as workers in the U.S. economy. This present-minded and vocationally oriented curriculum disturbed many who strove for a more well-rounded education for students. Skeptical of these changes, Johnson wrote:

> At the present time history seems to be losing rather than gaining in favor of school administrators. The demand is for social studies of direct and immediate concern to individual communities. Questions relating to public health, to housing and homes, to good roads and the like, in the present, are coming to be viewed as of greater importance than questions relating to how people lived in the past.[14]

Henry Johnson championed the central role of history in the curriculum. To him, history served as a base of knowledge for students and adults. History taught the use of language (both oral and written) and multiple causations, as well as the complexity of unintended consequences. Johnson believed that students could best express their ideas through the use of historical examples. The emphasis on "vital present problems" reduced history, from Johnson's perspective, to data for current discussions.

Thomas Jesse Jones devised a curriculum for African American students who wanted to be teachers. While at Hampton Institute in Hampton, Virginia, Jones implemented a vocationalized education for Hampton Institute students. The Hampton curriculum was meant to fit the students into the existing social order. Individuals were taught to accept the "conditioning realities," a term used at the time to describe social norms. These accepted realities included the racial, ethnic, and sexual discrimination of the times.[15] Jones pressed his plan on the educational scene, causing a change in terminology from *social sciences* to *social studies*. He influenced others to endorse his program, which integrated history and the social sciences into a single subject, to be called social studies.

As social studies caught on as a field of study, history lost its central role in education. The loss was not immediate, but occurred gradually. In part, professional historians (mostly academics) contributed to the loss of prestige history held in classrooms. University historians were concerned with research, writing, monographs, and teaching graduate students. They had little time and few professional incentives to become heavily committed to the improvement of history instruction in elementary and secondary schools. In 1921 the American Historical Association created the National Council for the Social Studies (NCSS). At times, historians such as Charles Beard actively participated in NCSS projects. For example, Beard joined with George S. Counts to report on social studies teaching in the

1930s. However, historians in subsequent generations participated less and less in such collaborations.

Within a decade historians had little incentive to remain steadfast in support of NCSS. Historians and NCSS were headed on a path of separation. In the 1940s historians complained about students' lack of historical knowledge. Civil War historian Allan Nevins lambasted social studies in the *New York Times* in 1942 and 1943. In 1942, Nevins was concerned that most colleges did not require U.S. history for admission or graduation. A year later he pointed directly at the social studies as being responsible for the historical ignorance in the United States.[16] In the 1950s and 1960s two prominent historians attacked social studies. In 1953, University of Illinois historian Arthur Bestor wrote *Educational Wastelands,* in which he attacked social studies for its lack of intellectual rigor, and educationists for their "interlocking directorate" that controlled the education of teachers and emphasized method over content. Richard Hofstadter, a Columbia University history professor, severely criticized educators for ignoring the intellectual purposes of education in his *Anti-Intellectualism in American Life.*[17]

History and the New Social Studies Projects

In the 1960s many projects were developed that were dubbed New Social Studies. History, again, took a back seat. Educator and psychologist Jerome Bruner established the direction of social studies in his 1960 work, *The Process of Education.*[18] The thesis of this work was that disciplines that were well organized within a structure of concepts would be memorable and applicable to new situations. Disciplines such as economics and political science appeared to possess such a structure, but history did not. Many critics opined that history lacked such structure and wondered whether historical knowledge was really important in a rapidly changing world. Concern with the present was a preeminent factor in determining the content of the social studies curriculum.

The New Social Studies projects did, however, create many excellent materials for teachers. New Social Studies projects, supported primarily by the federal government, numbered in excess of 50 by 1967. The majority of these projects reflected a discipline-based social science organization for the subject. Reformers pretty much ignored the role that history was to play in high school courses of study. The social studies were given priority. The New Social Studies projects did include the Amherst History Project, which focused on the use of primary sources.

Certain elements of the New Social Studies projects did stress intellectual inquiry, the development of students' thinking skills, and the transfer of these skills to new situations. Less attention was given to developing students' understanding of historical or social studies content.

The most prominent New Social Studies project, the Harvard Social Studies Project, stressed a jurisprudential model for discussion. The Harvard Social Studies Project incorporated factual and fictional documents, but emphasized students' reasoning skills rather than the documents themselves. For example, one featured document was a segment from Herman Melville's novel, *Billy Budd.* This fictional document served to engage students in the consideration of capital punishment during a time of war. The curriculum designers were unconcerned with the analysis of an actual historical event. Instead, they organized questions around policy making (Should Billy Budd be hanged?), values (Was Billy Budd's life of greater value than the security of the ship?), and the facts surrounding the case against Budd (Was Budd falsely accused?). The goals of the curriculum writers were to focus students' discussions on values, policies, and thinking skills. They hoped these skills would transfer to present situations. They were far less concerned with historical content.

From our perspective, one of the weaknesses of the New Social Studies projects was the belief that skills could be learned from almost anything (including fiction) and applied to new situations. This emphasis on the present frequently blinded curriculum writers to historical content. In the case of *Billy Budd*, rather than focus on the fictional story, the curriculum writers could have focused on historical decisions, which also involved questions of fact and value. *Billy Budd* was set in 1798. The curriculum writers could have used historical examples of the impressments of seamen, the Alien and Sedition Acts, and John Adams' decision not to enter war with France when the American public called for this war. Authors of the Harvard Social Studies Project chose not to immerse students in the historical fabric of 1798. Instead, they pursued the value of justice via the compelling tale. Good history can pursue these same purposes and at the same time promote historical understanding.

History and the Decision-Making Model

Another proposed form of instructional organization, the decision-making model, took shape in the 1960s. In part, this model was a reaction against the discipline-based New Social Studies projects. The primary architects were Shirley Engle and, later, his associate, Anna Ochoa.

Shirley Engle and Anna Ochoa's decision-making model provided a theoretical organization and instructional model for teachers to apply in their classrooms.[19] They drew on John Dewey's theories in creating an interdisciplinary framework that combined information from a variety of academic disciplines. This information, coupled with an analysis of values, supposedly enabled individuals to arrive at well-grounded decisions. Engle and Ochoa used a general model of thinking that was focused on contemporary, political choices. They did not acknowledge that historical thinking was something to be nurtured. History was simply a place to go for data.

Our differences with Engle and Ochoa focus on five issues. First, contrary to the decision-making model, we emphasize the importance of historical knowledge, *durable knowledge,* which students carry out of classrooms.

Second, we disagree with the violation of chronological time and periods supported by the Engle and Ochoa model of instruction. Advocates of the decision-making model disregard the context of events in historical periods. They describe the past as unitary, failing to note the subtle and not so subtle changes that occur over time. Decision-making advocates do not distinguish between *causation* and *change,* which are two of the central habits of mind of historians. We believe that effective history teaching raises problematic issues for students; however, these issues must be analyzed within the constraints of the time periods in which they occurred.

Third, comparisons between civilizations can occur with the helpful guidance of an individual who is well aware of the uniqueness and similarities of civilizations within a particular period of the past.[20] Cross-national comparisons of ecological issues such as deforestation can only be carried out within a framework recognizing the historical and social uniqueness of the various regions. The decision-making model holds historical experiences as inconsequential to current decisions.

Fourth, our emphasis is on *deliberation* among students rather than the decision making of the individual. We think that students need to be reminded that deliberation is not a contest to be won, but a process in which individuals join together to establish a better understanding of an issue and reason together.

And fifth, we believe historical thinking is domain specific; that is, historical thinking is neither a natural process nor something that automatically develops as a student matures. It is not customary. Students must learn historical thinking so they can make judgments regarding the meaning of the past.[21]

History on the Wane

Both the New Social Studies projects and Shirley Engle's decision-making model failed to totally displace history and civics in the high school curriculum. The teaching of history never disappeared in the 1960s and 1970s. U.S. history remained in part because state legislatures mandated its teaching. World history did not have such legislative protections. Few high school curricula listed social studies as a course. Courses listed under social studies departments usually included U.S. History, World History, Civics/Government, Economics, World Geography, Sociology, and less frequently, Problems of Democracy.

During both the 1960s and the 1970s, educational theorists did diminish the importance of history. In the 1960s history was no more and no less important than the other disciplines that comprised the social studies. In the 1970s values clarification and values analysis moved to the forefront of debates in social studies education as U.S. society grappled with three key issues: the Vietnam War, the Civil Rights Movement, and the belief that a generation gap separated young people from adults. The worth of content that dealt with the past was called into question when *relevancy* became the buzzword of the times. Many teachers at the secondary and university levels questioned whether ideas and events long removed from the time and the culture of students' lives were of any value to those students. These educators misunderstood the power of history to transport students into the lives and ideas of people in the past. They discounted the ability of students to connect these ideas and events with their situation in the present.

By the 1980s social studies educators' support of history continued to wane. World history nearly disappeared from the curriculum, in part because of the push for math, sciences, and vocational education. U.S. history maintained a position because most states mandated it by law, yet in many instances, the subject had been divided into a series of minicourses to meet the current interests of students. Many social studies educators, moreover, regarded history as merely one of the social sciences.[22]

History Makes a Revival

In the mid-1980s history made a revival in the curriculum. Led by history educator Diane Ravitch and historians and educators in California who created the California History-Social Science Framework, historians and educators reexamined the popular assumptions underlying the social studies curriculum. Most notably, they drew attention to the Expanding Horizons curriculum in the elementary school and the rationale for this curricular organization. In the 1930s Paul Hanna had popularized this curriculum, which began by focusing on the child in kindergarten and moved progressively to the family, the community, and the study of the state in fourth grade. Ravitch and her colleagues, most notably Charlotte Crabtree, questioned the major tenet of the Expanding Horizons curriculum, which is that children need to explore only the familiar. Ravitch relied on the work of psychologist Bruno Bettelheim to challenge the Expanding Horizons curriculum organization.[23] She and Crabtree observed that many children in fourth grade firmly believe that social studies deals with the same subject over and over again—the family and the community. Students arrive in the fourth grade with little concrete knowledge and the conviction that social studies is "social cruddies." Ravitch and Crabtree recommended that children not be confined to the present and the familiar. Historical narratives, Ravitch and Crabtree strongly suggested, transport students throughout time into exotic places and thereby nourish their young imaginations and intellect.[24]

By 1987 the Bradley Commission on History in Schools (now the National Council for History Education), in response to the ineffectual quality and quantity of history education in elementary and secondary education, proposed organizing historical content around six vital themes and narratives of history. This call echoed the ideas raised by the Committee of Seven in 1899 and historian Henry Johnson in 1916. The vital themes and narratives (see Figure 1.2 in Chapter 1) organized the broader patterns of historical understanding. These themes and narratives were designed to pull students into the stories of the past by organizing facts around larger themes that have permeated historical study and make history accessible and memorable.

The National Council for History Education also proposed 13 historians' habits of mind (see Figure 1.1 in Chapter 1, page 15). Historians' habits of mind help students think more critically about the past, both in accepting it on its own terms and considering how it has affected the present. These habits of mind illuminate the vital themes and narratives and serve as entry points for thinking about the past. Themes and habits of mind provide a broad framework to *reflect* upon the content and methods used in your classroom.

The habits of mind encompass historical thinking more broadly than do the traditional critical thinking skills. Historians' habits of mind provide important ways to ruminate about the past while providing intellectual enjoyment for students after they have completed their formal education.[25]

A funded national standards movement that grew out of the 1983 secretary of education report, *A Nation at Risk,* and a cooperative effort of national and state governments beginning in 1989 focused on raising the standards of history, civics and government, and geography. Lynne Cheney of the National Endowment for the Humanities provided initial support of history in schools with a pamphlet, *The American Memory,* which advocated that the humanities include history as a core subject for all students.[26]

The three disciplines of history, civics and government, and geography were reinvigorated as a federation of subjects that served as a core of social studies education in schools. These three core disciplines created national standards for states and schools to use as guidelines. The social studies did not receive funding for their standards.

Social Studies Defined

Social studies educators in the National Council for the Social Studies continued to define social studies as an integrated field in which history was simply one source of information. Perhaps this was a result of their desire to be inoffensive to any self-defined group, perhaps it was a commitment to finally initiate social studies as a school subject, or perhaps it was a combination of these and other purposes. In any case, the 1992 NCSS house of delegates almost unanimously (with only five members objecting) endorsed the following definition of social studies:

> Social studies is the integrated study of the social sciences and humanities to promote civic competence. Within the school program, social studies provides coordinated, systematic study drawing upon such disciplines as anthropology, archaeology, economics, geography, history, law, philosophy, political science, psychology, religion, and sociology, as well as appropriate content from the humanities, mathematics, and natural sciences. (The primary purpose of social studies is to help young people develop the ability to make informed and reasoned decisions for the public good as citizens of a culturally diverse, democratic society in an interdependent world.)[27]

History was part of an alphabetical definition of social studies with citizenship education as the primary, and perhaps sole, purpose for the curriculum. Lawrence W. McBride, a history educator from Illinois and one of the few dissenting voices, spoke to the NCSS house of delegates in opposition to the definition that was eventually overwhelmingly approved. McBride raised a question for the NCSS: Was this the "end of history"?[28]

History Makes a Revival Again

At the turn of the 21st century, three initiatives reinvigorated history teaching. First, U.S. history education received federal support when U.S. Senator Robert Byrd (Democrat, West Virginia) initiated legislation for two federal grants under the name Teaching American History. These grants provided $50 million initially (in 2001) and $100 million (in subsequent years) over 3-year periods to schools and agencies for the purposes of improving the teaching and learning of U.S. history. Second, the administration of President George W. Bush stressed the importance of history and civic education with its White House Forum on American History, Civics, and Service. In September 2002, this White House initiative spotlighted the need for a better understanding of U.S. history and civic education and drew attention to the best practices of teaching these core disciplines. And third, the Organization of American Historians (OAH), the American Historical Association (AHA), and the National Council for the Social Studies (NCSS) merged their efforts to promote better teaching of history and collaboration among schools and universities. In June of 2003 the OAH, AHA, and NCSS joined together to sponsor a conference called Innovations in Collaboration: A School-University Model to Enhance History Teaching. The OAH, long the home of professional historians, has witnessed a rather dramatic increase in the participation of high school history teachers. Such collaborations seem to signal the reinvigoration of history education in our schools.

Internal Disputes

History education, though, has not been without its internal disputes. A controversy over national standards in history erupted in the mid-1990s when former head of the National Endowment for the Humanities Lynne Cheney sharply disagreed with the standards that historian Gary Nash and others had published. Two major issues defined the positions of advocates and critics of the national standards. First, should history emphasize global or world history, or Western civilization and its narratives? Second, whose history should be included in a U.S. history course? Should history include the contributions and struggles of various racial and ethnic groups, or should history in schools introduce students to the achievements of Americans and the importance of American core principles and ideals in guiding the nation?

The first question caused history educators to consider whether U.S. history should be taught in isolation or situated in a world history context. History educators suggested various models of teaching world history, which will be discussed in a later chapter. The second question marked an evolution within history as an academic discipline. How should historians and history teachers organize political, cultural, and social history? These questions persist for history teachers today.

Teaching history in the 21st century will require you to meet multiple responsibilities. Wherever you teach, you will need to refer to the National Standards for History and the National Social Studies Standards. The state in which you teach will most likely have its own set of history or social studies standards as well. Although the respective states are encouraged to reference the National Standards for History when they create their own state standards in history, the social sciences, or the social studies, each state writes its own standards, which may or may not stress the importance of historical content and historical thinking.[29] You will have to draw on both national and state standards when preparing a curriculum or making out lesson plans.

In some schools, teachers and administrators still use the words *history* and *social studies* interchangeably. Others know there is a difference, and use their references to history and social studies purposefully.

Stephen Thornton, a well-respected social educator, recently summed up the issue facing history and social studies educators at the present in history and social studies education programs at universities:

> [C]urrent teacher education efforts appear inadequate. Perhaps most problematic is the division of responsibility for teacher education between social science departments and education schools and the lack of much coordination between them. The social science courses that teachers take may bear scant relationship to the school curriculum. Methods courses, on the other hand, often stress competencies for teaching but devote scant attention to how those competencies are conditioned by subject matter.[30]

History teachers need to combine their content knowledge and pedagogy that is domain-specific. The discipline of history requires a unique way of thinking. For students in school to understand historical thinking, their teachers need to understand it.

SUMMARY

The early purposes for teaching history centered on the moral and patriotic development of students. The Committee of Seven emphasized the use of primary sources, discussions, and other instructional activities. Progressive education challenged the traditional liberal purposes for teaching and learning history.

Advocates of history and advocates of social studies often disagree over the organization of school curriculum. History serves as an integrative discipline to organize social education, and it draws on the social sciences to analyze issues. History teachers need to understand the methods of historians in order to improve students' knowledge and understanding of history.

Activity 2.1   Interview a History, Social Science, or Social Studies Professor

Interview a history, social science, or a social studies professor. Make a list of questions and use a tape recorder or take notes. Try to write the responses as verbatim as possible. Then, write a brief history of the person you interviewed.

Activity 2.2   Interview a Parent, Grandparent, Relative, or Neighbor

Oral history interviews are a form of research. Normally, you set up an interview with a person who has information about a topic. Come to the interview with some background information and some questions. During the interview session, be a good listener. Be alert for comments that may lead you to new areas of discussion.

During the interview use a tape recorder, or video recorder, or take careful notes. After the interview, transcribe the information you have gathered. Then write a brief history of the person you interviewed. What did you learn about the person's life, where the person lived, and the different experiences the person encountered?

Here are some procedures you can follow:

1. Choose a topic (an idea).
2. Choose a person to interview.
3. Create a set of questions and practice interviewing.
4. Tell the person you are interviewing your purpose and make an appointment.
5. Set a proper climate during the interview. Ask the person if you can tape the interview and take notes.
6. Conduct the interview and take notes. Be a good listener and practice good manners.
7. Be prepared to ask questions that may lead you in a new direction.
8. Transcribe and edit the notes.
9. Show the transcript to the person you interviewed.
10. Write a brief history of the person you interviewed.

REVIEWING THE CHAPTER

1. What commonalities of thought are shared by "Parson" Weems and Lynne Cheney?
2. At what point do we shift from historical reverence to historical criticism? Should social criticism precede historical criticism?

3. How do you plan to use mimetic and transformative strategies in your classroom?

4. Analyze current newspapers to identify interest group views of education. What key ideas do these contemporary citizens express regarding the purpose and practice of schools?

5. David Snedden argued that students need to be "trained." How is education different from training?

6. Assess the definition of social studies and write your own definition.

7. What does it mean to be an integrative discipline? What makes history unique compared with social science disciplines?

3

Historical Thinking

I try to show that historical thinking, in its deepest forms, is neither a natural process nor something that springs automatically from psychological development. Its achievement, I argue, actually goes against the grain of how we ordinarily think, one of the main reasons why it is much easier to learn names, dates, and stories than it is to change the basic mental structures we use to grasp the meaning of the past. The odds of achieving mature historical understanding are stacked against us in a world in which Disney and MTV call the shots. But it is precisely the uses to which the past is put that endow these other aims with even greater importance.

— Sam Wineburg, *Historical Thinking and Other Unnatural Acts*, 2001

The influence of misapplied Piagetian ideas and shallow behavioristic learning principles . . . creates an interesting self-fulfilling prophecy: We believe that children are incapable of difficult acts of historical thinking and investigation, so we prevent them from having opportunities to do so, which in turn reinforces our assumptions that they are incapable because we do not see them perform as such.

— Bruce VanSledright, *In Search of America's Past: Learning to Read History in Elementary School*, 2002

*I*n this chapter we establish an instructional and cognitive framework for your teaching strategies. Historical thinking resides in the heart and mind of the historian and the effective history teacher. It is a unique way of thinking that avoids present-mindedness. The teacher who introduces students to primary sources reveals to them the building blocks of written history. It is based on facts, not fiction. Primary sources lay the foundation for students to understand the true nature of history and its corollary, historical thinking. The artful history teacher blends the use of primary sources with the use of a text in her teaching. Historical thinking is integrated in historical content.

Focus Questions

1. What is historical thinking?

2. Why is historical thinking important?

3. How can you improve historical thinking in your students?

What Is Historical Thinking?

The concept of historical thinking has been part of the history teacher's lexicon since at least 1899 when the American Historical Association issued its report, *The Study of History in Schools.*[1] Today, because historical thinking encompasses multiple ideas, we do not offer one simple definition of historical thinking. Instead, we draw from the contemporary writings of historians, history educators, and cognitive psychologists. For example, Chapter 2 of the *National Standards for History* identifies five types of historical thinking:

1. Chronological thinking
2. Historical comprehension
3. Historical analysis and interpretation
4. Historical research capabilities
5. Historical issues-analysis and decision-making.[2]

Some states have drawn from these five aspects of historical thinking in their state standards.[3]

The National Assessment of Educational Progress' (NAEP) *Framework for U.S. History* (1994, 2001) stresses historical thinking. The NAEP framework specifically states, "Historical study requires specialized ways of knowing and thinking, habits of mind and cognitive processes that typify historians' approaches to the past." These habits of mind include (a) historical knowledge and perspective and (b) historical analysis and interpretation.

Other professional organizations have described historical thinking and its importance. An article in the American Historical Association newsletter

FIGURE 3.1 Ten historical thinking benchmarks.

1. Analysis of primary and secondary sources
2. An understanding of historical debate and controversy
3. Appreciation of recent historiography through an examination of how historians develop differing interpretations
4. Analysis of how historians use evidence
5. An understanding of bias and points of view
6. Formulation of questions through inquiry and determination of their importance
7. Determination of the significance of different kinds of historical change
8. Sophisticated examination of how causation relates to continuity and change
9. Understanding the interrelationship among themes, regions, and periodization (establishing historical time frameworks)
10. Understanding that although the past tends to be viewed in terms of present values, a proper perception of the past requires a serious examination of values at the time

Perspectives identified a special committee's views regarding 10 "historical thinking benchmarks"[4] (see Figure 3.1). The National Council for the Social Studies' *Expectations of Excellence: Curriculum Standards for Social Studies* mentions the phrase *habits of mind* under one of its 10 themes related to history—time, continuity, and change. Habits of mind are more fully described by the National Council for History Education.[5] (You are already familiar with NCHE's 13 habits of mind. See Figure 1.1.)

Historical thinking is distinguished from critical thinking. Historical thinking is sensitive to time and space, while critical thinking lacks this important sensitivity. Historical thinking is embedded with content; historical thinking subsumes critical thinking.

Historical Thinking and Historical Consciousness

Historical thinking involves historical consciousness, which requires thinking back and forth in time. It involves rational thinking about time and change and recognizing the interdependence, as well as the uniqueness, of the past, present, and future. Historical consciousness is more than "personal memory." It entails a willingness to look at the world through the "memories of others" and to contemplate the world through the filter of their thoughts. Historical thinking includes thinking about each era of the past in terms of its own values, perspectives, and context (called *historicism*), rather than imposing present values on the past. It compels a constant reviewing and thinking about a view of life.[6] It requires a reflection on worldview. Human beings are temporally oriented. Thus, it entails a future aspect. Without consideration of the future, the past is reduced to nostalgia. Yet without the past, the future does not benefit from the human laboratory of past experiences. Historical thinking is an antidote to self-centeredness.

Historical Thinking and Causal Explanations

Historians are always examining causes for events, for instance 9/11, and for revolutions, such as the American, French, and Russian. Historians look for causes of immigration and emigration as well as other human experiences. It is natural for history teachers to explore causation in the history laboratory. For the history teacher, it is important to raise the question *why* and to denote to students that they can find causes working at three separate levels. Before distinguishing these three levels, we need an analogy to understand the levels of causation and the importance of time.

When you shake a grapefruit tree, grapefruit come dropping down. What causes the grapefruit to fall? Is it the shaking of the citrus tree? Is it the maturity of the grapefruit, so that they would fall to the ground even if there had been no shaking of the tree? Is it the infestation of a worm that causes the grapefruit to fall prematurely? Does gravity make the grapefruit fall? In which direction—left or right—do the grapefruit roll once they hit the ground? In dealing with the human experience, several similar levels of explanation make it nearly impossible to find out which of them determines the precise outcome. Some explanations are broadly general and some are quite specific. Usually, as in the instance of the grapefruit tree, historians find causation and time working in conjunction on three separate levels: the *longue durée,* the intermediate duration, and the very immediate.

The *longue durée* ascribes tendencies over which human beings cannot wield command. Neither individuals nor social groups can manage outcomes because processes, rather than events, move as slowly as glaciers. Causation as categorized under the *longue durée* take place over very long periods of time. As an example, the fall of Rome did not occur at one specific point in time. Its decline was part of a corrupt system, and the system finally succumbed to its own decay over time.

The intermediate time recognizes that individuals acting on their own or in concert do make a difference regarding what happens. For example, during the American Revolution and the writing of the U.S. Constitution, key individuals provided a trajectory for the role of national and state governments, the protection of individual rights, and majority rule.

Finally, causation can occur almost immediately—even by accident—in time. When the Bolsheviks came to power in late 1917, Lenin was the only person who seized the moment. Other Bolsheviks wanted to wait to seize power, because Marxism taught that certain stages had to be reached before revolution could occur. Lenin, having surfaced from the underground on the eve of the coup in October 1917, was stopped by officers on his way to Smolnyi, the command center of the Bolsheviks. Lenin feigned drunkenness so authorities did not keep him. We can only imagine what the outcome of the Bolshevik coup would have been had officers arrested him at that very moment. The October Revolution might not have occurred, the Bolshevik regime might never have come to power, and subsequent events of the 20th century might not have unfolded as they did—including National Socialism, perhaps World War II and decolonization, and the Cold War.[7]

Nothing is preordained in the history laboratory. Historical inevitability, often emphasized by Marxist historians, is not a reality of history. Nearly 2 months before the Russian tsar lost power in February 1917, even Lenin did not foresee that he and his followers would witness a Russian revolution in his lifetime. Hindsight provides everyone with vision about the past. But it should not be confused with predictability. If historical inevitability had validity, why was it that few foresaw the eventual dissolution of the Soviet Union in 1991? The disintegration of the Soviet Union was not inevitable, for it was as seemingly embedded in power as tsarist power had been more than 70 years earlier.[8] Both the fall of tsarism and the fall of the Soviet Union seemingly caught everyone by surprise.

Causation is not a unilinear explanation of historical events. There is no single explanation for events, though some explanations may carry more plausibility than others. The history laboratory provides opportunities to examine the multiple nature of causation. History recognizes that causation is neither a singular nor a unilinear explanation; events were not "meant" to happen. Historical thinking is an antidote to simple-minded, reductionist thinking.

Historical Thinking and Frame of Reference

Historical thinking requires more than just reading history or telling a story, although both are important. Historical thinking is framed by **positionality** (or frame of reference), which emanates from an array of cultural experiences to inform ontological (worldview), existential (who am I?), and epistemological (how do I know?) stances.[9]

Historical thinking is an act of thinking about a new experience with a set of temporal bearings. As teachers, we need to take into account the ontological, existential, and epistemological positions of our students (see Figure 3.2). In other words, we must probe and understand the positionalities of our students.

Researcher Linda S. Levstik found that, when young students discuss such topics as the settlement of America, the American Revolution, the Bill of Rights, the Depression, the Civil Rights movement, and the Vietnam War, they use words like *we, us, they,* and *them* to describe their perceptions of what took place. Students are defining themselves and the connection they have to the past by the use of their words. Teachers should recognize their students' frame of reference, which informs us of their perceptions regarding how they think about history.[10]

In addition, we must keep in mind that your students' frames of reference are grounded in the school curriculum and what they learn at home, from their peers, and from the media.

The Need to Teach Historical Thinking

History is a core content of any preparation for citizenship. It recognizes the role of human agency in the creation of change, and it can be viewed from multiple perspectives. Exposure to multiple explanations of the past and the critical examination of evidence help prepare the critical literacy informed citizens need as they encounter the massive deluge of media information. Historical thinking, then, prepares students for citizenship. Historical thinking (which is a domain-specific way of thinking) does not occur naturally, however. It must be taught.[11]

Cognitive studies researcher Sam Wineburg gained much deserved acclaim for his observation that "historical thinking, in its deepest forms, is neither a natural process nor something that springs automatically from psychological development." Wineburg, a leading researcher in cognitive studies, based his statement on empirical evidence. He wrote that the "achievement" of historical thinking "actually goes against the grain of how we ordinarily think."[12] Wineburg's book, appropriately titled *Historical Thinking and Other Unnatural Acts,* distinguishes professional historians from teachers and beginning students of history.

Wineburg had historians and advanced placement students "talk aloud" what they were thinking as they considered primary sources related to the Battle of Lexington. The historians' approach differed from that of the students untrained in the discipline of history.

FIGURE 3.2   Historical Thinking and History Education.

Source: Courtesy of Sarah Drake Brown. Used by permission.

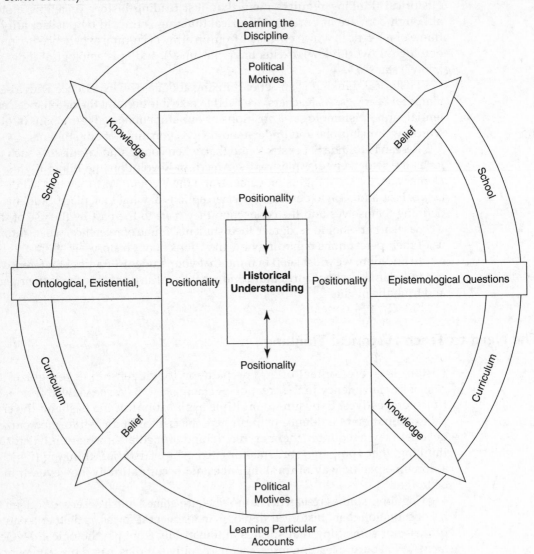

Wineburg used two key concepts—the **sourcing heuristic** and the **corroboration heuristic**—to explain how historians think as they read documents. These **heuristics** can also be defined as habits of mind. Before analyzing a primary source document, historians apply the sourcing heuristic by asking questions about the author's credentials, motivations, and participation in the events at the time the document was written. They also consider the audience for whom the document was intended. When you and your students use the sourcing heuristic, you create a distance between your own views and those of the people of earlier eras.

Historians use the corroboration heuristic to compare information learned from several documents. Historians apply layers of understanding to the analysis of new documents. Your students can gain historical sophistication as they engage in the analysis of documents. Practice and accretion of knowledge results in increasing competency in applying levels of historical understanding to the analysis of documents.

Historians contextualize the content of a document, which enables them to appreciate ways of perceiving and thinking that are quite different from conventional ways of perceiving and thinking today. At least two taxonomic (principles of classification) contextual levels—analogic and linguistic—exist. Historians might draw on analogic context when they read a speech of Abraham Lincoln at the time of the Lincoln–Douglas debates. How did Lincoln feel about slavery compared to Douglas? This analogic context comprises one of two levels of contextualization. How did Lincoln's attitude toward slavery compare to that of his contemporaries such as Douglas, slave owners, and abolitionists? Historians also understand a linguistic context, which considers the meaning of words at certain times in history. For example, the word *mere* in Shakespearean times meant "pure." In the 18th century, to be called "mere" Irish was an insult. Your students perceive language as atemporal, with meanings fixed for all time. Yet words rouse thoughts. Another example is the word *compromise*. During the 19th century, the United States had political leaders who sought compromises (for example, the Missouri Compromise and the Compromise of 1850) over serious issues. To "compromise" meant a willingness to face an issue and, after finding the opposition's position, work out the differences to achieve results. Each side would gain as well as give up something. "Compromise" connoted a positive quality about a political candidate, at least in most, not all, 19th-century circles. Today, to compromise is often a pejorative description of a political candidate. In most 21st-century circles, a candidate who compromises lacks principles and is willing to do anything for pragmatic reasons. "Compromise" is used disparagingly today to critique a political candidate. As you and your students read primary sources and come across the use of words, it will be important to discuss how words connote different meanings in time and place. How have such words as liberty, slave, trade, nation, protestant, and president shifted over space and time?[13] Your knowledge of history and its analogic and lingustic contexts will help your students gain more sophistication.[14]

Historians make intertextual links while reading documents, noting corroboration among primary sources as well as among historians' interpretations.[15] Historians also have a larger base of knowledge so they are constantly able to compare their analysis of a document with ideas and events in other parts of the world at that time.

Thus, Wineburg suggested that the sourcing heuristic (what historians do before reading for content comprehension); the corroboration heuristic (what historians do to relate one document to another document); **contextualization** (what historians do to describe the time frame and conditions locally, nationally, and globally); and **comparative thinking** (what historians do to describe conditions in other parts of the world at the time) are all central elements of historical thinking (see the Ideas for the History Classroom feature on the following page).

The need to understand progressively sophisticated thinking levels, as well as students' positionality (frame of reference), makes teaching history complex. As a teacher of history, you can use and develop your own understanding of the subject while introducing the views of historians to the classroom. Too often, there has been a "breach between school and academy."[16] You must "bridge across this breach," intervening to prompt students to internalize historical concepts and ways of thinking. Keep in mind that, although historical thinking is a domain-specific way of thinking, it does not prohibit historical thinking skills from being applied in concert with other content areas. Multiple teaching and learning strategies can be used to enhance students' historical thinking. The use of first-, second-, and third-order documents, a systematic approach we will elaborate on further in Chapter 7, helps bridge the gap by engaging students in the habits of mind of historians.

Structured Analysis Guides and Creative Historical Thinking

We introduce you now to two historical thinking analysis guides (see the Ideas for the History Classroom features on page 63 and 64) to use with your students when analyzing print documents and images such as photographs or paintings. Note that both guides (not intended to be worksheets) have the following five major headings, each of which contains more detailed component parts:

- Identifying the document
- Analyzing the document
- Determining the historical context
- Identifying the habit of mind and vital theme and narrative represented
- Determining the relationship to a discipline in the social sciences/social studies

---

Ideas for the History Classroom

Classification Framework of Historical Thinking

The analysis guides in the following Ideas for the History Classroom features provide a framework for thinking historically. The analysis guides emphasize what historians look for and think about as they analyze a document. They are not intended as a checklist or a worksheet. Instead, they focus the discussion on the credibility of historical evidence and historical understanding.

Create a Context

Ask an Open-Ended How/Why Question

Use a guide that emphasizes the following heuristics:

- **Sourcing heuristic**—what historians do before reading for content comprehension
- **Corroboration heuristic**—what historians do to relate one document to another document
- **Contextualization**—what historians do to describe the time frame and conditions both locally and nationally
- **Comparative thinking**—what historians do to describe conditions in other parts of the world at the time

Each guide is related to aspects of historical thinking suggested by Sam Wineburg: the sourcing heuristic, the corroboration heuristic, contextualization, and comparison. The overprinting in the guides illustrates the relationship between the concepts and the guides. The potential benefits of analyzing documents both contextually and comparatively moves students beyond consideration of themselves as isolated individuals and moves them into the role of individuals whose lives are contextualized in a historical fabric. You may use these guides to internationalize the teaching of U.S. history, thus offering a comparative dimension in historical thinking.

Each analysis guide is annotated; that is, each is keyed to the classification of historical thinking. In the print documents analysis guide, for example, sections 1 and 2 involve the sourcing heuristic, and the second question under section 2 and all of sections 4 and 5 involve the corroboration heurstic. Section 3 also involves contextualization. In the guide that deals with photographs and images, the sourcing heuristic applies to sections 1 and 2 except for questions beginning with the words *preceding conditions, relationship,* and *biases,* which call for the corroboration heuristic. The corroboration heuristic is also involved in the entirety of sections 4 and 5. Contextualization and the comparative heuristic are called for in section 3. Unlike most guides that serve as mere checklists, our guides are keyed to the cognitive studies research of Sam Wineburg regarding historical thinking.

The problem-solving questions (heuristic strategy) that historians use as they probe the meaning of a document—often before even reading the document—are lifelong habits of mind that will forever assist your students. These questions will engage you and your students in thinking about documents in historical contexts.

Once you have become familiar with the classification framework embedded in these guides, you can create your own analysis guides for analyzing maps, political cartoons, old radio and television programs, musical recordings, films, tables, charts, and graphs. Historical thinking is a unique inquiry that requires you and your students to engage actively in the analysis of documents and their contextualization in time.

Students' Minds Are Not Blank Slates

Most students come into your classroom with a number of preconceptions regarding the nature of history and expectations of you as their teacher. Your students' minds, in other words, are not blank slates. History's subject matter can be quite complex, which gives it richness. Its complexity, however, also requires careful consideration on your part as you organize its content and encourage your students to determine what it has meant to others as well as what it means to them.[17]

William Perry of Harvard University pointed to the individual differences among college students in terms of stages of cognitive development when they enter a classroom (see Figure 3.3). His schema has implications for teachers of secondary and middle school students as well.

FIGURE 3.3 **Perry's Student Stages of Cognitive Development.**

1. **Dualism Stage**
   - Students believe that all knowledge is known.
   - Students regard historical accounts as either true or false.
   - Students want the teacher to just "give them the facts."
2. **Early Multiplicity Stage**
   - Students believe that most knowledge is known.
   - Students believe that all knowledge is knowable.
   - Students believe that knowledge depends on a person's opinion.
3. **Late Multiplicity Stage**
   - Students realize that opinions are more valid when supported with evidence.
   - Students recognize the importance of criteria or standards when judging the credibility of a position.
4. **Contextual Relativism Stage**
   - Students understand that knowledge is contextual.
   - Students understand that interpretation (giving meaning to the past) is an act of intellectual creativity with restraint provided by standards of historical scholarship and inquiry.

Perry identified four stages, or what he called positions, of students: dualism, early multiplicity, late multiplicity, and contextual relativism.[18] In the lower position are students who possess a dualistic view of knowledge. Students at this stage believe that all knowledge is known. Historical accounts that you present to your students at this stage are either true or false, right or wrong. Your students in this position believe that you know the truth and the history textbook provides an "official" truth, which they are obligated to learn. Keep in mind, then, that some of your students will be frustrated if you do not just "give them the facts" and "tell them the truth."

Students at the middle stages of cognitive development—early and late multiplicity—understand that authorities and historical interpretations differ. Students believe that most knowledge is known, and that all knowledge is knowable. Students in the early multiplicity stage recognize that there is a paucity of established truth; they believe that knowledge is dependent on a possession of opinions.

In the late multiplicity stage, your students recognize that opinions are more valid when they are supported with evidence. Thus, at this cognitive position your students understand the importance of establishing criteria for a warranted position.

The final level of attainment in Perry's schema is contextual relativism. Students operating at this stage of sophistication understand that all knowledge is contextual. Very few middle and high school students reach this stage. Does this mean that we should postpone the teaching of history? We think not. You need a range of teaching strategies to accommodate students of varying levels of cognitive maturity.

Ideas for the History Classroom

Annotated Primary Source Analysis Guide to Historical Thinking: Print Documents (including Heuristics)

1. **Identifying the Document**
   Author(s) or source _____
   Date _____
   Type of document _____ *Sourcing Heuristic* _____

2. **Analyzing the Document**
   Main idea of the document _____ *Sourcing Heuristic* _____
   Relationships to other documents (How does the content relate to the first-, second-, and/or third-order documents?) _____ **Corroboration Heuristic** _____
   Preceding conditions that motivated the author _____
   Intended audience and purpose _____
   Biases of the author _____ *Sourcing Heuristic* _____
   Questions to ask the author _____

3. **Determining the Historical Context**
   Important people, events, and ideas at the time of the document
     Local/regional: people, events, and ideas of the time _____
     National: people, events, and ideas of the time _____ *Contextualization* ____
     World: people, events, and ideas of the time _____
   Conclusions about local/regional, national, and world context at the time ____ *Comparative* ____

4. **Identifying the Habit of Mind and Vital Theme and Narrative Represented**
   Habit of mind _____
   The way you used this habit of mind to analyze the document ___ *Corroboration Heuristic* ___
   Vital theme and narrative _____
   Evidence that the document represents this vital theme and narrative _____
   Evidence that the document relates to other documents (first-, second-, and/or third-order) through this vital theme and narrative _____

5. **Determining the Relationship to a Discipline in the Social Sciences/Social Studies**
   Discipline _____
   Evidence of relationship _____
   NCSS theme _____
   Evidence of relationship _____ *Corroboration Heuristic* _____

Ideas for the History Classroom

Annotated Primary Source Analysis Guide to Historical Thinking: Photographs/Images (including Heuristics)

1. **Identifying the Document**
   Photographer or source _____
   Title _____
   Date _____
   Type of document _____
   Sourcing Heuristic

2. **Analyzing the Source**
   Main idea of the source _____
   What do you see (people or objects) in the image? _____
   What are people, if any, doing in this image? _____
   Who do you think these people are? _____
   What does this image tell you about ways of living? _____
   When do you think this image was created? _____
   Why do you think this image was created? _____
   Sourcing Heuristic
   Preceding conditions that motivated the procedure of the image **Corroboration Heuristic**
   Intended audience and purpose ___ **Sourcing Heuristic**
   Relationship to other sources (how does the content relate to the first-, second-, and/or third order
      sources?) _____
   Corroboration Heuristic
   Biases of the image's producer _____
   Questions to ask the image's producer _____ **Sourcing Heuristic**

3. **Determining the Historical Context**
   Important people, events, and ideas at the time of the image's creation
      Local/regional: people, events, and ideas of the time _____
      National: people, events, and ideas of the time _____
      World: people, events, and ideas of the time _____
   Contextualization
   Conclusions about local/regional, national, and world context at the time ___ **Comparative**

4. **Identifying the Habit of Mind and Vital Theme and Narrative Represented**
   Habit of mind _____
   The way you used this habit of mind to analyze the image _____
   Vital theme and narrative _____
   Evidence that the image represents this vital theme and narrative _____ *Corroboration Heuristic*
   Evidence that the image relates to other source (first-, second-, and/or third-order) through this
      vital theme and narrative _____

5. **Determining the Relationship to a Discipline in the Social Sciences/Social Studies**
   Discipline _____
   Evidence of relationship _____
   NCSS theme _____
   Evidence of relationship _____
   Corroboration Heuristic

© Frederick D. Drake, 2001.

Teaching Scaffolds

The "cognitive revolution" of the 1970s and 1980s challenged the behaviorist practices in vogue at the time. Howard Gardner emphasized multiple intelligences, and Jerome Bruner stressed the importance of stories as a framework for meaningful learning. The cognitive revolution revived the importance of narrative in teaching history, which had been pretty much doomed by Piagetians and behaviorists.

Russian psychologist Lev Semenovich Vygotsky's ideas inform us that as teachers we need to provide scaffolds that support our students' cognitive advancement. Vygotsky argued that to help your students learn, you must identify and then operate within their "zone of proximal development." The zone of proximal development represents the disparity between students' varying abilities to solve problems on their own and their abilities to solve problems with your assistance. Scaffolding can help your students maneuver complex ideas within a provided structure.[19]

In addition to scaffolding, you will want to add an emotional and affective dimension to your classroom strategies. Engage your students in interactive strategies that include role-playing and imagining that they are someone else, dramatization of an event, and creating pictures and maps.

The questions you ask your students during discussions can include higher order questions that encourage them to think differently about an issue. For example, the following sequence of higher order questions can help your students think about James Madison and his role at the Constitutional Convention of 1787: What might have been on James Madison's mind? Remember, he's a leading Virginian at the Constitutional Convention and is concerned about liberty. What would be the problems for someone in his position? Such questions encourage your students to think in terms of someone else and are productive in engaging discussion.

Creating a Framework for Meaningful Learning

Cognitive psychologists David Ausubel and Jerome Bruner argued that higher level, more abstract knowledge is necessary to organize information in a meaningful way. In effect, your students will organize new learning according to understandings they already have. Your students' ability to make sense of new knowledge depends closely on their *a priori* knowledge or understanding.[20]

David Ausubel believes that lecture is an efficient way to teach (see the Ideas for the History Classroom feature on page 67). Ausubel prescribed "advance organizers" for a lecture (see Figure 3.4). They provide intellectual frameworks in which more discrete events are organized under larger ideas, themes, and generalizations.[21] Advance organizers are an excellent way to organize lectures because they focus your students' attention on large ideas and help them to organize the information learned via the lecture method. Thus, you could organize a lecture around one of history's vital themes and narratives or around one of the 10 themes of the National Social Studies Standards.

For educational psychologist Jerome Bruner, the narrative, or story, is essential to good history teaching. The narrative provides a meaningful framework that

FIGURE 3.4 Using an Advance Organizer to Structure Historical Understanding.

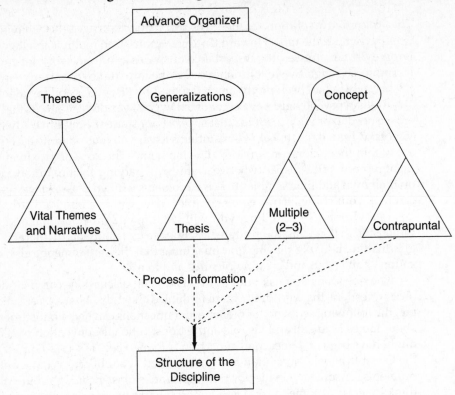

organizes students' individual experiences. Students use this narrative to make meaning of the world both past and present.[22] A library of stories exists for you and your students of history. You can bring in grand narratives dealing with national struggles for freedom or engage your students in micronarratives focusing on local or family histories.[23]

Bruner argued that students are at one of three stages when they consider the information contained in lessons: enactive, iconic, and symbolic.[24]

At the enactive stage, students can communicate and learn only through doing and imitating others. Role-playing and similar activities appeal to students at this maturity level.

At the iconic stage, students can learn and communicate through images. Students have preconceptions that influence their perceptions when they are presented with new historical information. Photographs, paintings, slides, PowerPoint presentations, and film excerpts are all important for students at this level of maturity.

At the highest level, the symbolic stage, students can communicate through abstract language, both oral and written. Students at this stage can think like professionals within the discipline of history. Although they have preconceptions, they are not limited by them. At the symbolic stage, they are willing to recognize interpretations, weigh them, and accept or reject them. The Ideas for the History Classroom feature, The Cone of Experience and Jerome Bruner's Stages, includes various general teaching strategies. These strategies are illustrated in the shape of a cone that is broad at the base and narrow at the top. The strategies appeal to students at the three levels of maturity. To reach all of your students, you will want to use materials and activities, as well as discussions.

Many of your students will not reach the third maturity level, the symbolic stage. In fact, many college students find the language of historians sometimes difficult to comprehend. Thus, part of your efforts need to be focused on the iconic stage, using images of various kinds as a foundation for the discussions that will hold the attention of students in your classes.

Ideas for the History Classroom

Dimensions of a Lecture

I. Purpose of a Lecture
  A. Motivational lecture
  B. Informational lecture
  C. Expansion or enrichment lecture
  D. Summation lecture
  E. Multiple goal lecture

II. Procedural Dimensions of a Lecture
  A. Introductory presentation (the hook)
  B. Content presentation
    1. Formal or informal
    2. Word or sentence outline
    3. Use of language
    4. Logical theme, illustrations, visuals
    5. Blends abstract and concrete
    6. Arrange content: beginning, middle, end
    7. Voice and position

III. Content Dimension of a Lecture
  A. Organized around a story
  B. Uses an advance organizer
  C. Organized around a vital theme
  D. Organized around a question or problem
  E. Uses one or more habits of mind

IV. Being an Effective Lecturer
  A. Friendly
  B. Confident
  C. Verbal skills
  D. Consider the audience (pacing)
  E. Prepare the audience (cueing)
  F. Use transitions
  G. Repeat
  H. Be planned and organized

Ideas for the History Classroom

The Cone of Experience and Jerome Bruner's Stages

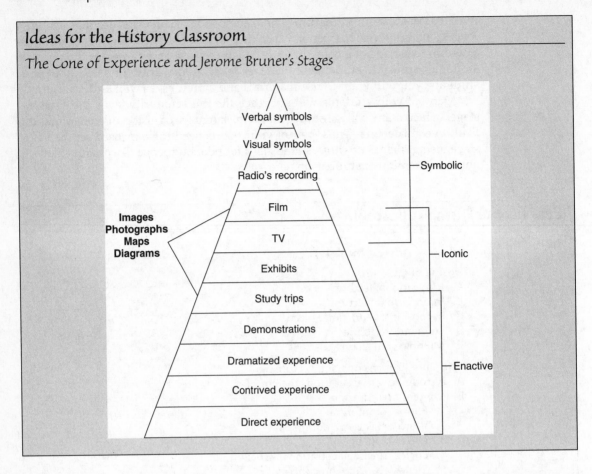

Images work especially well for elementary, middle school, and high school students, and they carry over for instruction with adults.[25] The use of narrative and images provide learners with comfortable means of organizing new information and remembering it. Your students learn these schemas when they are very young and never give them up. (In part III of this book, we identify three strategies that you can use to bring images into your classroom.)

SUMMARY

Historical thinking is a unique way of thinking that you must teach to your students so they gain autonomy as thinking individuals and citizens. Because your students are not blank slates, you will need to help them gain a more mature perspective and understanding of history and the ways historians think. Your students have some knowledge of history and a frame of reference when they enter your classroom. One of your tasks is to identify their frame of reference by discussing how they view the world and how they believe historical knowledge is created. You can use historical narratives as well as primary sources to improve your students' historical thinking. In later chapters (see part III of this book), we suggest a systematic approach as one of several methods to help students think historically.

In this chapter we emphasized the use of analysis guides that are keyed to the ways historians think. We also stressed the importance of using images to lead your students toward the sophistication of the symbolic stage and the language of history. Because most of your students will be at the iconic stage, the use of images should play a powerful role in your teaching. In part III we suggest teaching strategies that enhance the use of images in your teaching.

We now turn to part II—Planning and Assessment—which applies the theoretical background of part I to the organization of your U.S. and world history courses.

TRANSLATING HISTORY INTO CLASSROOM PRACTICE

Activity 3.1   Jerome Bruner's Three Stages of Thinking

Jerome Bruner believed that teachers need to let their students be creative and construct meaning regarding history. Bruner reminded us that students do not reach the same stages of thinking at the same time. Teachers need to provide scaffolds so their students can manipulate complex ideas.

Read the descriptions of the three stages—enactive, iconic, and symbolic—as described in this chapter. Consider the following question: How will you vary your teaching strategies to engage your students effectively at each of these stages of development?

Activity 3.2   Creating an Analysis Guide

Examine the analysis guides (textual and image) in this chapter. Both guides have five major headings that pose questions that historians ask themselves as they probe the meaning of a document. The headings are as follows:

1. Identifying the document
2. Analyzing the document
3. Determining the historical context
4. Identifying the habit of mind and vital theme and narrative represented
5. Determining the relationship to a discipline in the social sciences/social studies

Use the major headings to create your own analysis guides for one of the following:

- Maps
- Political cartoons
- Old radio and television programs

- Musical recordings and musical scores
- Films
- Tables
- Charts
- Graphs
- Legal documents

Then, under each heading, pose questions you believe historians would ask about a map, political cartoon, or other document. Finally, identify the problem-solving questions (heuristic strategy) that relate to your questions as a historian. Refer to the classification framework of historical thinking in the chapter (sourcing heuristic, corroboration heuristic, contextualization, and comparison).

Activity 3.3   Historical Thinking and Teaching

It seems more probable that a teacher who presents material in an original manner is not necessarily highly creative but simply more willing to spend time thinking about how best to convey information to a specific audience.

— James C. Schott and Laurel R. Singleton, *Teaching the Social Sciences and History in Secondary Schools*, 2000

Consider the times you were inspired by someone or some event from history and how you can make that historical moment more meaningful for you and your students. . . . Though it can at times be tumultuous, enjoy the ride and reap the numerous rewards along the way. In short make history.

— James Percoco, *A Passion for the Past: Creative Teaching of U.S. History*, 1998

Read the preceding quotes. Identify a topic in history you would like to teach and be prepared to discuss the following questions:

1. What teaching strategies have you seen that worked well with your topic (or any other topic)? What made them effective?

2. Describe a pedagogical technique or teaching strategy you plan to use. Why have you chosen this strategy?

3. What content knowledge will your students already have about your historical topic?

4. What sources are you planning to use to prepare for your topic?

5. How do you plan to make a historical moment more meaningful for your students?

REVIEWING THE CHAPTER

1. Give examples of how you engaged in historical thinking when you were a middle or high school student.
2. Of the *National Standards for History's* five aspects of historical thinking, which will you most likely emphasize? Why?
3. How are historical thinking and historical consciousness interrelated?
4. Why is presentism a problem in teaching history? What can you do to combat presentistic thinking in your students?
5. How do analysis guides (as keyed in this chapter) promote historical thinking?
6. Which of Samuel Wineburg's heuristics do you consider most essential to your teaching? Explain.

Planning and Assessment

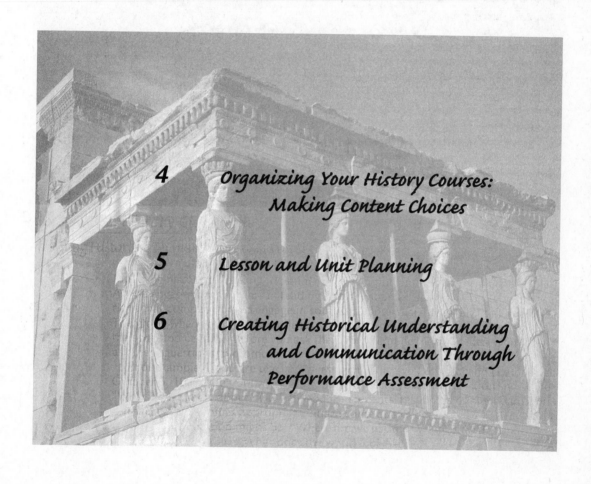

4
Organizing Your History Courses
Making Content Choices

Students [who] are new immigrants reinforce the necessity of organizing history around our nation's values, beliefs, and political system. We need to ensure that the students who will become citizens know the core values and guiding principles that unite us as a people.

—Veteran history teacher, spring 2002

Memory guides human action to a very great extent, and because different people have different memories their actions vary, sometimes in ways that surprise ignorant outsiders. . . . [We aspire to] careful teaching about the history of countries with cultural traditions and public memories different from ours. The mistake Americans make is to assume that everyone is, or at least wishes to be, just like ourselves.

—William H. McNeil, *Historical Literacy*, 1989

$\mathcal{A}$t a spring 2002 conference that brought together experienced history teachers, we overheard the following conversation:

"What we ought to do," quipped a well-respected female teacher, "is start with the historical perspective of the student. So many of our students are new immigrants to this country, and they cannot possibly appreciate or understand history unless we begin our courses from their cultural perspectives. Our traditional way of teaching just will not work with these students."

An equally well-respected male colleague countered, "I disagree. The very fact these students are new immigrants reinforces the necessity of organizing history around our nation's values, beliefs, and political system. We need to ensure that the students who will become citizens know the core values and guiding principles that unite us as a people."

These two highly regarded teachers approach the organization of their history courses from very different perspectives. As a teacher, you will be faced with this issue in every history course that you teach.

Focus Questions

1. How does chronology help organize your teaching of history?

2. How do themes help organize the content of your history courses?

3. How can diachronic and synchronic approaches become part of your teaching of history?

4. What models of world history can inform your teaching?

The Issue of Time

A basic problem you face as a history teacher is the scarcity of time. A yearlong course consists of approximately 180 days. However, you can subtract 10 to 20 of these days for standardized testing, assemblies and other programs, and teacher in-service days. In addition, you can subtract another 20 days for your own testing of what your students know and are able to do. You are left with as many as 140 days, perhaps only 130 days, to teach your courses in world history or U.S. history.

A pitfall that traps many veteran and beginning teachers is rushing to the text-book, beginning with Chapter 1, and trying to cover as much as possible before June. Many high school students recall courses in U.S. history that began with voy-ages of discovery and ended abruptly in the Great Depression. Many students in world history became acquainted with cultures in Mesopotamia and ancient Egypt, were immersed in the histories of Greece and Rome, and came to understand the circumstances of feudalism in the Middle Ages. However, they left the course with little understanding of modern history and only a passing acquaintance with the his-tory of Asian and African civilizations. This situation raises a couple of questions. First, What is the nature of world history? Is it really Western civilization with short side trips into the past of Africa and Asia? Second, What are the vital themes stu-dents will remember and draw upon to organize and elaborate their understand-ing of world and U.S. history?

The Purpose of History Education

The experienced history teachers quoted in the introduction of the chapter, in spite of their disagreements, share one very important commitment: Both teachers want their students to gain historical understanding. They do not view history simply as a required course, a ritual that students must endure to graduate from middle or high school. Nor do they appear to cater to state or school bureaucrats whose mantra is to teach to a state test. Their concerns take the form of two questions: What should my students understand about history (U.S. and world) at the end of my course? And what should my students appreciate and remember in the study of the human past long after they have graduated from high school?

The first teacher's emphasis is on engaging her students' interest in the study of history. She recognizes that students cannot be compelled to study history, but must be invited and engaged in history by being connected with the events of the past. The students' interests lie at the heart of her purposes for teaching. She wants to draw on her students' cultural experiences as an entry point into the study of U.S. and world history.

The second teacher recognizes history's role in the perpetuation of the U.S. democratic republic. Democratic principles are not perpetuated in documents, but are ingrained in the minds, hearts, and actions of U.S. citizens. Unless the docu-ments are carefully examined and discussed and the ideas incorporated into the world view of students, the principles are simply matters of the past. There is no guarantee that citizens of the United States will continue to be guided by the democratic principles of the past. Democracy is neither guaranteed nor a product of geographic location. Rather, democracy resides within citizens who learn and appreciate the principles that sustain democratic government. Thoughtful history teachers blend historical knowledge, historical thinking, and a positive disposition for history into their planning, instruction, and assessment. Although these two teachers are cognizant of the demands placed on them by statewide testing, these tests are simply one factor that enters into their curricular and instructional decisions.

Chronological Organization of History

As a U.S. and world history teacher, you will need to organize your courses. Your challenge is to organize courses that are meaningful, while not simplistic. For example, "progress" may be one theme to organize the understanding of history. While optimistic, it is such a partial view of the rich events of the past that include success and also failure. History includes regress and elements of "tragedy." Your students should be challenged to consider both "progress" and "tragedy" in U.S. and world history. A story of "progress" alone organizes a narrow, simplistic, and linear view of the past as if history as experienced by human beings is always one of improvement. Chronology is important for the accurate portrayal of people and cultures in successive events within a time frame. Chronology is not a sufficient substitute for the teaching of good history, however. Chronology alone neither constitutes good history teaching nor helps your students understand history. The teacher who defines history as chronology (that is, as a sequence of events in chronological order) implies that history is linear. This linear concept of history reduces history education to memorizing a sequence of events; a complex body of past events becomes a mere skeleton.

Chronological thinking resides at the core of historical reasoning. Unlike chronology, chronological thinking is more than the ordering of facts and events. Chronological thinking is a more complex phenomenon involving an understanding of cause and effect relationships and changes over time. For chronological thinking to occur, students must have a baseline of phenomena from which they can determine and interpret changes in beliefs, customs, institutions, technology, and values.[1] Thus, the history teacher emphasizes patterns of historical *duration* and patterns of historical *succession*.[2] Patterns of historical duration illustrate for students the continuity of principles and institutions over time. For example, the U.S. Constitution has survived as a living document for over 200 years. The U.S. Constitution can also illustrate patterns of historical succession; although its principles have endured for over 200 years, many political, economic, and social changes have occurred. Slavery has ended, women can vote, corporations have risen to positions of power and prominence, and presidents possess greater executive power.[3]

Chronological thinking, however, can never be reduced to an examination of either historical continuity or historical change. History involves the simultaneous consideration of continuity in beliefs and institutions and changes in the ideas and social organizations that occur within any period of time. For example, even the rapid changes that societies undergo during revolutions are accompanied by continuity in many beliefs and forms of social organization. Similarly, periods of history that seem on the surface to be defined by sustained beliefs and practices are filled with social changes if examined carefully. The good history teacher identifies key turning points without reducing history to earthquakes of change.

Organizing your course around chronology and chronological thinking has advantages. It disciplines students' thinking as they examine cause and effect relationships in particular time periods. Periodization (establishing historical time frameworks) affords an organizational framework to help students structure and remember historical events and help teachers organize individual lessons and unit plans. There are disadvantages, however. Teachers using periodization can be tempted to provide too many anecdotes, which detract from what they are trying to emphasize. In a U.S. history course, for example, minorities can be overlooked. Controversial issues can also be ignored even though they may relate to the main story. In world history, non-Western history is often given the short shrift.

Even though periodization has some difficulties, several sources will provide you with guidance. For example, you can organize your U.S. history course around larger periods of time as recommended by the National Assessment for Educational Progress (NAEP) Framework.[4] NAEP identifies eight periods of U.S. history:

Period 1: Three Worlds and Their Meeting in the Americas (Beginnings to 1607)

Period 2: Colonization, Settlement, and Communities (1607 to 1763)

Period 3: The Revolution and the New Nation (1763 to 1815)

Period 4: Expansion and Reform (1801 to 1861)

Period 5: Crisis of the Union: Civil War and Reconstruction (1850 to 1877)

Period 6: The Development of Modern America (1865 to 1920)

Period 7: Modern America and the World Wars (1914 to 1945)

Period 8: Contemporary America (1945 to Present)

NAEP's world history periodization is currently under development and has yet to be published in 2007. The National History Standards for World History suggest eight eras as a framework in which to organize your course:

Era 1: The Beginnings of Human Society

Era 2: Early Civilizations and the Rise of Pastoral Peoples, 4000–1000 BCE

Era 3: Classical Traditions, Major Religions, and Giant Empires, 1000 BCE–300 CE

Era 4: Expanding Zones of Exchange and Encounter, 300–1000 CE

Era 5: Intensified Hemispheric Interactions, 1000–1500 CE

Era 6: Global Expansion and Encounter, 1450–1770

Era 7: An Age of Revolutions, 1750–1914

Era 8: The 20th Century

As you examine the periods of U.S. history and the eras of world history, consider several questions: Why does the framework for U.S. history sometimes divide the past into periods, while the framework for world history divides the past into eras? Why is there a reference to BCE and CE in the world history eras? How does this designation change? Is there a noticeable difference in the political, geographic, economic, and social emphases of these two frameworks? How do the National Social Studies Standards relate to the frameworks of U.S. and world history?

Thematic Organization of History

Your courses can be organized thematically, stressing different topics and ideas to be examined over time. Two thematic organization approaches are the diachronic and synchronic approaches. (see Figure 4.1). The **diachronic** approach takes one theme and traces it from its inception to the present. For example, the diachronic approach might examine diseases as they affected people from 1500 to the present. Another example is tracing liberalism in U.S. history. Until the late 19th century liberalism focused on individual rights and liberties. In the 20th century the meaning changed from protecting the individual from government to concentrating on social welfare. Other examples are to trace technology from its origins to the present or to trace the family from one period to another.

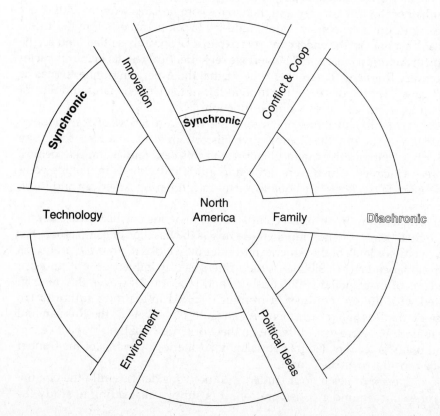

FIGURE 4.1
Synchronic and Diachronic Wheel for Thematic Teaching.

The **synchronic** approach examines several themes within a particular period. For example, you can integrate the themes of conflict and cooperation, political ideas, innovation, technology, and patterns of social change in examining the decade preceding the American Civil War. The synchronic approach considers the relationship of multiple political, economic, and social phenomena within a short period of time. The synchronic approach allows you and your students to focus on the uniqueness of past society. Figure 4.1 represents a "wheel" with one spoke symbolizing the diachronic approach (one theme) across time. The synchronic approach is represented by all of the themes spinning through a particular point in time.

Both the diachronic and synchronic approaches avoid the flatland of one fact after another. Instead, they provide students with larger organizing ideas that give them the **durable knowledge** to construct historical memory.

Comparative History Approach

The comparative approach to teaching and learning history holds a good deal of promise if the teacher is able to temper enthusiasm with caution. This caution is a product of understanding the uniqueness of historical circumstances and events. For example, there is a certain degree of seductiveness in contemplating the factors leading to American Pioneers to populate the Pacific Coast and the Great Plains in the latter half of the 19th century and then make comparisons with the settlement of the eastern frontier of Russia. Does Frederick Jackson Turner's Frontier thesis explain, at least in part, the effect of a great expanse of sparsely settled land on the formation of American character? Should we seek identical results in the character of 19th century Russians? If a teacher believes that the American frontier served as a "safety valve" for the discontented individuals in the United States, did Siberia and the Russian Far East serve a similar function?

Before we identify attributes of the comparative approach we offer the following cautions as issued by the Comparative History Project and a recent web site that describes Comparative History Failures, in this case feudalism.[5] We believe these three principles, which were written to guide individuals in making comparisons of feudal societies, are equally useful in comparing American and Russian frontiers.

One primary error in historical comparison is to define one historical example as the "normal" circumstance and then use this as the baseline of comparison. For example, your students of the American frontier may look for examples in Russia where the independence of Siberian settlers filters back to influence the attitudes of the residents of metropolitan St. Petersburg and Moscow. However, the freedom associated with life on the Russian frontier resulted in a strong authoritarian response by the Russian government. As a result, the effects of the Russian and American frontiers were very different on the world views of their respective citizens and political leaders. Neither Russian nor American variants of the frontier should be considered as the "norm."

A second error arises if your students do not consider carefully the circumstances of each case under consideration. It is simply misleading to study the

American frontier in detail followed by a cursory glance at the similarities in Russia. Geography is important, but it does not trump differences in Russian culture in explaining historical events. Given the time constraints placed on history teachers it is nigh impossible to engage all students in all of the historical ideas and events that we would like so that they can understand the similarities and differences that the frontier played in American and Russian history. The middle school, high school, and college teacher will each define the careful consideration of the American and the Russian frontier according to varying standards arising from the characteristics of students and competing curricular demands, but a balance must be struck in examining both frontiers if valid comparisons are to be made.

A third consideration centers on the time of events being compared. In our comparison of American and Russian frontiers, how do we consider the very different circumstances facing the Kievan Rus of the 12th century and the American settler of 1877? The obvious answer is: Only with great caution. It seems far more reasonable to limit comparisons to the effects of the 19th century frontiers on American and Russian life.

Having made the case for caution, we believe there are compelling reasons for comparison in teaching. We are constantly reminded that we live in a global society, but is this really a recent occurrence? A strong argument can be made that European colonization of the Americas was part of the global age that was already several centuries old in 1492. The founding of St. Petersburg in 1703 marks a pronounced turning toward Western thought, science, and technology by Tsar Peter the Great. Less well known is that the initial German Quarter (all foreigners were identified as German) was established in Moscow in the mid-16th century. While the exchange of ideas between people was not rapid by today's standards, it did occur and it changed the worldview of rulers and subjects.

Just as teaching gross generalizations that tend to explain phenomena across centuries of time and thousands of kilometers is deceptive, so too is the teaching of national histories in isolation. We offer two print documents for consideration. One is a "Call to the People," written by Eugene V. Debs in 1897 as miners and workers faced deplorable working conditions in the United States. The other is Vladimir Illyich Lenin's lengthy pamphlet "What is to be Done?" which was written in 1902 to sketch out a vision for the Marxist revolutionary party. There are numerous questions that require answers before you present these documents to your students.[6]

You need to consider the information necessary to provide the historical context surrounding these documents. Eugene V. Debs, while calling for radical change and expressing a distrust in American political leadership, affirmed his faith in the character and abilities of American citizens to reform society. Debs grew up with small-city, Midwestern values. The son of a keeper of a small store in Terra Haute, Indiana, he left school at the age of 14 to work in the local railroad shop and later as a locomotive fireman. Debs would organize the Brotherhood of Locomotive Firemen, and he switched from advocating craft unionism to founding the American Railway Union (ARU), which he organized along industrial lines. Against Debs' judgment, the ARU struck against the Pullman Company in 1894. Debs was subsequently arrested for obstructing the mail. When that charge was dropped, Debs served a 6-month prison sentence for violating a court injunction. Named for Eugene

Sue and Victor Hugo, Debs was fascinated by the ideals of French Romanticism and often quoted Hugo and French revolutionary songs in his writings and speeches. His radical rhetoric developed slowly, coming from personal experience rather than from persuasion by a social theorist. While in prison, Debs read Marx. Socialism for Debs, though, was more from the "heart than from the head" and was based more on his observations of living and working conditions than upon theory or doctrine.[7]

Hegel and Marx's thoughts would clarify Lenin's certainty that a revolution is required and that the revolution requires the leadership of intellectuals and not "wretched amateurs." Lenin wrote his long pamphlet in the context of a debate raging in European Marxist circles spirited in part by the ideas of Eduard Bernstein, the amanuensis of Engels. Bernstein was a revisionist who advocated integrating German workers in society. Bernstein watched current European developments. He observed the terrible living and working conditions of most German workers, and he recognized that an improvement was coming; organized labor was exacting concessions from employers and big business increasingly accepted collective wage bargaining. German political and economic elites aimed to integrate German workers in society, and Bernstein argued that workers should take full advantage of this opportunity. The German Social-Democratic Party should become involved in peaceful, legal activities aimed at improving the economic well-being of the working class. Bernstein was shocked by preoccupations with violent struggle and dictatorship. He saw changes developing in Europe that did not fit neatly into the divisions of bourgeoisie and proletariat. Intermediate social groupings were growing and he thought Marxism should adjust to the changes of capitalism of the time. Some Russian Marxists, known as "economists," were advocating Bernstein's approach to integrate German workers in society. Lenin's "What is to be Done?" was a response to Bernstein, and Lenin's booklet urged the need for strict rules in the party, to assure centralism, and to discipline and vet recruits.[8]

As the teacher, you may choose to contextualize the documents in lectures and discussions to highlight the similarities and differences in the ideas and historical context of Debs and Lenin. The outcome for students is an understanding and appreciation that conditions faced by workers and condemned by radical leaders were not encapsulated in national histories, but global changes faced by individuals who lived in the transition period as economies shifted from agriculture to industry/commerce as dominant structures affecting the lives of Americans and Russians.

For other examples of comparative lessons see the recent work of Stephen Schechter and Margaret Branson. These comparative lessons focus on civics and political history as one component of the Civics Mosaic grant funded by the United States Department of Education. This grant supports a network of American and Russian partners. The forty comparative lessons are organized around seven central questions:

- What are the historical and philosophical foundations for politics and government?
- What are the sources of political authority and political power?
- How does political culture influence institutions and practices?

- What are the rights and responsibilities of individuals and groups in different political systems?
- How do representation and participation vary?
- How are nations governed, and how is policy made?
- How and why is governance changing in a globalizing world?

The comparative focus of these lessons is not limited to the United States, but comparisons are made between governments past and present throughout the world.[9]

Content Choices for World History

According to some world historians, world history is the "study of human history around the globe through time." World historians "study global forces and large historical themes such as climatic change, the spread of religions, and the expansion of the market economy."[10]

The teacher of world history faces tremendous challenges when creating a narrative. Although there are many ways to think about world history, we offer three models proposed by Ross E. Dunn that you can use to organize your ideas for this subject: the Western heritage model, the different cultures (muticulturalism) model, and the patterns of change model (see the Ideas for the History Classroom feature on pages 85–87).[11]

The Western heritage model evolved after World War I. This model views the central mission of history education to be the transmission of shared heritage, institutions, and great ideas of Western European people. This model emphasizes the values of democracy and freedom. If you use this model, your primary purpose is to transmit to your students the rich heritage of European and ancient Mediterranean culture.[12]

The different cultures model, beginning in the 1960s and 1970s, charges that the Western heritage model is too Eurocentric. The different cultures model emphasizes diversity and the uniqueness of cultures. This model includes more Asian and African topics in units of instruction. Its critics, however, point to its tendency toward present-mindedness, and some critics charge that its origins are linked to racist ideas and group rights. In contrast to the Western heritage model, which stresses unity, the different cultures model fixates on cultural differences and particularities, which can result in advocating for the separation of unique cultural groups. If you use this model, you are following a path that many historians criticize.

The patterns of change model originated in the 1950s and 1960s with such historians as William H. McNeill and Leften Stavrianos. This model provides a global or comprehensive view of world history, which has been possible only during the past 500 years—the so-called modern era. During this period of modernity, ideas and forces emanating from the West and transcending cultures throughout the world have shaped world history generally. Thus, properly and accurately treated, the patterns of change during the modern era of world history have borne the heavy imprint of Western civilization.[13]

The patterns of change model emphasizes social and spatial fields of inquiry that are not predetermined by cultural categories. Cultures by themselves are not

static. One culture is not more historic than another. They grow and change in interaction with one another. The nation-state is a porous boundary that serves to provide political unity; however, even centralized governments cannot stop the flow
of ideas. Thus, the nation-state system is a partial, yet inadequate, framework
around which to organize a world history course. This model emphasizes large
patterns of change over time. These patterns transcend the boundaries of nation-
states or earlier political divisions.

The patterns of change model stresses comparisons of civilizations. Using this
model, you and your students identify the changes that have occurred and make
comparisons within the context of the times. Your analytical framework establishes
a baseline of ideas and events against which these changes are measured.[14] This
model requires that you engage your students in numerous meaningful writing
assignments. Your students will need practice writing comparative essays.

No matter which model you choose (the three models suggested or other models), you will face this question: When does *world* history begin? Perhaps you will
regard the Columbian exchange in the late 1400s as a starting point. Perhaps your
world history starts with Marco Polo in the 1200s. Or you might move the horizon
of world history back to changes in technology that began in Mesopotamia, Asia,
Africa, and other geographic regions of the world.

World history teachers face a major challenge: How to include major ideas and
human experiences while not reducing the past to a travelogue of all the nations of
the world in 140 days. This is no easy task. The historian David Christian's recent
world history book, *This Fleeting World: A Short History of Humanity* (2008), may
provide a helpful framework for world history teachers. Christian organizes human
history into three eras: Foraging (250,000–8,000 B.C.E.); Agrarian (8,000 B.C.E.–1750
C.E.); and Modern (1750–Present). While organizing the past into large eras, Christian provides supportive detail to broad generalizations. He emphasizes "inter-
connectedness" in the human experience and identifies turning points related to
ways people have produced and distributed foods, organized their communities,
interacted with the environment, and increased production and population. The
sequence of foraging, agrarian, and modern societies reflects the changing relations
human beings have with the environment. *This Fleeting World* counters the tendency to provide a superficial tour of many events, and David Christian provides
this large framework of world history in less than 100 pages.

Content Choices for U.S. History

Many narratives inform the organization of a U.S. history course. Some teachers
emphasize exceptionalism—the belief that the United States is unique among all
other nations in the world. Other teachers stress the links the United States has
with the trans-Atlantic community. Still other U.S. history teachers focus on the
American past within a global context.

We believe that the changing meaning of freedom can serve as a useful thematic framework for teaching U.S. history. After all, freedom and security are moti-
vators of human beings. The search for freedom breaks the bounds of context in

Ideas for the History Classroom

Three Models for Organizing a Global/World History Course

U.S. educators have repeatedly rewritten the definition of world history as a subject during the past century and half. Definitions of the past are inevitably revised.

I. **Western Heritage Model**
   A. **Definition:** This model encourages and explores the special personality of the Western world and the search for prized ideals and institutions as a model for the teaching of world history.
   B. **Central Mission:** To transmit to rising generations:
      1. A shared heritage of values and institutions
      2. Great ideas derived mainly from peoples of European and ancient Mediterranean descent
      3. A dedication to democracy, freedom, and a shared system of cultural communication
      4. The belief that Western civilization was self-generating and continues to be self-perpetuating
      5. The values of Christianity, pluralism, individualism, and rule of law
      6. The belief that Western civilization has been a generator of progressive historical change in the world since the 15th century
         a). Produced the idea of freedom
         b). Ended slavery
         c). Created the Industrial Revolution
         d). Invented modernity
   C. **Rationale/Aim**
      1. To revitalize Western civilization
      2. To demographically and socially unify the changing world
      3. To protect the Western world from rival ideologies, e.g., fundamentalism and state terrorism
   D. **Specific Assumptions**
      1. Western civilization generated and will keep its cultural traits and innate attributes.
      2. The continuing core of Western civilization includes Christianity, pluralism, individualism, capitalism, and rule of law, which made possible modernity and opportunities to expand throughout the world.
   E. **Advantages (Advocates)**
      1. Affirms the Western qualities of democracy and freedom
      2. Attempts to unify a diverse society of competing values under historical "Western" and "American" values
   F. **Disadvantages (Critics)**
      1. Assumes that Western civilization uniquely possesses "inborn characteristics" in contrast with other civilizations
      2. Anthropomorphizes Western civilization, giving it personality and agency to create ideas and values; becomes a search for origins
      3. Is a "single tunnel" model

(continued)

Ideas for the History Classroom   (continued)

Three Models for Organizing a Global/World History Course

II. **Different Cultures (Multiculturalism) Model** (began in 1960s and 1970s as a result of social and domestic upheavals)
   A. **Definition:** This model criticizes the Western heritage model as Eurocentric. It tries to exhibit various civilizations and artifacts of various civilizations instead of one.
   B. **Central Mission:** To teach the accomplishments and historical involvement of historic cultures from around the world rather than only those of Europe.
     1. Assimilates new faces, questions, and regions of the world
     2. Provides a fuller account of women, working people, and ethnic and racial minorities
   C. **Rationale/Aim:** Contributions to the world have been made by others besides white males. Linked to social history.
   D. **Specific Assumptions**
     1. Every culture has its own internal coherence, integrity, and logic.
     2. No one culture is inherently better or worse than another.
   E. **Advantages (Advocates)**
     1. Internationally minded, concerns all cultures
     2. Demonstrates the diversity of the world
     3. Tells distinctive stories
     4. Introduces "great figures" of various civilizations
   F. **Disadvantages (Critics)**
     1. As with the Western heritage model, it assumes that all cultures have their own internal coherence, integrity, and logic
     2. Historicism—does not adequately express change over time
     3. Can become very present-minded
     4. Many short, narrow tunnels (multitunneled)
     5. Fixates on cultural differences, particularities, and otherness
     6. Origins before 1960s and 1970s can be linked to racist ideas, group rights, and separation

III. **Patterns of Change Model**
   A. **Definition:** This model states that social and spatial fields of historical inquiry should be open and fluid and not predetermined by conventionally assumed cultural categories. The nation-state format is limiting. This model examines the interaction of the pieces (community, societal, or continental) in human history and assesses the experience of humanity through the study of those interactions.
   B. **Central Mission:** One culture is not more "historic" than another. Historical inquiry should be made from local to global.
   C. **Rationale/Aim:** This model attempts to be "culturally neutral" and encourages students to link developments of the past to their own experiences as human beings.
   D. **Specific Assumptions**
     1. It is a response to the globalization of our contemporary world.
     2. The rules and methods of history should be followed no matter how long the time and large the space.
     3. One culture is not more "historic" than others.

4. The nation-state model is an inadequate framework for understanding the sweep of the human past.
5. Scholars can venture to any part of the world to find answers to historical questions.

E. **Advantages (Advocates)**
1. Socially inclusive yet firmly based in the discipline of history
2. Historical events are viewed not from within one cultural setting but as a world-scale historical problem
3. Links the past to students' experiences
4. Emphasizes the idea of empathy
5. Discovers large patterns of change
6. Does not replace historical and abstract themes such as empire, imperialism, and nationalism
7. Promotes the comparison of civilizations within a historical context

F. **Disadvantages (Critics)**
1. Forces teachers to broaden their historical knowledge so that they can adequately demonstrate how the event fits in a broader context
2. Causes teachers to frame questions beyond cultural divides
3. Students may not see the patterns and larger significance of the curriculum
4. In the hands of the "wrong" teacher and "wrong" students, this model can get out of hand
5. May leave out lesser known areas
6. Topical themes tend to isolate historical events and obscure historical relationships

which we live. The following three interrelated questions can be used to organize a direction for your course in U.S. history or world history. What are the meanings of freedom in the United States and in the world? What are the political conditions and social conditions that make freedom possible in the United States and in the world? What are the boundaries of freedom in the United States and in the world, and how have they been reduced as well as expanded?

Two historians, Richard Hofstadter and Eric Foner, wrote compelling narratives of U.S. history in which the pursuit of the political, social, and economic ideal of freedom served as the central theme. Hofstadter's *The American Political Tradition and the Men Who Made It*[15] stresses consensus among leading political figures. Hofstadter emphasized the agreements rather than the tensions that defined U.S. political issues. Foner's *The Story of American Freedom* considered freedom a contested ideal with three compelling themes: the various meanings of freedom, the social conditions that contributed to freedom, and the borders to freedom—that is, who has been included and excluded from freedom in the United States.[16]

Whether you and your students choose to emphasize consensus or conflict, the search for freedom can serve as a powerful narrative for your course. This theme provides opportunities to include important documents and compare the application of this idea to the lives of Americans from the origin of our country to the present. Your first-order document (again, this approach will be explained more fully in Chapter 7) might focus on the ideals of freedom, and your second-order documents might concern the inclusion and exclusion of groups pursuing this ideal.

Certainly, freedom should not be the only theme of your U.S. history course. However, it is your responsibility to consider your organizing framework and its effectiveness in providing students with durable knowledge regarding our American republic.

In organizing your U.S. history course, you will need to consult national standards, state standards, the National Council for History Education, the NAEP framework, and the requirements established by your school district. Perhaps your starting point will be the convergence of three cultures in the Americas—red, white, and black.[17] Or you may choose to begin your course with the post–Civil War period to emphasize more recent history. No matter where you start in time, you should consult history's vital themes and narratives, history's habits of mind, periodization, the national social studies themes, national and state standards, and your district's objectives.

The analysis guides provided in Chapter 3 encourage you to investigate with your students what happened and why in the United States and in the world at large. This internationalizing of history does not mean that you forsake national history; it does mean that you have opportunities to establish a firm foundation of U.S. history and at judicious times analyze what was experienced throughout the world. To use international comparative history effectively, you will need a good deal of historical understanding.[18]

You should consider the intelligence of your students along with the quality of the materials they study. Also, the quality of your instruction will result in your students' acquisition of both knowledge and skills, which can be either elegant, elaborate, and durable or rudimentary, primitive, and ephemeral.

The Past as a Wooded Thicket

The past is like a wooded thicket. Although it has structure and form, much of the detail is not obvious or is even hidden from the casual observer, who often perceives only the simple outlines of the thicket. Trees are obvious, but the life in the shadows must be uncovered.

This analogy of the wooded thicket implies that history does not provide a uniform picture of the past.[19] Your students will require your help to gain understanding as they investigate primary sources and historical narratives.

The narrative frameworks of historians and the frameworks of history teachers in the classroom are multiple, frequently conflicting, and wide-ranging. All teachers face difficult choices regarding the frameworks in which to organize instruction. Two extremes undermine history. At one extreme is to celebrate past achievements while ignoring failures. The opposite is also possible.

We know from research in history education that students frequently "learn official history" in order to pass tests. This official history, students perceive, is the history the teacher (or the school or textbook authorities) dispenses to them. Official history knows no ideological or national borders and is often learned from the ritualistic study of politically palatable views of the past. In the United States, racial and ethnic groups feel dispossessed or alienated from a history that fails to include their ancestors *or* a history that conspires to elevate every minority group to pre-eminent status in the forging of historical events. Neither approach accurately portrays the ideas and views of the past.

The teaching of history in Eastern Europe during the Soviet occupation, for example, branded its own style of "official history," with a "single, monolithic view of the past" that "was strictly enforced in the public sphere." History merged with ideology, and the result was public cynicism focused on both the past and the present.[20]

We encourage deliberative discussion, in which students engage in examinations of first-, second-, and third-order documents and are aware of various interpretations. This approach avoids the extremes of celebratory or cynical history. This means that as a teacher you should have a narrative to organize your instruction. At the same time you should provide opportunities for students to interpret documents and to construct well-informed interpretations regarding the past.

SUMMARY

Organizing U.S. and world history courses is a thoughtful process. Liberal democracy is broad and deep, offering a wide variety of intellectual currents. Your students can examine ideas developed by 19th-century conservatives opposing women's suffrage and at the same time analyze the arguments supporting the suffrage movement. Guided by the principles of rationality and historical inquiry, this method using a variety of sources and deliberative discussion balances the use of narrative and primary sources in teaching history. Students examine particular issues and sources and contextualize these issues and sources within larger narrative frameworks.

The teaching of history is well served when you offer students multiple primary sources organized systematically; a narrative from which they can gain a patterned understanding; and alternative narratives to avoid indoctrination and reductionism.

TRANSLATING HISTORY INTO CLASSROOM PRACTICE

Activity 4.1   The Ecology of Teaching

Discuss how you would apply knowledge of content, pedagogical skills, and the learner to the teaching of a U.S. or world history course. Identify the knowledge you need to be successful.

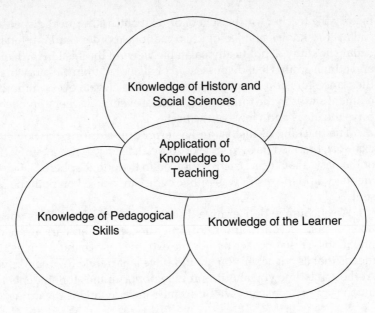

Activity 4.2   Knowledge of Political History

Discuss what comprises knowledge of political history. What are the essential qualities students should know to understand political history (as illustrated in the diagram)? What would you add to the diagram?

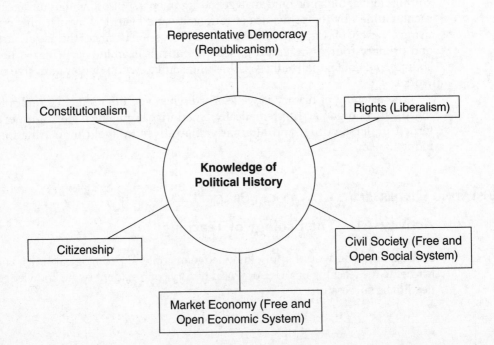

Activity 4.3   Political History at the Core of Teaching

Political history dominated teaching, lost its emphasis, and has made a recent come-back. In the 1960s through the 1990s, social history dominated. Why has political history been revived? How can you develop a nexus between political and social history? What are the advantages of students' knowing political history? Are there disadvantages? What elements in the following diagram are important to political history? How would you change the diagram?

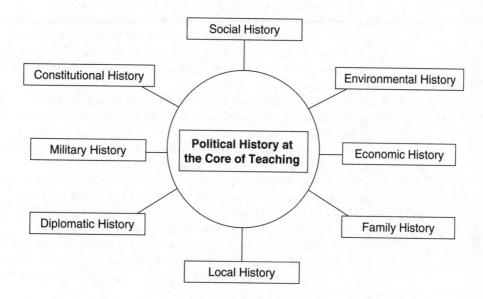

Activity 4.4   Ten Essential Elements of Education for Democracy in Schools

Of the 10 essential elements of education for democracy, which do you think you could put into practice immediately? How do these 10 essential elements relate to the two teachers described at the beginning of this chapter?

I. **A systematic and continual emphasis on teaching and learning democracy, democratic government, and democratic society**
   A. Students should know what a democracy is and what it is not.
   B. Students should know the standards or criteria by which democratic governments and societies are distinguished from those that are not democratic.
   C. A government is minimally democratic if:
      1. The people's representatives in government are elected in free, fair, open, and competitive elections.
      2. The electorate is inclusive so that a large majority of the people who live under the government's authority have the right to vote.

3. There is a people's government, limited by the supreme law of the people's constitution, for the purpose of protecting equally, through the rule of law, the rights of everyone in society.
4. There is a constitutional protection for individuals' rights to think, speak, decide, and act freely to influence the policies and actions of the government.
5. There is majority rule with protection of the human rights of everyone, including individuals in the minority.
6. There is recognition to act for the common good.
7. There is equal justice under the law for all in the society.

II. **Teaching and learning about the constitution and institutions of the democratic government and civil society in which the students live**
   A. Students should know the principles of the constitution, the institutions of government under this constitution, and the nongovernmental institutions that constitute the civic society.
   B. Students should compare their government and civil society with the government and civil societies of other nations in terms of the generally accepted criteria for democracy.

III. **The development of the students' capacity to apply or use knowledge to think and participate competently in a democracy**
   A. Students apply basic knowledge of democracy—its principles, practices, and history—to the civic and political events of the past and present.
   B. Students' cognitive skills enable them to respond to their experiences reasonably and effectively when confronted by public issues.
   C. Students' participatory skills in concert with cognitive skills enable them to cooperate with others to monitor and influence the actions and decisions of government and to make their representatives accountable to them.
   D. Students' participatory skills with cognitive skills enable them to cooperate with others as leaders and followers in nongovernmental organizations that constitute their civil society and thereby to act for the common good.

IV. **The development of civic virtue and the behavioral dispositions of the good citizen in a democracy**
   A. Students develop the civic virtue of subordinating personal interests to the common good.
   B. Students exhibit democratic dispositions that include temperance or self-control, fortitude or courage, commitment to justness or fairness, prudence, charity or compassion for others, hope or optimism about the future, honesty or fidelity to the truth, civility in dealings with others, tolerance, and respect for the equal worth and dignity of each person in recognition of the equal humanity of all.

V. **The systematic connection and integration of basic knowledge, skills, and dispositions in the curriculum and instruction presented to students**
   A. Knowledge of democracy should be integrated with skills of cognition, participation, and moral dispositions.

     B. Knowledge, skills, and dispositions should be connected through activities that apply knowledge.

     C. Core content is the indispensable foundation of an effective education for democracy, and should include representative government, popular sovereignty, constitutionalism or the rule of law, human rights, responsible citizenship, civil society, and market economy.

  VI. **The teaching of knowledge, skills, and dispositions of democracy throughout the curriculum of the school**

     A. Lessons about democracy should begin in the primary grades and continue at every grade or level to the completion of high school.

     B. Lessons about democracy should be in various school subjects.

     C. Lessons about democracy should be about the history of democracy in courses on world history, European history, and the history of particular countries, especially the student's own country.

  VII. **The involvement of students in extracurricular activities that can be connected to the formal teaching and learning experiences required by the curriculum and conducted by teachers in the classrooms**

     A. Participation in student government activities provides opportunities for learning democracy by doing it.

     B. Democratic skills and dispositions through extracurricular activities enhance an ethos or spirit of democracy when the organization demonstrates these skills and dispositions.

  VIII. **Teacher-led discussions of current events and issues in an open classroom in which the environment is conducive to and supportive of a free exchange of information and ideas, and where there is mutual tolerance for diverse opinions**

     A. The teacher should establish a democratic ethos in the classroom, which encourages free and open expressions of ideas, security for freedom of inquiry, and respect for the dignity and worth of each person in the group.

     B. Discussions should emphasize the primary importance of content or subject matter of current events and public issues anchored in core concepts.

  IX. **The teaching of democracy and democratic citizenship comparatively and internationally**

     A. Teachers teach democracy in schools realistically and responsibly by teaching it globally and internationally.

     B. The main method of teaching and learning is the comparative method of analysis and appraisal.

     C. Teachers compare the wide range of institutional and constitutional designs and political practices across many different countries of the world.

     D. Teachers examine various examples from different countries, which represent variations on the common themes or principles by which we distinguish democratic and undemocratic governments.

     E. Comparative methods develop a useful method of inquiry among students.

     F. Three main types of comparisons can be made in global and international studies of democracy:

1. Warranted categories by which to distinguish a democracy from a nondemocracy
2. Justifiable categories (concepts) to compare and contrast various democratic countries and thereby to appraise the extent to which particular countries are more or less democratic
3. Compare and contrast constitutions, institutions, and participation of citizens in various democratic countries to understand the various ways democracy is practiced

X. **The effective preparation of teachers in terms of the knowledge, skills, and virtues of democratic citizenship**
   A. University-based teacher education programs should emphasize education for democracy.
   B. Teachers must be well prepared to teach democracy and democratic citizenship.

Source: From John J. Patrick, ed., "Essential Elements of Education for Democracy: What Are They and Why Should They Be at the Core of the Curriculum in Schools?," http://www.civiced.org/pdfs/EEOEforDemocracy.pdf

Activity 4.5   Teaching English Learners: Moving the Past into the Present

This chart provides four broad ways to help English language learners. Identify two suggestions in each category that will be most helpful in your teaching situation. What additional strategies would you include? How might the suggestions be utilized with respect to Ross E. Dunn's "Patterns of Change" Model for course organization? How might the strategies be incorporated under John Patrick's core concepts in Activity 4.4? How might the strategies be related to the NAEP U.S. history framework or the world history National Standards?

Incorporate Students' Point of View	Extra Help	Teacher Strategies/ Awareness	Providing Written Material
Have students bring an artifact(s) from their country related to a lesson and let them share it.	Spend time with students outside or after class.	Spend more time educating teachers in a second language, i.e., Spanish.	Give students guided notes for lectures and guided reviews for written assignments.
Talk about global events in class to eliminate racial sterotypes.	Encourage other students to serve as tutors.	Promote diversity within the teaching profession.	Create reading guides that include key terms and people.
Encourage students to speak about issues studied in class.	Involve translators and ESL assistants in the classroom.	Be patient with English language learners' language skills in addition to teaching history.	Make sure all directions and expectations are written and state them three times.
Assign research topics that help students think and write.	Practice English through small-group (first) and large-group	Do not assume that everyone has the same background knowledge.	Give students copies of overheads or notes from the board.
		Use images and visual aids (e.g., maps, artifacts, content/ graphic organizers) because they are a universal language.	Modify tests/quizzes

Incorporate Students' Point of View	Extra Help	Teacher Strategies/ Awareness	Providing Written Material
Practice English through small-group (first) and large-group discussions. Assign a "daily question" that helps students practice language skills.	discussions. Use technology such as automatic translation via headsets. Find a textbook in the student's language.	Look for outside help with English language learners. Have students paraphrase instructions/assignments in class to ensure understanding. Use various means of assessment (e.g., role-plays, posters, oral testing) to allow for learning differences. Use technology (e.g., software for ESL students). Make students take notes before giving them a written handout to ensure that they practice writing and are attentive in class. Repeat all directions in writing aloud three times.	with word banks. Modify assessment (e.g., less choices or multiple-choice exams or giving students extra time).

REVIEWING THE CHAPTER

1. Create a Venn diagram to illustrate the similarities and differences between the two teachers mentioned at the beginning of this chapter.

2. What role does chronology play in the organization of history courses?

3. Based on the history courses you have completed, which vital themes will you use to organize your courses?

4. What are the advantages and disadvantages of diachronic and synchronic approaches in teaching history?

5. Which model of world history do you find most appealing? Why?

5
Lesson and Unit Planning

Look, the school gives you a textbook. That's my lesson plan. The school pays a lot of money for those books. Teaching history is simple. You teach a chapter a week—most of the time. And each chapter has sections. I can have students read one section on one day, maybe two sections on another day. I vary my teaching by using the review questions at the end of each section.

—Eighteen-year experienced teacher, 2001

I plan my lessons every day. I believe it is important for me to write out what I want my students to know and be able to do. Lesson plans help me teach conceptually and thematically. I can ensure that I vary my instruction and that my students and I can see the bigger picture. I have taught for five years, and I have a lesson plan for every lesson I have ever taught.

—Five-year experienced teacher, 2003

*T*he previous statements of teachers illustrate two very different views regarding lesson and unit planning. Some teachers reject outright the writing of lesson plans. Others regard lesson plan writing as essential to their reflective teaching. In every lesson, some planning should be evident if it is to be successful.

In this chapter we make several suggestions concerning the writing of lesson and unit plans. Although our suggestions blend well with formats in most methods courses and school districts, we do offer several unique aspects of lesson planning.

Focus Questions

1. What are the common features of all lesson plans?

2. How can history's vital themes and narratives and habits of mind help you prepare your lessons?

3. How are unit plans developed?

4. How does a unit plan matrix help you in your teaching?

Textbooks and Standards

Most students want to do well when they come into your classroom; you may be amazed at how many students actually enjoy history, especially when it engages them initially. Your planning is essential to maintain the sincere interest of motivated students. Your planning will also attract those groggy and unsteady class members and help them immediately start to think about the meaningful past.

A textbook, as you well know, can serve as a starting point. However, many reviewers of textbooks point out several frailties.[1] They are bland. The spice of human experience is diluted. Authors of textbooks rarely offer interpretations and many slam the door to uncertainty. The "metadiscourse," or suggestions of judgment, points of emphasis, doubts, and uncertainty are absent.[2]

Historians, in contrast to textbook authors, rely greatly on interpretation. When historians write monographs, they communicate with their readers by giving meaning to the past. They recognize uncertainty. Historians "hedge" with such words as *might, seem, appear, possible,* or *perhaps.* Well-written books of history imply that history is an investigation and that readers are co-investigators with the author.

When designing your lessons, use relevant portions of the textbook to supplement your teaching, but do not relinquish the scholarship you bring to the classroom. Consider integrating excerpts from well-written books published by historians.

National and state standards can also help you plan your teaching.[3] Keep in mind, however, the purpose of standards: to provide a basic framework that ensures that all students are exposed to content knowledge and ways of thinking and knowing. Although you should look to national and state standards for guidance in lesson planning, you cannot translate them directly into your lessons. The standards are not a mind-numbing checklist to plow through. Nor are they the great panacea. Rather, they should serve as powerful reminders of important core concepts, ideas, documents, and ways of thinking and knowing.[4]

A very bright preservice teacher once asked if every standard should constitute a lesson. He wanted to know how standards (and textbooks) could help him become a better teacher. Through discussion, he came to understand that standards are guidelines that highlight the ideas, documents, and ways of thinking and knowing that all students in a democracy should face and deliberate on.

Lesson Plans

There are many ways to write lesson plans. Nevertheless, lesson plans share some common characteristics no matter where you are teaching. As you write your lesson and unit plans, you should consider yourself a curriculum maker; that is, you need to write detailed plans that are so clear that someone else could use them to teach your lesson. Your plans should include lecture notes and key questions to ask your students when you lead discussions. Your plans should also include copies of your textual primary sources (edited) and image primary sources as well as analysis guides.

An ideal lesson plan should:

1. Have a title
2. Have a two-paragraph focus statement
3. Identify one of the vital themes and narratives or NCSS themes
4. Identify a habit of mind and/historical thinking skill
5. Include instructional and expressive objectives (especially the latter)
6. Make connections to your state's learning standards
7. Include procedures for the lesson, which include an introduction, the body of the lesson and major activities, and a conclusion frequently including a means of assessment
8. Identify the method of assessment
9. Provide a list of sources and supporting materials

Keep in mind that vital themes and narratives as well as habits of mind serve respectively as organizers of content knowledge and ways of thinking to help your students enter the past. You need to consider the interactive instructional strategies you will use and the formal as well as informal ways you will assess your students. All should be interwoven seemlessly into your lesson.

Focus Statement

The Ideas for the History Classroom feature illustrates the format for a formal lesson plan. Once you have decided on a title for your lesson, write a focus statement. We prescribe that you write two paragraphs.

Your first paragraph should clearly identify how the content of your lesson relates to a vital theme. The vital theme organizes the larger ideas of the lesson and helps in the analysis and synthesis of those ideas.

Your second paragraph should identify a habit of mind you plan to emphasize as your students enter the past. The habit of mind you choose illuminates the content and vital theme because you are asking your students to read a primary source or to engage their historical imaginations as a historian would. You may want to stress the avoidance of present-mindedness as the habit of mind that you want your students to apply as they consider what James Madison and others endured to bring about the U.S. Constitution and the Bill of Rights. Your students will know that there are three branches of government. How will you help them recognize the complexities of the executive and legislative branches? Madison had no fixed idea of what the executive branch would look like. Would it be one, two, or three executives? The Virginia Plan was not explicit. Madison also proposed a federal negative (veto) on state legislative acts. Did he make such proposals because he was an overzealous nationalist? Or was his intention to protect the rights of minorities in states where there were abuses? Madison thought many states' bills of rights to be mere "parchment barriers." Originally, he opposed a bill of rights in the Constitution. Yet it was he who argued before the First Congress in June of 1789 for just such a bill of rights.

Ideas for the History Classroom

Lesson Plan Format

Title of Lesson

Focus   Two paragraphs should summarize the purpose of your lesson and discuss appropriate themes and habits of mind. One way to discuss the themes and habits of mind is to follow this procedure in writing the paragraphs: The first paragraph summarizes the content of the lesson and organizes the content around a vital theme and narrative, a social science concept, or an NCSS theme; the second paragraph explains how students will enter the past by way of one or two habits of mind and become historical thinkers.

Vital Theme   Drawn from one of the six vital themes and narratives of NCHE.

Habits of Mind   Drawn from one or two of the habits of mind as identified by NCHE.

NCSS Theme   Drawn from NCSS standards.

Objectives   Generally, two types of educational objectives are written: instructional and expressive. Instructional objectives specify unambiguously a particular behavior (skill, item of knowledge) the student is to acquire after completing a learning activity. An instructional objective is observable. The behavior is isomorphic; that is, all students will do approximately the same thing. An expressive objective does not specify the behavior the student is to acquire after a learning activity; rather, an expressive objective describes an encounter by identifying a situation or problem to cope with. The encounter provides an invitation to explore. Diversity is expected to occur rather than homogeneity. An expressive objective serves as a theme around which understanding and skills learned earlier can be expanded.

Here are examples of both instructional and expressive objectives:

Instructional: Describe the three authors of the *Federalist* essays. Explain the differences between federalists and antifederalists.

Expressive: Interpret the meaning of the Tenth *Federalist*. Visit a museum and discuss what was of interest there.

Some suggestions: Write two to three objectives. Avoid beginning objectives with the words *list* or *name*. Objectives beginning with *list* and *name*, are low level and do not cause thinking. Objectives should cause students to think.

Students will be able to:

1. Explain . . .
2. Create . . .

Learning Standards	Identify and explain the state learning standards that relate to this lesson. Identify one type of historical thinking from the National Standards for History.
Procedures	Every lesson should have at least three parts: a beginning (sometimes called the set induction or cognitive set), a middle, and an end. The lesson might begin by showing a picture for students to analyze or having students read a brief quote and asking them to identify a central idea or think about the meaning of the quote. The middle might include a lecture (notes are included here) or a discussion (questions are included here) or a debate or a simulation. The end might include students creating a poster related to the content of the lesson. The end pulls together the lesson and bridges the lesson for today to the lesson for the next day. The end also serves as a way to assess what students know and can do. Although quizzes are typically used to assess students, you might consider other ways to assess. For example, have students analyze a picture (different from one shown at the beginning of a lesson). Or students can analyze a cartoon or a quote from someone who is famous or not so famous. Or students can create their own picture or cartoon or write a paragraph reflecting on what they learned.
Assessment	Assessment should inform you and your students of the students' knowledge, reasoning, and communication; that is, your students should be able to communicate what they know and how they think about a topic, idea, or event.
Sources, Materials, and Accommodations	Provide a list of the sources you used to create this lesson and appropriate materials and accommodations. Please note that all photographs, political cartoons, excerpts from documents, and maps (for example) should be attached at the end of the lesson. All documents attached should look professional; that is, all black markings on the edges from photocopying should be removed.

He was booed and reportedly said that it was one of his worst experiences. He prevailed, however, undaunted by the criticisms. A bill of rights eventually was proposed by the 1789 Congress and ratified in 1791 by the necessary three-fourths of the states. Many of your students will think a bill of rights in the U.S. Constitution was a surety. How will you engage your students in the complexities of events so they can experience how others felt at a particular time and place?

Objectives

Your lesson plans should include both **instructional** and **expressive** educational objectives.[5] An instructional objective specifies unambiguously a particular behavior, skill, or item of knowledge that *all* students should acquire after a learning activity. The behavior is isomorphic in that all your students are expected to do approximately the same thing. Your expectations for instructional objectives are a homogeneity of answers. The following are two examples of an instructional objective: Describe the three authors of the *Federalist* essays or explain the differences between federalists and antifederalists.

An expressive objective does not specify the behavior the student is to acquire after a learning activity; rather, an expressive objective describes an encounter by describing a situation or problem with which your students must cope. The encounter invites your students to explore and construct an interpretation. Diversity is expected to occur. All your students' thinking is not expected to be the same.

An expressive objective serves as a theme around which understanding and learned skills can be expanded. The following is an example of an expressive objective: Interpret the meaning of the Tenth *Federalist*. "Interpreting" the meaning of the Tenth *Federalist* compels your students to emphasize the importance of such words and sentences as "faction," "Liberty is to faction, what air is to fire," and "Extend the sphere, and you take in a greater variety of parties and interests." Your students will emphasize varying points as they give meaning to Publius' (James Madison's) words and phrases. What was James Madison thinking in November 1787 when he wrote the Tenth *Federalist*?

Beginning, Middle, and End

Every lesson should consider state standards, of course, and every lesson usually follows a format. Usually lessons have at least three parts: a beginning (sometimes called a set induction or cognitive set), a middle, and an end. Your lesson might begin by introducing a primary source such as a picture for students to analyze. Or it might begin with you asking your students to read a brief quote and calling on them to identify a central idea or to think about the meaning of the quote in the context of its period. You might use a think-pair-share strategy (details in a later chapter) as a way to elicit a discussion about your primary source, an image, or a brief quote.

The middle of your lesson might include a 10- to 12-minute lecture using an advance organizer as a generalization, theme, or concept. You might arrange your students at stations to discuss and analyze documents in relation to your primary source. Or you might involve your students in a discussion, debate, or simulation.

The end of your lesson might include having your students create a poster related to the content of the lesson. Or your students might look for documents using the Internet. The end pulls together the lesson, and makes a bridge to the next day's lesson, a key component that beginning teachers often forget.

Assessment

At the end of the lesson you must also assess what your students know and can do (keep in mind that you can also assess throughout your lesson as you listen to discussions and watch your students interact). Although quizzes are typically used to assess students' knowledge and understanding, you might consider other ways to assess. For example, you might have your students analyze a picture (different from the one shown at the beginning of the lesson). Or you can have students analyze a political cartoon or a quote from someone who is famous or not so famous. You might have students create their own political cartoon or draw their own picture and write about it, reflecting on what they have learned. Or your students might find something in a newspaper or magazine. Assessment should inform you and your students of their knowledge and reasoning and their ability to communicate what they know and think.

Finally, you should make a list of the sources—primary and secondary—that you are using for your lesson. You should also identify the ways in which you will accommodate students with special needs in your classroom.[6]

Creating a Unit Plan

Unit plans, like lesson plans, are creative endeavors. Unit planning is important in teaching and learning and is part of all courses that are offered at schools. Creating your unit plan entails more than identifying a chapter from a textbook and the various sections of a chapter. Successful unit planning requires organization, thinking, and planning. Following are some general areas you might consider as you develop your unit plan.

Once you know what your course assignment is and how long it will be (a year, a semester, a quarter, or another time period), you have to make decisions about the content, themes, concepts, values, and skills you want your students to learn in your course. Ask yourself, what do I want my students to take away with them from this course? How will the course I teach affect my students' lives? Is this unit important in history or in the social sciences? How will I go about ensuring that this course is organized and that it ties together important content and skills? How will I assess what my students know, think, and are able to do? You can always draw from the National Standards for History and the National Assessment for Educational Progress framework to help you determine the importance of your periods and eras of history.

Within the time frame of the course, you must determine how much time to give to each unit. You will need to give attention to the sequencing of learning experiences: Will the learning experiences be presented in chronological sequence? As selected themes? Using the first-, second-, and third-order documents? (In Chapter 7 we describe this systematic approach.) As problems-focused topics? As area studies? Or in some conceptual order? Most likely, your instruction will include combinations of these arrangements.

You will also need to decide how you will carry out your instruction: Will you lecture? Lead discussions? Involve your students in group activities? Use cooperative learning? Written primary sources? Pictures? Poems? Music? Tables and graphs? Docudramas? Will you integrate literature into your history class? Will learning technologies be part of your unit plan? Your students need to experience a variety of sources. What sources such as pictures, political cartoons, maps, charts and graphs, letters, and diaries will you include in your lessons? History is not a ritual to be practiced in school; nor is teaching history a ritual of worksheets. Reflect thoughtfully upon your choices so they blend purposefully and artfully with the content of your lesson.

Finally, each state has developed learning standards for history and the social sciences. How will you make sure your students meet the standards of the state in which you teach? What are the outcomes you expect of your students? How will you assess what your students know and can do? What vital theme and narrative organizes the content of the lesson? What habits of mind serve as entry points into the lesson? What critical thinking skills will you emphasize in the lesson? Which of the 10 NCSS themes does your lesson address?

Units vary in length. Most are a minimum of 2 weeks long; some are much longer. We suggest that you create a unit for at least a 2-week period. It should consist of six to nine lessons and various forms of assessment. Each lesson should follow the lesson plan format mentioned previously. Your completed unit plan should include the following:

1. A title page for the unit with unit title, your name, and the course in which the unit plan will be taught
2. A summary (a minimum of one page and a maximum of five pages) explaining the following:

   Why the content matters to students

   What content preceded this unit and what content will follow

   A list of primary sources important in this unit

   Major projects or activities for the unit

   Unit objectives related to standards, usually written as expressive objectives

   A capsule summary of each lesson plan

   Methods of assessment

   Sources and materials
3. A completed unit plan matrix
4. Individual lesson plans
5. A unit assessment

In your summary you should identify a vital theme and narrative (or if you prefer, a social studies theme) to organize the content of your unit. Make sure to describe your theme and habits of mind clearly. You should also identify core primary sources in your unit plan.

Unit Plan Matrix

A unit plan matrix is a helpful reminder of the varieties of themes, objectives, sources, and assessments you can use when you create a unit plan. The Ideas for the History Classroom feature illustrates a unit plan matrix.

The unit plan matrix serves two purposes. First, it reminds you to address the learning styles of your students in various ways. The matrix identifies visual and print sources of information to organize a variety of different types of learning activities. For example, the teacher is reminded that some students learn best through the interpretation of graphs and charts. It also reminds teachers that some students learn best when they create charts, graphs, or other visual representations of their understanding. Second, it captures visually the variety of ways you integrate historical content and thinking in your unit. The unit plan matrix is a convenient way to show principals or district officials your plans for teaching history.

Unit Reviews

A creative, interactive way to conduct unit reviews is to use stations with individual prompts that engage your students in content. Write questions on butcher-block paper and post the paper at stations around the classroom (on the walls, table, or desks). Organize your students into groups of two to four and have them move from station to station. Give each group a different colored marker

---

Ideas for the History Classroom

Unit Plan Matrix

	Lesson 1	Lesson 2	Lesson 3	Lesson 4	Lesson 5	Lesson 6	Lesson 7	Lesson 8	Lesson 9
Vital Theme and Narrative									
Habits of Mind									
Historical Thinking Skill									
NCSS Theme									
State Learning Goals/Type of Historical Thinking in National Standards for History									
Textual Primary Sources									
Secondary Sources									
Pictures/Photographs									
Political Cartoons									
Literature, Novel, Poem									
Music/Lyrics									
Maps									
Graphs and Tables									
Technology: Internet and CD-Rom									
Assessment: Objective and Alternative									

so that you can determine which group contributed to the ideas at each station. Tell your students that they will have 2 minutes to read the prompt at the first station and then respond as a group. After 2 minutes, groups rotate clockwise to the next station. Students must now read the prompt and the response of the group that preceded them. Each group should place a star next to the response they believe is best and then add to the list. This procedure continues until every group returns to its original station. The groups now review the lists at their original station and summarize the responses. In the summary students should point out the most important ideas.

Here are questions we use in the station activity. Please note that you can alter the wording in the prompts so they are germane to the content in the courses you teach. The subject of this activity is the Cold War.

1. In this box ⬛ are people, ideas, and events that all students and teachers think about when they discuss the Cold War. What is in the box?

2. The Cold War is like an iceberg [draw an iceberg]. Above the surface are visible characteristics of people, ideas, and events. What is above the surface? What is below the surface? That is, what is less evident to the public at the time in which the events occurred?

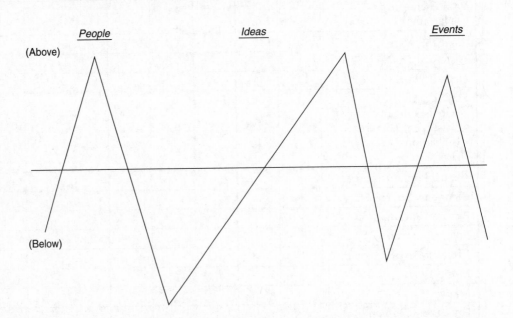

3. In the left-hand column list the central ideas of these primary sources: George F. Kennan's Long Telegram, Nikolai Novikov's Long Telegram, and Frank K. Roberts' Long Telegram. In the right-hand column list the evidence each man used to support his central idea.

George F. Kennan

Central Idea _____|_____ Evidence

Nikolai Novikov

Central Idea _____|_____ Evidence

Frank K. Roberts

Central Idea _____|_____ Evidence

4. There are many ways to explain to others how much you know about the start of the Cold War. Write the first sentence you would use in an essay to explain how the Cold War started or create a picture that illustrates how the Cold War started.

5. During the Cold War we lived in a bipolar world. What rules of behavior were followed during the Cold War? What rules were not always followed?

6. What are the key ideas you think all citizens should know about the Cold War?

7. Twenty-five years from now Americans will look back at the Cold War as a period of history. What will they remember?

8. The Cold War is like (name an animal or insect) because (explain).

Animal/Insect   Explanation

9. What essential skills did a Cold War leader/policy maker need to be effective?

10. Among your readings are primary sources and secondary sources. List the name of the primary source you think is most important. Explain why it is important. List the title of a secondary source. Explain why it is important.

Primary Source   Explanation

Secondary Source   Explanation
[might be your text
so have students select
a sentence/passage]

11. During the Cold War a great deal of tension existed between liberty and order. At what key turning points did liberty dominate order? At what key turning points did order dominate liberty? Explain.

Liberty over Order   Explanation

Order over Liberty   Explanation

12. In the left-hand column list positive adjectives that describe how primary sources tell us about the past. In the right-hand column are problems we have with primary sources and the story of the past.

Positives   Problems

Of course, you can modify the previous prompts for your unit review. You can use all or a few of the prompts. The station strategy avoids the overuse of the game "Jeopardy" as a review strategy or a long list of people, terms, and events. You may want to use study sheets to supplement the station strategy.

The station strategy can be used in other ways as well. For example, some teachers use stations to introduce a unit or to give a lecture. At each station are key ideas, themes, and concepts for the lecture. Students move from one station to the next to take notes that are organized around these larger ideas.

SUMMARY

Planning your lessons into the larger framework of a unit helps your students organize the past. Of course, you will always make adjustments in your unit plans and daily lessons.

First, lesson plans and unit plans are logical extensions of the knowledge, skills, and values you wish to teach students regarding a particular historical topic—such as the Cold War example.

Second, plan to integrate a complementary vital theme and narrative in your plans. This vital theme helps your students see a bigger picture and retain knowledge after instruction has been completed.

Third, use a habit of mind to actively engage students in historical thinking.

Fourth, use a variety of teaching strategies. In the next chapter we explore ways to assess what your students know and think about history and their abilities to communicate clearly their knowledge and understanding of the past.

TRANSLATING HISTORY INTO CLASSROOM PRACTICE

Activity 5.1   Lesson Plans and Effective Teaching

Some teachers scoff at formal lesson plans and believe that teaching history consists of merely covering the pages in a text. Consider the following statement of a teacher regarding the use of the textbook, films and film worksheets, or sources from the Internet.

> Look, the school gives you a textbook. That's my lesson plan. The school pays a lot of money for those books. Teaching history is simple. You teach a chapter a week—most of the time. And each chapter has sections. I can have students read one section on one day, maybe two sections on another day. I vary my teaching by using the review questions at the end of each section. The textbook company has great worksheets with tons of materials for me to give my students. I photocopy some of them and give them to the kids. Every once in a while, I show a movie. I like the 3-day movies. I make a worksheet for students on those days. My worksheets usually have 50 or so questions. I also use the Internet now. If I need a source—say, a court case

or a famous speech—I can find one, download it, and print it out for the kids. Sometimes they're pretty long. But everything all together keeps the kids occupied. The kids know what to expect. They're happy, and so am I.

1. If you were to advise this teacher, what suggestions would you make?
2. How does the statement violate the purposes of effective teaching?

Activity 5.2   Creating Prompts for a Stations Strategy

Decide on a unit you want to teach in U.S. or world history. Then read the prompts in the station strategy at the end of this chapter and modify the questions so they fit your unit. Create one of the following:

1. A review for the unit with questions at each station
2. A lecture with key ideas, themes, concepts, and primary sources at each station

REVIEWING THE CHAPTER

1. Describe the teaching strategies you encountered in your high school U.S. history course. Compare your experiences with those of your fellow students.
2. Compare the teaching strategies you encountered in high school with those described in this chapter.
3. What learning styles were most emphasized in your high school U.S. history course? How were they similar and different from your middle school history course?
4. What are the advantages and disadvantages of a station approach?

6 Creating Historical Understanding and Communication Through Performance Assessment

It isn't always easy to explain to my students (and their parents) how I assess their essays, posters drawn, role-playing, and participation in debates and discussions. After all, there is a degree of subjectivity. I needed a rubric to give my students structure while feeling they have ownership and creativity. I shared this rubric with my students and even at parent–teacher conferences. It gave me confidence when I met with a parent who happened to be a lawyer. I listened as he told me how to teach and how to grade essays. I then shared this rubric. He treated me differently from then on.

— Five-year experienced teacher, 2001

*W*hen teaching history or the social studies, you will be assessing your students in numerous ways. You will undoubtedly meet students who disagree with your judgments about what they know. You will also meet parents who may doubt the fairness of your evaluation, especially if you do not use standardized multiple choice tests.

This chapter provides a model and a rationale for the assessment of student learning of history. This model will reinforce your efforts whether you are a new teacher or a veteran who is rethinking what students should know about history and how they should be evaluated.

Focus Questions

1. How do means of assessment other than the traditional multiple-choice test help you assess your students' knowledge and understanding of history?

2. What are you expecting of your students when you assess them?

3. How can you create an effective authoritative rubric that you can share with all of your students?

Your curriculum planning, choice of classroom methodology, and means to assess student learning are inextricably linked. Forms of assessment that involve only recall of discrete information are likely to encourage teaching methods that emphasize low-level cognition. Further, traditional forms of assessing students' knowledge of history neither prompt students to reveal all they know about the subject nor challenge them to learn more. Thus, the traditional methods of assessments must be complemented by new methods that can reinvigorate and improve the teaching and learning of history in your classroom.

Traditional forms of assessing students' knowledge of historical facts—true–false, fill-in-the-blank, matching, short identification, and multiple-choice questions—should be complemented, if not supplanted, by new methods of assessment (see Figure 6.1 for definitions of four types of assessments). If you have a plan of assessment in mind as you develop your objectives for a course, unit of instruction, or lesson plan, you will be in a better position to select the best means of evaluation.

Often identified by educators as performance-based assessment or authentic assessment, performance assessment consistency in the history classroom requires students to accomplish complex and significant tasks by applying their prior knowledge and skills within a predetermined amount of time.[1] Although reformers in history education disagree over terminology, they agree on two ideas. First, they want students to think seriously about the past. And second, they want to engage students in meaningful activities that indicate a reasonable grasp of subject matter.

Performance assessment activities provide you and your students with the opportunity to do just that. Performance assessment accompanied by a history rubric can be both a *diagnostic* and an *instructional* tool.[2]

Performance Assessment and Historical Literacy

Performance assessment can be a diagnostic tool to improve both your instruction and your students' understanding of history. Performance assessment activities reveal information about three dimensions of your students' historical literacy. First,

FIGURE 6.1 Four Types of Assessments.

1. **Standardized:**	Multiple-choice, fill-in-the-blank, matching, true–false
2. **Alternative:**	Applies to any and all assessment that differs from multiple-choice, one-shot approaches that characterize most standardized tests and many classroom assessments
3. **Authentic:**	Conveys the idea that assessment should engage students in applying knowledge and skills in the same way they are used in the real world
4. **Performance:**	A broad term encompassing both alternative and authentic assessment

students who complete performance assessment activities demonstrate their *knowledge* of historical facts, themes, and ideas. Second, students demonstrate their ability to *reason;* that is, to analyze, evaluate, and synthesize historical evidence. And third, students demonstrate their ability to *communicate* their historical knowledge and reasoning to a wider audience.

In short, performance assessment provides an excellent opportunity to assess the traditional cognitive development of students. Moreover, it offers a wide variety of effective teaching and learning techniques that engage your students in history lessons while at the same time tapping their powerful minds and allowing them to use their multiple intelligences to communicate what they know and how they think.[3] Performance assessment is a perfect vehicle for developing a pedagogy that addresses the different ways your students learn. Using a rubric with which students are familiar, you can inform your students how they can improve their knowledge, reasoning, and communication skills.

Performance assessment with a rubric serves an additional purpose. It can become an *instructional* device in your teaching. A rubric that includes the three dimensions of historical knowledge, reasoning, and communication can be used as a ladder of success through which your students can ascend in their historical literacy. By letting your students know in advance the standards and levels in your rubric, you can coach them to greater levels of historical sophistication. Finally, performance assessment helps each of your students develop a foundation of durable historical knowledge to draw on in the future.

Knowledge Dimension

Each dimension of a student's historical literacy has its own characteristics. *Knowledge* of historical evidence is the prerequisite your students need to demonstrate their ability in the other two dimensions. Students who have developed historical knowledge are able to identify, define, and describe important concepts, facts, and details. The study of history, however, must extend beyond the acquisition of discrete pieces of historical information. Although mastering the contours of a given narrative and knowing about significant individuals and events are important, students must also know about the universal themes and ideas that cut across the human experience. These themes and ideas help students differentiate between what is significant and what is insignificant in the historical record. The National Council for History Education has identified what it calls six vital themes and narratives[4] to help teachers organize the knowledge domain of a history curriculum. We identified these themes in Chapter 1 (see Figure 1.2).

The six vital themes and narratives set the context for both explaining historical processes and events and understanding why they matter. These themes and narratives serve as a schematic framework that your students can use to organize historical knowledge that they may draw on in the future.

Reasoning Dimension

Historical facts and themes, approached through informed questions, are a point of departure for demonstrating your students' ability to reason. *Reasoning* makes the facts and themes meaningful, thereby bringing about a deeper understanding of the subject. Reasoning is an active process, an intellectual transaction between a student and information. Reasoning involves varying levels of thought: the translation, interpretation, application, analysis, synthesis, and evaluation of information. Reasoning requires your students to discover relationships among facts and generalizations, and values and opinions, so they can solve problems, make judgments, reach logical conclusions and organize historical knowledge in their memory. You will recognize these abilities from lists of critical thinking skills. However, just as a distinction can be made between isolated, inert facts and more fully developed historical knowledge, a distinction must also be made between critical thinking skills and historical reasoning or thinking. Thoughtful reasoning ought to be the principal aim of historical study. The National Council for History Education provided a useful explanation of historical reasoning in its description of 13 habits of mind.[5] In Chapter 1 we identified these habits of mind (see Figure 1.1 page 15).

The National Standards for History (Basic Edition, 1996) identified five Standards in Historical Thinking that require students

> to raise questions and to marshal evidence in support of their answers; to read historical narratives and fiction; to consult historical documents, journals, diaries, artifacts, historic sites, and other records from the past; and to do so imaginatively—taking into account the time and places in which these records were created and comparing the multiple points of view of those on the scene at the time.[6]

The five Standards in Historical Thinking are: chronological thinking, historical comprehension, historical analysis and interpretation, historical research capabilities, and historical issues analysis and decision making.[7]

Communication Dimension

Effective *communication* of historical knowledge and historical reasoning requires students to organize their thoughts. Effective communication also involves a historically literate listener or group of listeners. One hallmark of effective history teaching is a classroom in which the ideas of one student spark a conversation among students using the currency of historical knowledge. In recounting the story of the past, a student must have a clearly defined thesis and an interesting narrative that tells what happened in an informed way. A well-organized presentation also supplies relevant examples to support main ideas and offers conclusions and a synthesis based on an analysis of historical sources. Furthermore, evidence of your student's knowledge and reasoning must always be apparent in an effective presentation. Performance assessment in history offers a wide variety of ways for your students to communicate their knowledge and reasoning with one another, including analyzing a primary source, drawing political cartoons, creating newspapers, participating in historical simulations, and writing research papers. As an imaginative history teacher, you can create dozens of additional activities that are appropriate for assessment at the end of a class session, during a unit of study, or at the conclusion of a semester.

Many teachers, however, do not take advantage of performance assessment activities to evaluate their students' levels of knowledge, reasoning, and communication, and as a means to initiate meaningful student discussions. Some teachers do not realize the full potential of their current instructional activities as a reliable means for assessment. Others are uncomfortable using multiple assessment activities because they do not have a systematic means to assess a variety of student performances. Teachers may have a general sense of what constitutes an outstanding report or historical exhibit, but they lack established criteria or a rubric that provides specific feedback about their students' abilities in each of the three dimensions. Moreover, teachers sometimes use rubrics borrowed from other subjects, which are inappropriate for teaching history.

A History Rubric

In A History Rubric for Performance Assessment, we offer a **rubric** and general criteria that you can use to assess your students' historical knowledge, reasoning, and communication.[8] This model is an analytic rubric: It allows you as a history teacher simultaneously to assess student performance in each of the three interrelated dimensions. Each level is defined by several criteria, which reflect each of your students' abilities and skills. Collectively, levels 6, 5, and 4 describe students whose knowledge, reasoning, and communication skills are *developed*. Collectively, levels 3, 2, and 1 describe students whose knowledge, reasoning, and communication skills are still *developing*. Level 6 describes the work of a student who exhibits the most developed skills; level 1 describes the work of a student with the lowest level of developing skills. The gap between level 3 and level 4 is wider than the gap between any of the other levels because it differentiates between students whose skills are still developing and students whose skills are developed.

An analytic rubric is especially appropriate and useful for assessment in history education. You and other teachers know that students may perform at a more or less developed level in one dimension than they do in another. For example, when a student analyzes a primary source document, he or she may demonstrate knowledge at a level 6, reasoning at a level 5, and communication at a level 3. An analytic rubric allows you to take these differences into account when assessing your students. An analytic rubric also benefits your students. It shows them their strengths and weaknesses in each dimension, thereby indicating areas they must work at to improve their historical knowledge, reasoning, and communication.

Students who have developed knowledge—levels 6, 5, and 4—are able to demonstrate their ability to identify, define, and describe key historical concepts, themes, issues, and ideas; they show their awareness of the connection between key

A History Rubric for Performance Assessment

KNOWLEDGE	REASONING	COMMUNICATION
Knowledge of evidence from history: facts/ supporting details, themes, issues, and concepts/ideas	*Analysis, evaluation, and synthesis of evidence*	*Demonstrates knowledge and reasoning through oral, written, visual, dramatic, or mixed media presentation*
6	**6**	**6**
▪ Key concepts/vital themes and narratives/issues/ideas are thoroughly identified, defined, and described ▪ Significant facts/supporting details are included and accurately described ▪ Has no factual inaccuracies	▪ Identifies and logically organizes all relevant evidence ▪ Uses appropriate and comprehensive historical thinking skills including habits of mind to analyze, evaluate, and synthesize evidence ▪ Reaches informed conclusions based on the evidence	▪ All ideas in the presentation are expressed in a way that provides evidence of the student's knowledge and reasoning processes ▪ Presentation is well focused with a well-defined thesis ▪ Presentation shows substantial evidence of organization ▪ Presentation shows attention to the details of specific performance conventions
5	**5**	**5**
▪ Key concepts/vital themes and narratives/issues/ideas are considerably identified, defined, and described ▪ Facts/supporting details are included ▪ Has only minor factual inaccuracies	▪ Identifies and logically organizes most of the relevant evidence ▪ Uses appropriate historical thinking skills including habits of mind to analyze, evaluate, and synthesize evidence ▪ Reaches informed conclusions based on the evidence	▪ Most ideas in the presentation are expressed in a way that provides evidence of the student's knowledge and reasoning processes ▪ Presentation demonstrates a focus and thesis with minimal narrative gaps ▪ Presentation shows sufficient evidence of organization ▪ Presentation has minor mistakes in attention to the details of specific performance conventions
4	**4**	**4**
▪ Key concepts/vital themes and narratives/issues are partially identified, defined, and described ▪ Some facts/supporting details are included	▪ Identifies and organizes some of the relevant evidence ▪ Uses partial historical thinking skills including habits of mind to analyze, evaluate, and synthesize evidence	▪ Some ideas in the presentation are expressed in a way that provides evidence of the student's knowledge and reasoning processes ▪ Presentation demonstrates a focus and thesis with several narrative gaps

- May have a major factual inaccuracy, but most information is correct

3
- Some key concepts/vital themes and narratives/issues/ideas are identified, defined, and described
- Few facts/supporting details are included
- Has some correct and some incorrect information

2
- Few key concepts/vital themes and narratives/issues/ideas are identified, defined, and described
- Facts/supporting details are not included
- Information is largely inaccurate or irrelevant

1
- Key concepts/vital themes and narratives/issues/ideas are not identified, defined, and described
- Facts/supporting details are not included
- Information is inaccurate or absent

- Reaches informed conclusions based on evidence

3
- Identifies some of the relevant evidence but omits other evidence
- Uses incomplete historical thinking skills including habits of mind to analyze, evaluate, and synthesize evidence
- Reaches incomplete conclusions based on the evidence

2
- Identifies little relevant evidence and omits most of the evidence
- Uses unclear or inappropriate historical thinking skills including habits of mind to analyze, evaluate, and synthesize evidence
- Reaches inaccurate conclusions based on the evidence

1
- Important evidence relevant to the problem is not identified
- Historical thinking skills including habits of mind are absent
- Conclusions are lacking or unclear

- Presentation demonstrates adequate evidence of organization
- Presentation has mistakes in attention to the details of specific performance conventions

3
- Few ideas in the presentation are expressed in a way that provides evidence of the student's knowledge and reasoning processes
- Presentation demonstrates an inadequate focus and thesis
- Presentation demonstrates inadequate evidence of organization
- Presentation has insufficient attention to the details of specific performance conventions

2
- Most ideas in the presentation are not clearly expressed
- Presentation demonstrates insufficient focus and a poorly defined thesis
- Presentation demonstrates insufficient evidence of organization
- Presentation has multiple mistakes in attention to the details of specific performance conventions

1
- Expression of all ideas in the presentation is unclear
- Presentation demonstrates little focus and lacks a thesis
- Presentation demonstrates little evidence of organization
- Presentation has no attention to the details of specific performance conventions

m Frederick D. Drake and Lawrence W. McBride, "Reinvigorating the Teaching of History through Alternative Assess- History Teacher 30, no. 2 (February 1997): 145–173. Used with permission.

facts and supporting details; and they are accurate in their use of facts and details. The levels are differentiated by the degree to which students can demonstrate their knowledge, that is, by being thorough, inclusive, and accurate. Similarly, students who are developing knowledge—levels 3, 2, and 1—are unable to demonstrate their ability to identify, define, and describe key historical concepts, themes, issues, and ideas; they show an inadequate awareness of the connection between key facts and supporting details; and they are largely inaccurate in their use of facts and details.

To demonstrate developed reasoning abilities, students must be able to organize evidence and select and apply an appropriate method for analysis, evaluation, and synthesis. To begin the effective analysis and evaluation of historical evidence, whether that evidence is located in a printed document, song, poem, picture, or statistical table, students must ask relevant questions. Similarly, they must be able to analyze effectively assertions made by classmates in discussions. Students with developed reasoning abilities also demonstrate the use of the habits of mind, which are continually nurtured by the study of history. These habits of mind not only demonstrate how the student thinks about historical sources, they also reveal aspects of your student's intellectual character. That is, students who possess habits of mind display self-discipline as thinkers and can interpret historical content and engage in thoughtful discourse about their inquiry. Although all developed students must be able to reach an informed conclusion, there are several ways to differentiate among students' historical reasoning skills at levels 6, 5, and 4. Differentiation among these higher levels is a matter of the degree to which a student can identify, analyze, and organize evidence and then construct a new historical synthesis.

Ultimately, students at level 6 methodically analyze and evaluate the evidence, thereby linking themselves with historians who seek answers to two fundamental questions: How has the past affected the present? and Why does history matter? Students at a level 6 understand the significance of historians' questions and the tentative nature of their judgments. They recognize how historians' interpretations rest on differing assumptions, constructing a past that changes over time, and they recognize that each preceding generation's inquiries about the past carry forward the implications of its predecessors' knowledge and reasoning. A student at level 4 identifies and analyzes the evidence from one perspective—but one that is still sufficient for them to evaluate successfully the sources and combine their new knowledge with what they have already learned.

Students who are still developing their reasoning ability show important deficiencies. They fail to organize information for proper analysis and may omit evidence. A developing student may also select an inappropriate method for analyzing, evaluating, and synthesizing evidence. Students who are in the process of developing reasoning skills have difficulty thinking critically and applying the habits of mind when answering historical questions. For example, when reading a newspaper editorial from a Radical Republican newspaper dealing with the impeachment of Andrew Johnson in 1868, they may accept the editorial's declarations at face value, as opposed to students with developed reasoning who recognize the difference between fact and conjecture, and evidence and assertion. Finally, the inability to reach a reasonable, informed conclusion is indicative of a student who is still in the developing stage of historical reasoning.

Your choice of teaching methods plays a central role in nurturing historical understanding in individual students and facilitating the communication of this understanding among students. As a history teacher, sometimes in conjunction with your students, you establish the context, or audience, for your students' presentations: an in-class or out-of-class essay, an oral report presented to classmates, a letter to the newspaper, or an exhibit or model placed on display at a local business or historical society. Your students may wish to develop a history project to enter in local, state, or national academic competitions such as National History Day. Other academic competitions, for example, the Model United Nations and *We the People . . . The Citizen and the Constitution* provide avenues for students to communicate significant historical knowledge and thinking. Each communication technique has its own convention, which you should take into account. For example, when assessing an oral report, you may want to consider the effective use of voice, gestures, eye contact, and visual aids. When assessing a student-made exhibit, you may want to consider the use of color, neatness, captions, and the selection of appropriate pictures, photographs, maps, and other materials.

The student who has developed ability in communication presents historical knowledge and reasoning in a clear and organized fashion. The presentation also takes into account the appropriate conventions for the selected activity. A historical essay, for example, has everything from a clear thesis statement to the appropriate use of footnotes or endnotes and bibliographical citations. A higher assessment, levels 6, 5, and 4, is determined by the degree of clarity and organization, the quality of illustrations and supporting examples, and the power of the conclusion. That is, the main ideas and reasoning processes are well developed and clearly articulated. Finally, a presentation at the highest level of development meets all the convention standards.

Students who are still developing their communication skills lack the ability to present historical knowledge and reasoning clearly and effectively in an organized presentation. That is, a student who is developing does not successfully provide a thesis or a clearly written narrative that is supported with evidence. Moreover, the student does not present an informed conclusion and demonstrates greater difficulty in responding to the ideas of other students. Lastly, a developing student neglects the details of the performance convention that he or she has selected as a means to communicate his or her historical knowledge and reasoning. The differences among students performing at levels 3, 2, or 1 are also a matter of degree in each of the criteria.

Recommendations Regarding the Use of Rubrics

Our recommendations regarding the use of rubrics are based on our own experiences.[9] As you create assessment activities, you should ask the following questions:

- Does the activity reflect my teaching goals?
- Does the activity adequately reflect the historical content and habits of mind that I expect my students to learn and use?

- Does the activity enable my students to demonstrate their development in historical knowledge, reasoning, and communication?
- Does the activity motivate students to demonstrate their capabilities?

You should reveal the rubric to your students because it contains the criteria that your students will have to meet. Both you and your students should know in advance the criteria you are looking for in each dimension. Students should be informed about a lesson's or unit's content; they should be advised about which combination of habits of mind provide the entry point for thinking about that content; and they should consider which performance medium affords them the best opportunity to demonstrate what they know and can do. For you as a teacher, therefore, the rubric serves as a *diagnostic* tool; for students, it establishes the parameters for attaining success. However, although rubrics serve as a foundation for historical thinking, they should not serve to constrain students' thinking. Creative historical thought cannot be organized into a pattern that is simply replicated in each new situation. You will need to practice using the rubric, and you will need to coach your students about the best ways to demonstrate their abilities in each of the three categories.

Samples of Performance Assessment

We conclude this chapter with representative samples of a performance assessment activity and show how the history rubric can be used to assess student work.[10] On page 123 we provide a "prompt," or directions, for an activity in world history. An *unedited* student response to the prompt is shown on pages 123 to 126. On page 126 is a prompt for the same activity applied to U.S. history. Four *unedited* student responses to the U.S. history prompt are shown on pages 127–131. The four student responses illustrate various levels of the knowledge, reasoning, and communication dimensions. Briefly, in establishing the criteria for knowledge in the Theodora activity (see pages 123 to 126), and when discussing its particulars with students, you should insist that the key facts and important details of Theodora's life be accurately recorded for a student to achieve the highest assessment at the knowledge level. (Some readers might think the task of applying for Secretary-General of the United Nations is anachronistic; however, the teacher wanted the student to apply his or her knowledge to a contemporary leadership position.) Students should also draw on the vital themes and narratives, such as values, beliefs, political ideas, and institutions, to place the life and times of Theodora and the Byzantine Empire into a wider historical context. Moreover, you should expect accurate information about the job requirements for the Secretary-General of the United Nations.

In the reasoning dimension, a developed student would use one or more of the habits of mind to explain why Theodora's life continues to be relevant. For example, the student would have to show that he or she had developed historical empathy as opposed to present-mindedness by perceiving past events as they were experienced by people at the time. In the communication dimension, the style and format of the resume and the letter of application should reflect a clear presentation of what the student knows and thinks about the past.

Experienced 10th-grade teachers used the history rubric to review this student's energetic attempt to come to terms with the life of Theodora. First, they concluded that the student was developed in all three dimensions: There was a good deal of accurate information; there was evidence that the student had thought about the significance of Theodora's life; and there was evidence that the student understood how to write a letter and construct a resume. Second, the teachers used the rubric to determine with more precision the developed student's performance. Based on the student's cover letter and resume, the teachers determined that this 10th-grade student of world history demonstrated knowledge at level 5, reasoning at level 4, and communication at level 4.

Like the Theodora activity, the George Mason activity calls on students to apply for a position, this time as a delegate to the Constitutional Convention of 1787 in Philadelphia. In this particular activity students should emphasize the beliefs of Mason as an 18th-century gentleman endeavoring to attend the Grand Convention

Ideas for the History Classroom

Prompt for Famous Personalities, World History

One of the most important aspects of applying for many jobs is the preparation of a resume and a letter of application. A resume is a brief outline of the most important aspects of a person's life. It is designed to make a person attractive to a prospective employer. A typical resume includes (a) the person's name and address, (b) the title of the job he or she is seeking, (c) an outline of the person's background and work experience, (d) a list of past achievements, (e) a list of the person's strengths, and (f) the name of at least one person who is familiar with the person's abilities. A letter of application explains why a person is applying for a position and why he or she should be hired.

Part A

Following is a list of some individuals who have had an important influence in world history. Choose one name from the list and prepare a resume that describes the person at the high point of his or her career.

Theodora	Michelangelo
Christopher Columbus	Attila
Martin Luther	Richard the Lionheart
Montezuma	Mansa Musa
Jeanne d'Arc	

Part B

Write a letter of application for the individual you chose. Explain why he or she is an outstanding choice for the job.

Ideas for the History Classroom

Famous Personalities World History

Student Sample 1 Grade 10

To Whom It May Concern:

Greetings! My name is Empress Theodora of the Byzantine Empire. I am interested in the job, as the Secretary-General of the United Nations. I feel I am best qualified for this job, because first and foremost, I am known as the definite leader, a sole ruler, recognized now as one of the most powerful women in the history of Byzantine, and served a total of twenty-one years as the empress of this large kingdom. Part of being the secretary-general of the U.N. is to have good communication skills with many different kinds of people. I have excellent communication skills with many kinds of people, both verbally and written. I even talked with foreign envoys and rulers about important issues which is something usually reserved for the emperor. When I was the empress of Byzantine, I had, and still have, superior intelligence and the ability to deftly handle political affairs, this, in result, caused many people to think that it was I, rather than Emperor Justinian I (my husband), who ruled Byzantine. I even saved my husband's crown and his empire with my excellent advice, during the Nika revolt in January of 532. Also, during my reign, I wrote many laws of religious and social policies that were in my favor. This, in turn, became good decisions for the people of Byzantine. With my charming, gentle personality and strict moral life, I also became Justinian I's most trusted adviser, an excellent advocate of decisions and even one of the first rulers who helped the rights of women and girls, who were especially being mistreated in that day and age.

I, myself, was even one of those women who was mistreated as a young girl. However, I educated myself and overcame this state in my life. All of this led me to have great intelligence and political aptitude, despite how unusual it was to the public eye. Then I met Justinian and soon after we got married; but before that incident ocurred, Justin had to tell his uncle (who was king at the time) to repeal the law forbidding marriages of senators with actresses. Justin had to confront and overturn the law, in order to marry me, Theodora.

As the secretary-general of the United Nations, I will not, I repeat, will not just idly enjoy the splendor and fame. As empress of Byzantine, I did a lot of effective and important things, and I assure you, I will do the same for the United Nations. If I am selected as chief administrative officer of the U.N., I will absolutely make sure to bring before the organization any matters that threatens international peace and security of the world. I will also administrate peacekeeping operations so every generation, everyone of any race, creed, color, ethnic, religious, etc. background, now and in the future, can live in a world of peace, instead of hostility and war. I will make sure that countries will be able to have proper education for children, so they can learn, and have the intelligence and knowledge. I will also make sure women, or other people, of all countries are treated equally and fairly, and also, have proper education. I will pursue to help the small countries of the world and its people, who have constantly been bullied by other countries. I will organize international conferences and treaties, and provide mediation in resolving international disputes, so enemy countries can get along in peace, instead of war. I will prepare surveys of world economic trends and problems, study rights and natural resources, compile statistics, and maintain the communication medias of the world with information pertaining to the U.N. Those are just a few samples of what I plan to do if I am selected. I have many other ideas and suggestions that will be effective and excellent for our world if I am chosen as secretary-general. However, overall, if I am selected as secretary-general of the United Nations, I will make it my first priority and I will try my absolute best to maintain international peace and security for the organization, the world, and its people.

Sincerely,
Empress Theodora of Byzantine

Empress Theodora
I Royal Castle of Byzantine
Constantinople, Byzantine Empire

Objective: *Secretary-General of the United Nations*
Date of Birth: c. 500 A.D. in Constantinople

Marriage Status: I am married to Emperor Justinian I (reigned 527-565) of the Byzantine Empire.

Summary of Qualifications

- I am a definite leader, sole ruler and served twenty-one years as Empress of Byzantine.
- I am recognized now as one of the most powerful women in the history of Byzantine.
- I became Justinian I's most rusted adviser with my great intelligence and political ability.
- I have excellent communication skills with many different kinds of people, both verbally and written.
- I have "superior intelligence and deft handling of political affairs, (it) caused many to think that it was rather than the Emperor, who ruled Byzantine."
- I was a member of the legislation of Byzantine.
- I am excellent in organization, commitment and peacefulness.
- I "talked with foreign envoys and rulers, which was usually reserved for the emperor."
- I am an expertise in political affairs—e.g., the Nika Revolt in January of 532—"The two political factors in Constantinople, the Blues and the Greens, united in their opposition to acts of the government and set up a rival emperor." The advisors of Justinian feared that there was trouble, and told him to flee, but it was I who told him to stay and save his empire and his crown. This, in result, did save his empire and his crown.
- I was one of the first rulers who helped the rights of women.
- I have a charming and gentle personality which makes me able to work with everyone.
- I lead a strict moral life.
- I am an excellent advocate in making decisions.

Employment History

527–548 A.D.—I became the Empress of Byzantine Empire: Justinian's most rusted adviser: enrolling myself in the legislation, social and political affairs.

525 A.D.—I became a mistress of Justinian, who was a senator at the time, and also, I had the rank of a patrician.

(?) 525–520—I was an actress at the Hippodrome in Constantinople, and also, a wool spinner. I had these jobs in order to make money for my poor family.

Additional Activities (e.g., Volunteer Work)

During my life, I also did additional activities. I instituted homes for prostitutes and on the occasion, I helped out or sent money to them.

(continued)

Ideas for the History Classroom (continued)

Famous Personalities World History

Other Interests

Some of my other interests include reading books, magazines, etc., keeping up-to-date on the latest news, and also, legislation, politics, peace, religion and social structures and policies.

References

There are two people that especially know me, as a person, and what went on during my life:

Justinian I—He is my husband also a valued friend. We got along very well, and I became his most trusted adviser. He knew about what I was doing and had not only a husband-wife relationship, but also a team-cooperation relationship.

Procopius of Caesarea—He wrote the Secret History of Procopius of Caesarea, which recorded some of the early years of my childhood.

Ideas for the History Classroom

Prompt for Famous Personalities, U.S. History

One of the most important aspects of applying for many jobs is the preparation of a resume and a letter of application. A resume is a brief outline of the most important aspects of a person's life. It is designed to make a person attractive to a prospective employer. A typical resume includes (a) the person's name and address, (b) the title of the job he or she is seeking, (c) an outline of the person's background and work experience, (d) a list of past achievements, (e) a list of the person's strengths, and (f) the name of at least one person who is familiar with the person's abilities. A letter of application explains why a person is applying for a position and why he or she should be hired.

Part A

Following is a list of some individuals who have had an important influence in the history of the United States. Choose one name from the list and prepare a resume that describes the person at the high point of his or her career.

Abigail Adams   George Washington
Thomas Jefferson   Alexander Hamilton
Charles Pinckney   George Mason
John Adams   James Wilson
James Madison

Part B

Write a letter of application for the individual you chose. Explain why he or she is an outstanding choice for the job. You have three days to complete this assignment.

Ideas for the History Classroom

Famous Personalities U.S. History

Student Sample 1

Grade 11

Honorable Governor of Virginia.

This letter is to serve as written documentation of my request, to be sent to Philadelphia as a delegate to the Federal Constitutional Convention. I intend to represent our glorious state of Virginia and support and serve the wonderful people of this state.

As you know, I have attended many other conventions and have served on quite a few committees. I believe I possess the expertise to understand and participate in conventional protocol.

In addition to my strong desire to serve my fellow Virginians, there are a few items I wish to address to the members of this convention regarding the pending constitution.

I intend to oppose sectional compromise relative to slavery, tariffs and slave trade. I will favor the gradual emancipation of the slaves. I will object to the extensive but vague power given to congress.

For the above mentioned reasons, and the opportunity to share my ideas, I again formally request, that I be selected to attend the Federal Constitutional Convention in Philadelphia.

Thank you for your kind and prompt consideration to this manner.

Sincerely,
George Mason

George Mason
Fairfax County, Virginia

Position: Seeking position of Delegate to the Constitutional Convention in Philadelphia.

Background:
  Born in 1725
  Living in Fairfax County, Virginia

Work Experience
  1759: Member of the Virginia House of Burgesses
  1774: Member of the Virginia Committee of Safety
  1775-1776: Member of the State Constitutional Convention
  1776-1788: Member of the Virginia Assembly

Last Achievements
  1769: Drew up Nonimportation Resolutions
  1773: Published Extracts From the Virginia Charters

(continued)

Ideas for the History Classroom (continued)

Famous Personalities U.S. History

> 1774: Wrote the series of 24 Resolutions (Fairfax Resolves)
> 1776: Drew up the Virginia Declaration of Rights and most of the Virginia
>   Constitution

Personal Strengths
  Honest
  Reliable
  Consistent
  Student of Politics

Reference
  Neighbor and lifelong friend, George Washington.

Student Sample 2
Grade 11

Dear Governor,

I am writing this letter to encourage you to choose me as a representative for the great state of Virginia in the upcoming Constitutional Convention. I feel it is extremly important for me to be present because of the need for this country to have a Bill of Rights. As you know I was largely responsible for the Virginia Bill of Rights, and feel as though our national government needs something similar. I will be one of the older men there and feel as though my life experiences, and knowledge will contribute greatly. Perhaps most importantly I do not consider myself a politican or lawyer, even though I have held many political positions. I am honest, straightforward, and care greately about this new country, and its people. The contributions I have already made to this new country speak for themselves. This includes everything from serving as Fairfax County's Justice of the Peace with George Washington, to helping with the militia, and organizing Maryland's and Virginia's plan for British boycott.

I trust you will not overlook my accomplishments, and grant me my wish. The importance of this convention is well known. It will change all our lives like nothing before in history. I feel it is my responsibility to represent the averageman, and his rights the government should not be able to touch. If chosen I will represent Virginia in a manner to be proud of. My actions and past history show what I am capable of, and what I plan on doing in the future. Thanks again for taking the time to consider me as a delegate, and remember above all I will fight for the addition of a Bill of Rights. I will not sign or support any document that does not contain one.

> Respectfully yours,
> *George Mason*

George Mason
Address
Gunston Hall, Dogue's Neck, Virginia

SEEKING A SEAT IN THE CONSTITUTIONAL CONVENTION

Personal Information:

Born:
    December 11, 1725 to Anne Thomson Mason, and George Mason III—oldest of three

Married:
    April 4, 1750 to Ann Eilbeck. She died in March of 1773—nine children 1780, remarried Sarah Brent

Occupation:
    Land owner, planter/farmer

Hobbies:
    Reading—favorite book: *Every Man His Own Lawyer*

Previous Achievements:

- Own thousands of farm acres in Virginia, and Maryland, over 1000 acres of uncleared land to the west
- Justice of the Peace, Fairfax County
- Trustee and co-founder of the town of Alexandria
- Treasurer of the Ohio Company
- 1759 elected to the House of Burgesses
- Drafted Maryland's and Virginia's plan for British good boycott
- Helped organize the Fairfax Militia
- Served in the colonial Militia

**Member of Virginia Convention:

- largely responsible for the Virginia Declaration of Rights
- largely believe in a man's natural right
- feel a Bill of Rights is extremely important
- should be certain areas government cannot interfere

**Longtime Member of Virginia House of Delegates

References:

George Washington
Richard Henry Lee
Patrick Henry
Charles Pinckney
George Wythe
Thomas Jefferon
James Madison

(continued)

Ideas for the History Classroom (continued)

Famous Personalities U.S. History

Student Sample 3

Grade 11

Dear Governor of Virginia—

   I, George Mason, am writing to you to express my deep concern for the future of this country we are building. I feel we must work together and pool our strengths as individuals to help create a nation for all to live in that is fair and just. I feel that my strengths are greatly needed at the Constitutional Convention that will be held in Philadelphia, Pennsylvania. Thus, I feel that I would be a superb choice as a delegate representing the state of Virginia.

   To create a fair and just nation, I feel we must secure the rights of the individual. Upon writing the draft that was accepted as the Virginia Bill of Rights, I have come to see that certain ideas are prevalent with many individuals. As a delegate, I will be sure to push for the rights of the individual. I believe that we must create a document to serve all fairly.

   We must make the outline of a national government that may overpower the state government but never infringe on the rights of the state. Our Virginia Bill of Rights can play an important role in the development of the Constitution. I will bring such ideas to the Convention as all men are created equal and free, all are entitled to the pursuit of life and liberty, all shall have rights to acquire and possess property, no citizen shall be compelled to testify against themselves, cruel and unusual punishment shall not be allowed, men shall receive a trial by jury, prescribed freedom of religion, and a peneral guarantee of people's freedom against the government. For these reasons and my genuine concern for this country, I feel I am a superb candidate as Delegate to the Constitutional Convention representing the state of Virginia. Thank you for your time.

Sincerely,
George Mason

Resume of George Mason

1786

George Mason

Gunston Hall

Virginia

I, George Mason, an applying for the job of the Delegate to the Constitutional Convention representing the state of Virginia.

Background & Work Experience:

- born in Virginia in 1725
- studies politics as a youth
- held a public office for the state of Virginia
- single-handedly run mansion, Gunston Hall
- own over 75,000 acres of land and 90 slaves
- wealthy squire
- worked on Virginia Bill of Rights

Past Achievements:

- served on the committee to work out a government for the state of Virginia
- produced the draft that was accepted as the Virginia Bill of Rights
- produced a fair and just document for the people of the state of Virginia to live by

Personal Strengths:

- independent
- clear and precise thinker
- honest
- careful student of politics
- reliable
- truly believed in the preservation of the rights of the individual
- consistent

Reference:

- George Washington

Student Sample 4
Grade 11

To the Governor:

   I believe you know me. I have lived in Virginia all my life. I have lots of money. I have slaves too. Rights are important to me. I have done many things to help this country. I have respect from many leaders.

   I should go to Philadelphia because I have spoken about rights before. I have friends in my state who want me to be there. I don't know what to say but I'll do the best I can.

Very truly yours,
George Mason

George Mason
Gunston Hall
Virginia

Owned slaves
Had 75,000 acres of land
Leader of Rights
Married two times with 9 children
Planter and farmer

References:

   James Madison

Frederick D. Drake and Lawrence W. McBride, "Reinvigorating the Teaching of History through Alternative Assessment," *The History Teacher* 30, no. 2 (February 1997): 145–173. Used with permission.

within the context of a resume and letter of application. They should also emphasize Mason's role as the architect of the Virginia Declaration of Rights (1776) and his insistence on a bill of rights at the Constitutional Convention (although he did so only in the last 2 weeks of the convention). To demonstrate proficiency in the knowledge domain, students should stress Mason's contribution to this belief in rights—organized around the vital theme and narrative of values, beliefs, political ideas, and institutions. A student who has knowledge about Mason must emphasize this important contribution in protecting rights.

A student who has the highest level of knowledge of Mason would also point out that Mason contributed greatly to the Constitutional Convention in no fewer than three ways. First, he contributed to the writing of the Virginia Plan, although primary responsibility for the Virginia Plan rested with James Madison. Second, Mason spoke to the convention delegates in early June 1787 about a "partly national, partly federal" government, a distinction that had an effect on the thinking of the Father of the Constitution, James Madison. Madison would acknowledge the contribution of Mason in making this distinction regarding the role of a new central government, a role that had not been made prior to the Grand Convention in Philadelphia and had not been articulated prior to June 1787. And third, Mason warned Thomas Jefferson (in Paris, when the Constitutional Convention took place) in a postconvention letter that "There is no Declaration of Rights." Mason's letter helped launch the antifederalist campaign to challenge the veracity of the Constitutional Convention and the documents the delegates had created.

In the reasoning dimension, a student would be expected to use one or more of the habits of mind to explain why Mason's dedication to protection of rights has meaning and importance. For example, students should empathize with Mason's dedicated pursuit of protection of rights, a dedication that prevented him from signing the Constitution when delegates refused his offer to preface the new plan of government with a declaration of rights. A student who truly empathizes with Mason might construct a letter of application that appreciates Mason's position. Certainly you would want students to recognize that George Mason was a significant individual whose dedication to protection of rights helped pave the way for a national bill of rights. In the communication dimension, students should present in proper format a resume and letter of application that expresses clear knowledge and reasoning about the contributions of George Mason.

Four teachers scored each of the four student samples of the George Mason activity. The consensus was that sample 1 was level 4 in knowledge, level 4 in reasoning, and level 4 in communication. Sample 2 demonstrated knowledge at level 5, reasoning at level 4, and communication at level 5. Sample 3 was assessed at a level 4 in knowledge, a level 5 in reasoning, and a level 5 in communication. Sample 4 showed a level 1 in knowledge, a level 2 in reasoning, and a level 1 in communication.

None of the high school students met the highest level of achievement of knowledge, reasoning, and communication about George Mason and the Constitutional Convention. And yet, except for sample 4, these students constructed a resume and letter of application for George Mason that demonstrated that they did recognize and understand several of his important achievements. The results of this activity can be explained by such variables as differences in teacher preparation, student ability, and access to information. Nevertheless, the value of the rubric is that it provides a framework for both you and your students to know in advance what is expected in knowledge, reasoning, and communication, given the variables that affect learning in all schools.

Finally, we know that you and other teachers will probably want to transfer the six levels of each dimension to a grade. We offer this advice: 6 and 5 are considered an A, 4 is a B, 3 is a C, 2 is a D, and 1 is a grade of F. You can derive a cumulative score by adding the score from each level and dividing by 3 (for example, knowledge = 5, reasoning = 4, and communication = 4 for a total of 13, which divided by 3 is 4.3 or 4. A 4 is a grade of B. The decision to translate the rubric levels to letter grades is up to you, and you may find other ways to provide assessment through grades if it serves your purpose.

SUMMARY

Assessment is a form of instruction. We encourage you to take seriously the engagement of your students in meaningful assessment activities. Performance assessment activities provide you and your students with the opportunity to do just that. Performance assessment accompanied by a history rubric can be both a diagnostic and an instructional tool.

A rubric for performance assessment is especially appropriate and useful for history education because the rubric benefits you and students alike. A rubric is not a checklist. It is not a list of tangential characteristics such as turning work in on time. Although timeliness may be factored into a student's ultimate grade, it should not be incorporated into a rubric. Rather, it is a guideline for assessing differing levels of knowledge, reasoning, and communication skills.

The effective use of a rubric requires planning and practice. You should share your rubric with your students because it contains the criteria that your students will have to meet as they construct historical knowledge, engage in historical reasoning, and communicate what they know and understand. To successfully acquire knowledge and skills in reasoning and communication, students should know in advance the criteria sought in each dimension and be coached about the best ways to demonstrate their abilities.[11] A rubric, such as the one offered in this chapter, provides a floor to durable knowledge; it does not place limits on the ceiling of historical literacy.

The rubric also serves a purpose when you meet with the parents and guardians of your students. During parent–teacher conferences the rubric facilitates clear communication regarding your expectations for and the achievements of your students.

In recent years an enormous amount of energy has been spent thinking about how best to reinvigorate the teaching of history. Certainly, the results of the National Assessment of Educational Progress (NAEP), published in November 1995 and in 2002, warrant the conclusion that, in general, students' knowledge, reasoning, and communication of historical content has not improved.[12] Performance assessment activities and a rubric that is especially designed for use in history classrooms combine to address the continuing demands that teachers become more selective in their content and imaginative in their teaching of history.

Knowledge, reasoning, and communication are contextual, but students must be held to rigorous standards that counter miseducative visions of doing whatever students think is proper. The criteria for assessing student learning of historical knowledge, reasoning, and communication should be determined and directed by those who know and understand the subject, that is, you, the teacher/historian. Effective performance assessment activities and a history rubric will help to set these standards and criteria, motivate performance, provide feedback, and help you evaluate students' development in the three dimensions of historical literacy.

TRANSLATING HISTORY INTO CLASSROOM PRACTICE

Activity 6.1   Remembering the Louisiana Purchase

Imagine the following situation: You represent a marketing company. The National Endowment for the Humanities has put you in charge of its marketing campaign for remembering the Louisiana Purchase. Prepare a presentation that demonstrates your marketing strategy and ideas for the NEH board of directors. Your presentation should explain how the strategies you developed will make the Louisiana Purchase memorable. Begin by naming the campaign, design an image for the public to remember, and draw a logo. Then, explain to the NEH board of directors the following:

- How you will target the public
- How you will determine the content you want the public to remember
- What you will emphasize in a 30-second advertising spot

You may complete this activity with two or three fellow students.

Activity 6.2   Creating Your Own Performance Assessment Strategy

Create your own performance assessment strategy that accompanies a lesson or unit plan. Some tips:

Prompt:
- Write a prompt that puts students in a situation.
- Make sure students apply content to the situation.
- Make sure there is a reasoning (thinking) dimension to your prompt.
- Make sure students must communicate what they know and think by writing, speaking, drawing, or dramatizing.

Rubric:

- Create a rubric (see pages 118 to 119, which show a three-dimensional, analytic rubric stressing knowledge, reasoning, and communication, or consult other rubrics).
- Fill in the details of your expectations in such categories as knowledge, reasoning, and communication.
- Share your expectations with your students in advance of the assessment.

REVIEWING THE CHAPTER

1. Describe the assessment strategies you encountered in your high school U.S. history or world history course. Compare your experiences with those of your fellow students.

2. Identify a historical topic that you are currently studying or have studied. Draw a political cartoon that illustrates a central issue.

3. From the cartoon you have drawn, create a rubric based on the three dimensions—knowledge, reasoning, and communication—described in this chapter.

4. In your field/clinical placement, work with your cooperating teacher to create a rubric that assesses a student assignment. Apply the three dimensions—knowledge, reasoning, and communication—to the rubric that you develop.

5. Why should teachers be concerned with students attaining higher levels of knowledge, reasoning, and communication?

7

Using Primary Sources
The First-, Second-, and Third-Order Approach

This approach has made me think more carefully about the way I think about primary sources. Many primary sources are available from textbook companies and the Internet, as if they [all primary sources] are all equal. They are not. This method makes me think like a historian.

— Veteran teacher of 34 years, summer 2002

It works! I may have to edit my primary sources, depending on my students' abilities, but the method helps them know content. Students relate sources one to another when they use this method.

— Student teacher, spring 2002

Primary sources are important as a first-order document. But secondary sources are also just as important. I like to mix a secondary source with other primary sources as my second-order documents. Secondary sources help my students see what was taking place and to understand change for better or worse.

— Veteran teacher of 12 years, summer 2002

$\mathcal{R}$esearch on historical thinking demonstrates that students who analyze and work with primary documents acquire valuable thinking skills. Although many approaches to teaching with primary sources are available, we advocate the first-, second-, and third-order approach.[1] Informal interviews with teachers who use this approach reveal that it increases student engagement and teaches valuable thinking skills.

The aim of this chapter is to provide you with a helpful strategy to improve your students' use of historical content and to help them develop historical thinking. We introduce a systematic approach that is consistent with best practices in pedagogy and involves the teacher in the "doing of teaching history" and students in "doing history" in the history laboratory." Experienced history teachers as well as novices will find this chapter meaningful.

Focus Questions

1. What types of primary sources can a teacher locate and use in the classroom?

2. What are some conventional practices that teachers employ when using primary sources?

3. How are first-, second-, and third-order primary sources used in teaching?

4. Give an example of the first-, second-, and third-order approach.

5. How can this approach help teachers assess students' historical knowledge, thinking, and dispositions?

Five Typologies of Primary Sources

Primary sources are the raw materials of the historian and a basic tool for the history teacher. They are, so to speak, the ore from which we mine meaning from the past. Primary sources are such documents as speeches, memos, letters, diaries, telegrams, cooking recipes, maps, school yearbooks, grocery lists, colanders, photographs, paintings, musical scores, legal wills, washboards, and political cartoons. We propose a process of imagining the landscape of primary sources and using them as a way to enhance historical thinking—by walking its parameters, roughing out some of its contours, and casting at least a few glances toward its center.

Teachers are always looking for a useful way to categorize primary sources. The five typologies of Gerald A. Danzer and Mark Newman, found in *Bring History Alive!* (see Figure 7.1), can serve as a helpful frame of reference as you think of documents you will use to teach about the past. Share this helpful typology with your students.

The first type of primary source consists of **print (or textual) documents** such as letters, diaries, and speeches. The second type of primary source comes from the **electronic media** such as videotapes and film clips. A third category is **folklore, folkways, and mythology,** which are passed down through the oral tradition. A fourth type consists of **images** that come from the fine arts and graphic arts, such as paintings, maps, political cartoons, photographs, charts, graphs, and posters. And a fifth type includes primary sources in the **physical environment and material culture** such as architecture, landscaping, and household artifacts.[2] For example, a Frank Lloyd Wright home with its furnishings intact is a veritable time capsule of life in the United States in the 20th century. It demonstrates the ways a human-made structure affects the natural environment. A visit to such a place is a perfect opportunity to introduce your students to the interrelationship between history and the geographic landscape. It is also an opportunity to take your students on a walking tour, a journey into the past.

Here are some helpful rules for using primary sources:

1. Select age-appropriate sources.
2. Make sure *selections are readable and edited* properly.
3. Provide *background* to help students "decode" the source.
4. Have *students work in groups* with primary sources.
5. Provide *purpose and motivation* for reading a primary source.[3]

Conventional Practices in Using Primary Sources

From observing student teachers and classroom teachers, we found that most history teachers use primary sources—particularly, textual sources—in one of two ways: using a *single source* approach or using a *multiple source* approach. Some teachers intersperse a single primary source within a historical topic, often to validate to students that the information they present is correct. Other teachers provide students

FIGURE 7.1   Five typologies of primary sources. Used with permission.

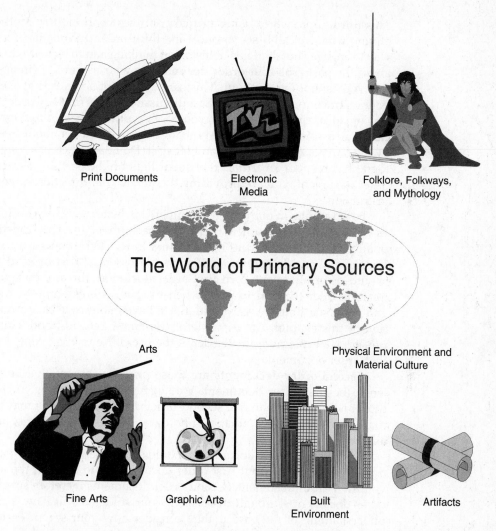

Print Documents

Electronic
Media

Folklore, Folkways,
and Mythology

The World of Primary Sources

Arts

Physical Environment and
Material Culture

Fine Arts   Graphic Arts   Built   Artifacts
                                            Environment

Source: Gerald A. Danzer and Mark Newman, *Tuning In: Primary Sources in the Teaching of History.*
Chicago: The World History Project, 1991. Used with permission.

with multiple primary sources to help them discover for themselves what the
teacher already knows. This second way is more complex, usually involving jig-
saw learning or other group techniques (for example, placing one or more sources
at stations around the classroom), because a variety of sources are brought to bear
on a topic.

Although these approaches (use of a single source to validate the teacher's
information and multiple sources for students to discover conclusions of historians) are valid and useful, we suggest a third way to extend the use of primary
sources.

Using First-, Second-, and Third-Order Primary Sources

This third approach to using primary sources is an inquiry method designed around what we call first-, second-, and third-order documents. It is a systematic way to engage your students in historical thinking and to increase their knowledge about the past. The **first-order document** is your essential primary source, one that you cannot live without. This core document should be at the epicenter of your instruction. You should lead a discussion of this first-order document based on a broad, open-ended question you pose to your students. A first-order document can be an inspiring speech by Abraham Lincoln or a letter about freedom written by the famous African American Frederick Douglass. It can be a significant photograph, a map, or an artifact that sheds light on the past. In selecting your first-order document, you are providing the intellectual direction in your classroom instruction.

For example, in our own teaching of U.S. history we use the Tenth *Federalist* as our first-order document when we teach about the U.S. constitutional and political experiences in the 18th century. In the 20th century, we use George F. Kennan's "Long Telegram" of 1946 as our essential first-order document. You should determine your own first-order document for different periods of history. We offer these as examples because they are essential to the knowledge and understanding we want students to have in our own classrooms. In the section of this chapter, An Example of the First-, Second-, and Third-Order Approach, we explain in greater detail the use of Kennan's "Long Telegram" as a first-order document.

Second-order documents are those primary sources that support or challenge the first-order document. We suggest that you bring in a minimum of three and no more than five second-order documents, which may comprise textual (print) documents, images (photographs, paintings, charts, and tables), or artifacts.

Your second-order documents should serve one of two purposes—to corroborate ideas found in your first-order document or to contrast the ideas found in your first-order document. Second-order documents therefore surround the first-order document. Through discussion, your students will have a more nuanced understanding of the past as they consider how your second-order documents support or challenge your first-order document.

Third-order documents are primary sources students eventually find themselves. At one time or another all teachers experience the moment when a student enters class and exuberantly describes a primary source (perhaps a family photograph, a letter, an old newspaper article, a family story, or a primary source found on the Internet) that relates to a topic or idea recently discussed in class. Because this experience is all too infrequent, we argue that it should be made more systematic. A third-order document, therefore, is a primary source that the student finds to be important. We emphasize, however, that students must find third-order documents that relate to your first-order document.

Ideas for the History Classroom

Defining First-, Second-, and Third-Order Documents

> *First-order document*—The most essential primary source for the teacher on a particular topic in history.
>
> *Second-order document*—Three to five primary or secondary sources that challenge or corroborate the central idea in the first-order document. At least one source should challenge the first-order document. These documents, selected by the teacher, provide a nuanced understanding of the topic by offering multiple perspectives.
>
> *Third-order document*—Additional primary or secondary sources that students find to challenge or corroborate the first-order document. Ultimately, students should select a third-order document to serve as their first-order document.

Selecting First- and Second-Order Documents

You should choose your first-order document based on three key criteria: its historical value, its potential contribution to your students' historical knowledge, and its potential to help them develop their historical thinking. When determining a document's historical value, consider at least two essential qualities. First and most important, the source should represent the heart of a historical issue or period in history. The selection of a first-order document is an act of interpretation. It determines the intellectual direction of subsequent discussions.

Your first-order document should also express a position so vividly that other documents can be found that challenge or corroborate the position. Your first-order document should have the quality of bonding with other documents. The best first-order document is one that contributes to your students' historical knowledge and thinking.

Here are several questions that will assist you as you determine your first-order document:

- Will the document be of interest to my students?
- Will the document enable students to draw on their prior knowledge?
- Does the document allow my students to relate the concept, idea, or event to knowledge with which they are familiar?
- Does the document allow my students to examine change over time?
- Is the document appropriate cognitively for my students?
- In what ways might the document deepen my students' contextual understanding of the past?
- How will the document affect my students' preconceived historical narrative?
- How will the document contribute to my students' abilities to deliberate and make informed decisions?

- In what ways does the document require students to use one or more of history's habits of mind?
- How does the document relate to one or more of history's vital themes and narratives?
- How does the document relate to state and local standards and performance indicators that call for the development of historical thinking?

Use similar criteria in the selection of second-order documents, keeping in mind that a central purpose of your second-order documents is to make sure they support or challenge your first-order document.

As you engage in the process of determining your first-order document and three to five surrounding second-order documents, you will discover numerous other sources. Do not discard other documents that you find. Instead, create a list of potential third-order documents.

This list of potential third-order documents serves two purposes. First, you can use it to give seed reluctant students examples of documents to look for. Second, you can use it to "seed" students who are willing to look for primary sources but need direction for their work.

An Example of the First-, Second-, and Third-Order Approach

We suggest that you intersperse the first-, second-, and third-order approach with other teaching methods throughout the semester. You might use this approach as you and your students investigate the period of the Cold War. You can readily access primary sources on the Cold War period through the Internet. For example, the "Cold War International History Project" (http://cwihp.si.edu/) provides a wide range of both documents and links to other related websites and sources. The U.S. National Archives and Records Administration (http://www.archives.gov/) also provides sources and teaching strategies, including the Digital Classroom, which you can draw on to incorporate sources and teaching strategies.[4]

Internet sites provide only the raw intellectual material for creative lessons, however. You now need to consider the issue of document selection, and we suggest you organize selections around the framework of first-, second-, and third-order documents. Let's consider George F. Kennan's "Long Telegram" of February 1946 as a first-order document. A question to ask your students as they read Kennan's "Long Telegram" is, How did American leaders view relations among the Grand Alliance (U.S., U.S.S.R., U.K.) members? How did they view the international balance of power between the United States and Soviet Russia?

George F. Kennan, the U.S. charge d'affaires in Moscow, wrote a secret 8,000-word telegram to officials in Washington, D.C., on February 22, 1946. His telegram, which assessed Soviet behavior within a historical context, led the Truman administration to formulate the policy of containment. Kennan warned,

"We have here a political force [the Soviet Union] committed fanatically to the belief that with [the] U.S. there can be no *modus vivendi* [arrangement between people who agree to cope with matters over which they disagree], that it is desirable and necessary that the internal harmony of our society be disrupted, our traditional way of life be destroyed, the international authority of our state be broken, if Soviet power is to be secure."[5]

Kennan's assessment represented the widely shared U.S. objective of containment in the post–World War II period. His assessment of how to achieve containment became an important issue in the Truman administration and succeeding administrations. Would containment of Soviet expansionism be limited to Europe? Would containment be global?

To enrich your students' historical understanding, you will want to introduce second-order documents next. You may decide to include Nikolai Novikov and Frank Roberts' telegrams of 1946, respectively. Soviet Ambassador Novikov's cable assessed the United States from the Soviet perspective. Novikov's cable is informative and captivating to both a reader whose knowledge is limited and to one who is more knowledgeable and well grounded. The Soviet cable was first published publicly in November 1990 during the era of glasnost and perestroika. It appeared in an issue of *Mezhdunarodnaia zhizn'*, an official publication of the Soviet Foreign Ministry. British charge d'affaires Frank Roberts' cable, also written in 1946, provides a British perspective of Soviet and U.S. objectives; Sean Greenwood described its significance over 15 years ago in the *Journal of Contemporary History*.[6] You may also want to include as a second-order document an image, perhaps a picture taken of the Allied leaders during the Potsdam Conference of July 1945.

Several third-order documents your students might find include Winston Churchill's 1946 "Iron Curtain" speech given in Fulton, Missouri; a May 17, 1946, speech by the general secretary of the Hungarian Communist Party at the meeting of the central committee; Kennan's 1947 "X" article; the Truman Doctrine of 1947; the Marshall Plan of 1947; a Henry Wallace speech; and the 1950 NSC 68, to name a few. All documents can be found on the Internet.

The Importance of Asking Questions

You cannot simply give students first-order documents with instructions to read them and answer some questions. Intellectual enjoyment and engagement are the products of a co-investigation involving intellectual interaction between teachers and students. History, after all, is to a great extent an investigation. History is a process of interrogating primary sources and secondary narratives. Historians primarily ask questions when they "do" history, often prefaced with *why* and *how*. History teachers also ask questions, though perhaps for different purposes. The historian's purpose is to give meaning to historical facts. As a discipline and course of study, history insists on "meaning over memory."[7] History teachers ask questions (and encourage their students to ask questions) to help students think historically and to "give meaning to their historical experiences."[8] History teaching is a co-investigation in which the teacher and students shape and reshape their interpretations about the past.

You will need to ask these basic questions common to historical thinking (see the Ideas for the History Classroom features.) Note that in Chapter 3 we provided annotated versions of these same guides to assist you in knowing the categories and heuristics of historical thinking): Who is the author? When was the source written? What type of document is it? Who was the intended audience? What factors motivated the author to create the source? Was Kennan, in our example, writing the "Long Telegram" because he had been asked to assess the relationship among the members of the Grand Alliance? Did he take the initiative to write the persuasive cable? These are questions historians ask and students need to practice asking. By encouraging your students to speculate on these questions, you enable them to weave this first-order document into their historical frameworks of understanding.

After considering these questions, you should then discuss with your students the central meaning of the document and how Kennan supported his argument. During this deliberative discussion, ask students to suspend judgment regarding whether Kennan was right or wrong. This suspension of present-mindedness is essential to deliberation. It is also difficult and will take a good deal of practice. You should also ask your students to consider events and ideas that were taking place regionally, nationally, and internationally at the time the document was written. And you should ask your students to relate the document to a theme of history (such as conflict and cooperation) and to other disciplines in the social sciences. In effect, you are engaging your students in the dual process of examining a particular document and simultaneously relating that document to a larger historical context (see page 147).

Discussion of second-order documents, like that of first-order documents, requires analytical questioning. (Use the analysis guide on page 147 for both first- and second-order documents.) Again, ask questions that help your students identify the document and analyze its significance and relationship to your first-order document and larger events. In this example, the three textual documents and the image document provide your students with a nuanced understanding of the Cold War from the perspectives of three countries—the United States, the then Soviet Union, and Great Britain. How did relations among the Grand Alliance nations of World War II change? How did relationships among the citizens of each nation change relative to their allegiance to their national governments? How did the three nations establish objectives? How do the three telegrams compare in style, substance, and significance?[9] These comparative questions serve as portals into a coinvestigation of the Cold War.[10] When you have students look at a photograph, ask them these five initial questions:

- Was this photograph taken east or west of the Elbe River (or another appropriate geographic feature)?
- Who are the people in this photograph?
- What year/decade/century was this photograph taken?
- What does this photograph tell us about the lives of the people it depicts?
- What were the motives of the photographer?

Ideas for the History Classroom

Primary Source Analysis Guide to Historical Thinking: Print Documents

1. **Identifying the Document**
   Author(s) or source _____
   Title _____
   Date _____
   Type of document _____

2. **Analyzing the Document**
   Main idea of the document _____
   Relationship to other documents (How does the content relate to the first-, second-, and/or
     third-order documents?) _____
   Preceding conditions that motivated the author _____
   Intended audience and purpose _____
   Biases of the author _____
   Questions to ask the author _____

3. **Determining the Historical Context**
   Important people, events, and ideas at the time of the document _____
     Local/regional: people, events, and ideas of the time _____
     National: people, events, and ideas of the time _____
     World: people, events, and ideas of the time _____
   Conclusions about local/regional, national, and world context at the time _____

4. **Identifying the Habit of Mind and Vital Theme and Narrative Represented**
   Habit of mind _____
   The way you used this habit of mind to analyze the document _____
   Vital theme and narrative _____
   Evidence that the document represents this vital theme and narrative _____
   Evidence that the document relates to other documents (first-, second-, and/or third-order) through
     this vital theme and narrative _____

5. **Determining the Relationship to a Discipline in the Social Sciences/Social Studies**
   Discipline _____
   Evidence of relationship _____
   NCSS theme _____
   Evidence of relationship _____

These questions encourage your students to view the creation of an image as having purpose and meaning (see guide on page 149). The questions will elicit your students' thinking about people in the dimensions of time and space.

Editing First- and Second-Order Documents

The first-, second-, and third-order documents discussed in the previous section are examples we have used in our classrooms for a U.S. history survey course in middle and high schools or universities and for a university course on American

Ideas for the History Classroom

Primary Source Analysis Guide to Historical Thinking: Photograph/Image

1. **Identifying the Document**
   Photographer or source _____
   Title _____
   Date _____
   Type of Document _____

2. **Analyzing the Source**
   Main idea of the source _____
   What do you see (people or objects) in the image? _____
   What are people, if any, doing in this image? _____
   Who do you think these people are? _____
   What does this image tell you about ways of living? _____
   When do you think this image was created? _____
   Why do you think this image was created? _____
   Preceding conditions that motivated the producer of the image _____
   Intended audience and purpose _____
   Relationship to other sources (How does the content relate to the first-, second-, and/or third-order
        sources?) _____
   Biases of the image's producer _____
   Questions to ask the image's producer _____

3. **Determining the Historical Context**
   Important people, events, and ideas at the time of the image's creation _____
        Local/regional: people, events, and ideas of the time _____
        National: people, events, and ideas of the time _____
        World: people, events, and ideas of the time _____
   Conclusions about local/regional, national, and world context at the time _____

4. **Identifying the Habit of Mind and Vital Theme and Narrative Represented**
   Habit of mind _____
   The way you used this habit of mind to analyze the image _____
   Vital theme and narrative _____
   Evidence that the image represents this vital theme and narrative _____
   Evidence that the image relates to other sources (first-, second-, and/or third-order) through this vital
        theme and narrative _____

5. **Determining the Relationship to a Discipline in the Social Sciences/Social Studies**
   Discipline _____
   Evidence of relationship _____
   NCSS theme _____
   Evidence of relationship _____

diplomatic history. We determine the length of the textual documents depending on the nature of the course. In the American diplomatic history course, we read the entire primary sources. In the U.S. history survey course, we edit them. Students have then asked us how they can find the entire document, which we regard as a sign that their interests have been aroused.

Although the Internet and textbook companies make documents readily available, these sources do not absolve you from the responsibility of editing the sources for your students. You must make careful choices in selecting a document and then think wisely about what to delete or what to maintain. Editing is an act of interpretation, and many teachers find it to be a difficult task. Just as the selection of a document is an interpretive act on your part, editing a document involves interpretation that draws on your historical knowledge. One of your priorities must be to maintain intellectual honesty. You should never distort the meaning of a document through the use of ellipses (. . .) or other editorial devices. (For example, you should never delete such words as *not, never,* or *always.* As obvious as this point may appear, scholarship has sometimes violated this canon of the discipline.) Students trust your intellectual honesty, and you can quickly lose their confidence if you deliberately falsify a document through ellipses, link multiple documents as if they were one, or make up a false document.

When editing a primary source, consider these questions:

- Can you edit the source?
- What do you know about the document that will help you edit it appropriately?
- What do you need to know about the document to edit it appropriately?
- How does this document enhance your teaching and your students' learning?
- What are the essential parts of this document?

Although these questions serve as a guide, the final decisions are based on good judgment. You must keep in mind when selecting passages from a textual document that your students may ask what parts have been omitted. Instead of responding defensively, you should regard your students' questions as reflecting curiosity and interest. Encourage your students to read an entire, unedited document and ask them to select key sections of the source.

Historical Narrative; The First-, Second-, and Third-Order Approach; and Analysis Guides

All of us know that effective history teachers blend narrative and primary sources. Although this chapter focuses on a strategy for using primary sources, we do not want you to think we are overlooking the power and importance of narrative in teaching. The recent study conducted by Kathleen Medina and her research team points to problems that occur when teachers overemphasize either primary sources or interpretative narratives in their teaching.[11] Educational psychologist Jerome Bruner informs us of the power of narrative to help students construct the past. For Bruner, the narrative, or story, helps individuals create meaningful frameworks that organize their experience and make meaning of the world both past and present.[12]

We provide two analysis guides for organizing your discussions of documents, both print (page 147) and image (page 148). These guides are unlike most guides, which serve as mere checklists. The analysis guides offered in this text are keyed to the cognitive studies research of Sam Wineburg regarding historical thinking. Both guides are organized around five major headings, which are in turn informed by more detailed components. The headings are as follows:

1. Identifying the document
2. Analyzing the document
3. Determining the historical context
4. Identifying the habit of mind and vital theme and narrative represented in the document
5. Determining the relationship the document has to a discipline in the social sciences/social studies

Each guide is also related to aspects of historical thinking as suggested by Sam Wineburg. (In Chapter 3 we provided two annotated or keyed analysis guides related to historical thinking.) Having students analyze documents both contextually and comparatively moves them beyond consideration of themselves as isolated individuals and into consideration of themselves as individuals whose lives are ensnared in a fabric of historical ties. These guides will also help you to internationalize the teaching of U.S. history as your students embed particular historical experiences within a larger and more meaningful historical context.[13]

Wineburg's work and the work of others defined the problem of historical thinking. Few, however, have offered a solution to the problem other than to provide students with multiple sources and a narrative account of the past and to use active teaching strategies to engage students in the past. We have no quarrel with these suggestions.

We believe, however, that our systematic approach—which stresses discussion of first-, second-, and third-order documents and the use of analysis guides (one for textual sources and the other for images)—adds an additional dimension of active engagement in historical content and historical thinking. First, it encourages students to engage in sourcing. Second, it promotes the discussion of central ideas using a core document and relates the central ideas to supporting and contrasting documents. Third, it encourages a discussion of central ideas within the concept of space and time, emphasizing habits of mind. And fourth, when students find a third-order document, this document becomes their own first-order document. They will attach their document to an important idea in a particular time in history. Their document then becomes the epicenter for their understanding of history, transforming their narrative.

Assessing Historical Knowledge, Understanding, and Dispositions

Because the concepts of historical knowledge, understanding, and dispositions are inextricably linked, you will want to assess your students' development in both the cognitive and affective domains. As students relate their third-order document to your first-order document, the content becomes more meaningful to them. You can assess your students' historical understanding (the cognitive dimension) by engaging in conversations that require them to examine their documents in relationship to your first-order document. Cognitively, the third-order document intertwines with the first- and second-order documents within the process of historical inquiry and deliberation. Assess your students' abilities to communicate the relationship their third-order document has to your first-order document. Does the student's document challenge or corroborate yours? How so? Does the student relate the essential qualities of his or her document to the issue or historical

---

Ideas for the History Classroom

Classification Framework of Historical Thinking

Before giving students first-order and second-order documents, raise a question that is of historical importance—one that poses a central problem and piques students' curiosity, giving purpose to their examination of the sources. The question should be a How/Why question. Avoid initially a Should/Would question because it encourages presentism.

Discussions have an aim, which is to come to a consensus of the meaning of the document while initially suspending judgment. Ask questions that are prefaced by *what, how,* and *why.* Deliberative discussion is the heart of the discussion process.

The analysis guides in the Ideas for the History Classroom features provide a framework for thinking historically. The analysis guides emphasize what historians look for and think about as they analyze a document. They are not intended as a checklist or a worksheet. Instead, they focus the discussion on the credibility of historical evidence and historical understanding.

Create a Context

Ask an Open-Ended How/Why Question

Use a guide that emphasizes the following heuristics:

- **Sourcing heuristic**—what historians do before reading for content comprehension
- **Corroboration heuristic**—what historians do to relate one document to another document
- **Contextualization**—what historians do to describe the time frame and conditions both locally and nationally
- **Comparative thinking**—what historians do to describe conditions in other parts of the world at the time

period? Having your students discover third-order documents allows them to take ownership of the historical period or issue and to reconfigure their narrative of history in a more informed way. Such ownership lies at the heart of historical thinking because students are engaging in the doing of history with historians' habits of mind. This skill is their portal to an illuminated knowledge of the past.

To understand history, students must learn to value and enjoy historical thinking. This process of examining first-, second- and third-order documents enables you to assess your students' disposition toward inquiry, their capacity to engage in historical inquiry, as well as their historical understanding.

You can assess the affective dimensions of your students in at least three ways. First, some students will demonstrate their enthusiasm for history by voluntarily bringing in newspaper articles related to a topic, artifacts from home, and primary sources they find from research in the library or on the Internet. These activities indicate a positive disposition regarding the study of history. Are they willing to relate their finding to your first-order document?

Second, some students will not voluntarily locate sources on their own. You may then have to resort to showing them your list of third-order documents. In so doing, you "seed" students' interests and provide a structured starting point for inquiry. Some students will require this structure to feel confident and secure in historical inquiry.

And third, once a student begins to work with a third-order document (from their perspective, now a first-order document), you can determine the student's willingness to ask questions historians pose when they examine documents. Is the student willing to ask questions, to participate in a co-investigation of the past?

SUMMARY

Even though teachers and students are not confounded by the use of such terminology as *primary sources* and *secondary sources,* our terminology (*first-, second-, and third-order documents*) does confuse some teachers and some students at first. To avoid this initial confusion, you can define first-order documents as the teacher's essential documents, second-order documents as supporting and contrasting documents, and third-order documents as the documents students find.

This systematic approach, used at times you deem appropriate, effectively compels you to think more carefully about primary sources and narratives. It also improves your students' historical knowledge and thinking.

The selection of a first-order document and surrounding second-order documents is a creative act on your part. You will apply and enlarge your historical understanding as you determine the essential core documents that comprise your historical interpretation. Remember, at least one image must serve as a first- or second-order document, thus assuring access to information for students who learn through visual images.

Students become engaged in creative scholarship as they make meaningful connections between ideas contained in first-order and second-order documents and apply their historical understanding as they investigate third-order documents. This systematic approach makes history meaningful, encourages the use of historians' habits of mind, and shapes and reshapes the historical narratives linked to primary sources. We believe this approach will contribute to the renascence of using primary sources in history classrooms and will assist teachers at all levels in developing historical thinking among their students.

TRANSLATING HISTORY INTO CLASSROOM PRACTICE

Activity 7.1   Doing History Research Kit

Create a first-, second-, and third-order research kit. Organize it as follows:

Contents

- Table of contents
- Introduction to topic

I. Themes/habits used and type of historical thinking from National Standards for History (Reference to state learning standards is optional.)

II. Key question to engage students in inquiry
- *How* or *why* question
- Do not use a *should* or *would* question

III. Identify a first-order document for teaching your group's topic. (Written reasons for why this is a first-order document: Why does this document deserve to be a first-order document? What kind of source? What qualities does this document have that make it essential to your teaching and to your students' knowledge and understanding of history? How is it tied to the overall theme or subtheme?)

Include the actual first-order document and an analysis of the document. (References to an analysis guide will help. Using the sourcing heuristic, corroboration heuristic, contextualization, and comparative approaches will be helpful.)

IV. Identify second-order documents (three to five documents; at least one is an image), and write a rationale for why they are second-order. How does each of the second-order documents support or challenge the first-order document? Following are some additional considerations that might be helpful:

■ Show evidence that you have used the Internet in your research.

■ Provide a list of a primary sources and secondary sources.

■ Provide at least three types of primary sources (print documents; electronic media; folklore/folkways/mythology; arts (fine or graphic); physical environment/material culture).

■ A list of second-order document(s)/material

(Following the list explain how and why the second-order documents are related to the first-order document. References to the sourcing heuristic, corroboration heuristic, contextualization, and comparative approaches will be helpful.)

V. Include a list of third-order documents (potential documents for your students to find), and a rationale for why they are third-order.

■ List of third-order documents, anticipating documents/materials students might find.

You may also include:

■ A plan for using the documents in the classroom

■ A mechanism to assess the classroom plan

VI. Bibliography/references for first-, second-, and third-order documents

Activity 7.2   Doing History Research Team Kits

Organize into teams of three or four. Team members work together to develop the team's research kit (outlined in the previous activity), and present these documents to other history teaching methods students. Each team begins with all members bringing three primary sources (one of which must be an image). Team members reach a consensus regarding their first-order document. Team members also reach a consensus regarding the three to five second-order documents. The distinctions of first-, second-, and third-order documents will be valuable to you, and to your students, as you think about, study, and teach history.

REVIEWING THE CHAPTER

1. Choose a time period in U.S. history or world history. Identify and explain your rationale for a first-order document. Of the five typologies of primary sources, did you decide on a print, recording, tale, image, or artifact? Why?

2. Define the various heuristics proposed by Samuel Wineburg (see Chapter 3). Apply his heuristics (sourcing, corroboration) to the analysis guides in the chapter or to an analysis guide that you have created.

3. Why should one of the first- and second-order documents be iconic?

4. Speculate on third-order documents your students will find that relate to your first-order document. Will they find a print, image, or other type of document? Why?

5. Speculate on the questions your students will ask as they inquire about the document they find and relate to your first-order document.

8

Considering and Doing Discussion in History Teaching

Deliberative discussion should serve as the primary means by which students translate historical and social science knowledge into civic understanding. Deliberative discussions share characteristics that are consistent with democratic theory of practice: Students are engaged in analysis of powerful texts that examine content ideas and issues of American society and government; students examine their ideas and the ideas of their colleagues; and students engage at the very core of the democratic process, the understanding of texts and public issues throughout the co-investigation of those texts, their contexts, and issues with other students.

— John J. Patrick and Robert S. Leming, *Principles and Practices of Democracy in the Education of Social Studies Teachers*, 2001

*I*n the popular movie, *Ferris Bueller's Day Off*,[1] a hilarious scene depicts a history, social science, or social studies teacher attempting to lead a discussion of economic policies. The setting is a classroom in Ferris Bueller's high school in the Chicago suburbs, and Ferris Bueller has happily arranged for his own absence from this class as well as other classes.

If you have seen the movie, you will recall the memorable words ("Anyone? Anyone?") spoken by the teacher whose lesson on the Hawley-Smoot Tariff and the Great Depression lacked student involvement on even the most superficial level. This "discussion" (which is not a discussion) is boring to say the least. Students are not disruptive. They are comatose. Some are sound asleep and drooling. Others appear angry, and still others view the class through glazed eyes, unaware of the teacher's comments about the depression and the contemporary economy. The teacher fails throughout the scene to ask a question, and he fails to elicit any response from students.

Focus Questions

1. What is the popular conception of a discussion?

2. What is meant by a deliberative discussion?

3. How can you conduct deliberative discussions in your classroom?

The script of the teacher's monologue in *Ferris Bueller's Day Off* is shown in Figure 8.1. As you read this script, note that the italicized passages are the teacher's answers to his own questions. No student answers his questions.

The "Anyone, Anyone?" was a classic call of distress in far too many classrooms long before this movie was ever made. The mistakes of the teacher in *Ferris Bueller's Day Off* are obvious and sadly familiar. Actor Ben Stein as a teacher portrayed a stereotypical notion of classroom discussion. Discussion was nominal. It was a guessing game requiring students to read the teacher's mind and fill in the blanks. In this scene no elaboration on any issue occurred beyond the mere recognition of a tariff. No documents were introduced. No photographs were used. All the viewer can assume is that some assignment preceded this classroom discussion. Knowledge was superficial and disconnected. The teaching methods made it impossible for students to want to participate. At best, the class was reduced to a game of trivial pursuit.

Additionally, Ben Stein tried to make an artificial connection between the conditions during the Great Depression and the current conditions of the 1980s. He tried to make his lesson relevant. The movie was produced in 1986 at a time when the Laffer Curve was of great interest to the public and of potential relevancy to students. After all, the United States had suffered through double-digit inflation and a double-digit unemployment rate in the late 1970s and early 1980s. Ben Stein's reference to the Laffer Curve meant little to his students, however. What little relevance there was quickly dissolved in light of the teaching methods he used. Again, no documents were introduced. Ben Stein only talked at the kids and seemed to pray for some response.

Moreover, Ben Stein's content was superficial and insufficient. He compared an economic policy, the Hawley-Smoot Tariff of 1930, with a tool of economic analysis, the Laffer Curve of the 1980s.

FIGURE 8.1   Type-script from the film *Ferris Bueller's Day Off.*

Standing behind a podium in front of the class, the teacher (Ben Stein) drones:

In 1930, the Republican controlled House of Representatives in an effort to alleviate the effects of the . . . (pauses, waiting for a response) Anyone? Anyone? (then, the teacher answers his own question) . . . *The Great Depression* passed . . . (pauses, waiting for a response) Anyone? Anyone? (then the teacher answers his own question) . . . *the tariff bill, the Hawley-Smoot Tariff Act,* which . . . (pauses, waiting for a response) Anyone? Raised or lowered? (then, the teacher answers his own question) . . . *Raised* (pauses) in an effort to collect more revenue for the federal government.

Did it work? Anyone? Anyone know the effects? (pauses, waiting for a response then answers) *It did not work and the United States sank deeper into the Great Depression.* Today, we have a similar debate over this. Anyone know what this is? Class? Anyone? (pauses) . . . Anyone? Anyone seen this before? (then, the teacher answers) . . . *The Laffer Curve.* Anyone know what this says? *It says that at this point* (screech on the board from teacher using chalk) *on the revenue curve you will get exactly the same amount of revenue* . . . (pause) *at this point.*

This is very controversial. Does anyone know what Vice-President Bush called this in 1980? Anyone? . . . (pause as a student pops her bubble gum) *Something 'd-o-o' economics? 'Voodoo economics.'*

Furthermore—and this is important—he expected the impossible. His students were expected to guess a relationship between the Laffer Curve and the Hawley-Smoot Tariff of 1930 as if they were filling in blanks with no contextual clues whatsoever. Of equal dubious value were his methods of asking questions. "Anyone, Anyone" was a plea for students to say something; it was not a question.

The Importance of Discussion

One conception of discussion is the image of Ben Stein's so-called discussion. The teacher asks questions that require students to recall information from prior classes or prior readings. If the students answer the question, the teacher moves on to the next question. If students fail to respond to the teacher's questions, the teacher answers his own questions and moves on. Students quickly learn to wait for the teacher to answer his own questions.

In this type of discussion, some educators suggest that if teachers simply use "wait time," magic will occur. Ben Stein could have given his students time to consider their answers. But wait time works only if the students are prepared to discuss. Otherwise, waiting turns into coercion, and the teacher threatens the students if they are not prepared next time. Or, in Ben Stein's case, the teacher simply answers the questions himself. Neither solution is satisfactory.

Observers of history classrooms have long remarked that discussions serve as the staple of history and social studies instruction.[2] Discussion is such a broad concept, however, that it is difficult to define.

Before we go on to suggest how to encourage successful discussions in your classroom, consider this portrait of a history classroom: Your classroom is full of well-prepared, eager students who engage in lively discourse concerning a historical period; you are equally well prepared and ask insightful questions that spur your students to think deeply about the historical issue. You provide your students with opportunities to consider central ideas and issues, and they reflect on the meaning of these issues. You and your students engage in an inquiry with your students interacting and their observations based on primary sources. Each student has read one or more secondary sources, which help them provide narratives and elaborate on the historical context of the primary sources.

Variations of Discussions

Discussion is one of several centerpieces of history teaching. We offer four variations of discussion, with the fourth being our preferred method.

Recitation

The first variation of discussion is simply recitation. Students regurgitate textbook information in response to teachers' predictable questions. Students who experience this form of discussion learn to equate history with "the covering of past events."

Blather

A second form of discussion is labeled "blather." Students express opinions without feeling compelled to explain the reasons for their beliefs. Opinions are plentiful; evidence is sparse. The blather consists of one student saying "I believe. . . ." followed by a series of other students' belief statements. Students do not listen to each other; nor do they feel listening is necessary.

In this blather discussion there is no direction. No peaks of understanding are transformed into durable knowledge. Students are left with faintly interconnected ideas that quickly disappear at the end of class or at the end of an exam. In the students' minds, they have "covered" the historical terrain, but remembering this terrain beyond an exam is unimportant. The discussion is merely a formality. Teachers take comfort in the fact that students are at least interested and talking. However, the sound and the fury signify nothing.

Debate

A third variation of discussion is really a debate in which students defend a position, which is sometimes assigned. It begins with the teacher asking an evaluative question: Should the United States have dropped the atomic bomb? Should the South have seceded from the Union? Should the Cartheginian Hannibal have crossed the Alps and invaded the Roman Empire? Such questions are provocative and invite students to take positions and to support those positions. A poorly prepared teacher will rely on a textbook and quickly discover that most textbooks provide only a thin narrative description. Unless students are well prepared, this technique can lead to mere arguing or ill-informed, rambling discussions.

If the debate is well structured, the teacher asks an evaluative question (such as those in the preceding paragraph) and then has students read about all sides of the question. These readings, written by experts, are valuable both in terms of historical knowledge and in stimulating interesting classroom activities. Typically, the teacher assigns students to a yes or no position in the debate. This assignment is then followed by the gathering of information, sometimes in the form of research and sometimes in the form of documents distributed by the teacher. Students then use this information to support their assigned positions.

A variation of the debate strategy is to let students read the views of experts and then take a position themselves. Students are compelled to take a yes or no position on the evaluative question without having the opportunity to consider or reconsider their initial position. Once every student has determined his or her initial position, their efforts are devoted to gathering information that supports their position.

We do not dismiss debate as a productive method of teaching. It certainly has its merits. However, we offer several cautions. First, the debate begins with the assumption that there are right and wrong positions. Second, the debate is combative in nature, which often results in the truth being relegated to secondary importance. Third, debate plays an important role in classrooms, but has limitations that if unrecognized seriously undermine the development of historical understanding and dispositions on the part of students. The ethos of debate is to defend the "rightness" of a position. This tactic may result in students concealing information that does not support their position. Students seek flaws in their opponents' arguments and focus only on their opponents' weaknesses. And fourth, the ultimate goal of the debate is victory rather than the establishment of plausible truth.

Teachers often resort to debate because it appears good to outside observers and because it involves students in an intellectual activity. We are not condemning debate as a teaching strategy to elicit discussion. Rather, we urge you as a teacher to use debates in tandem with deliberative discussions. Figure 8.2 compares debate and deliberative discussion.

Deliberative Discussion

A fourth form of discussion, which we encourage, is what we call **deliberative discussion. Deliberation** involves your students in reasoning and choice. The choice, or decision, students make regarding their position on issues occurs subsequent to the discussion of a number of historical sources. Deliberation requires you and your students to engage in a rigorous discourse in which sources, ideas, values, and conversations are held up to analysis. (Note how this contrasts with Ben Stein's class.)

Deliberation cultivates reasoning and choice while also fostering virtues necessary in a democratic society. Political theorist Amy Gutmann asserted that "the

FIGURE 8.2   Comparison of Debate and Deliberative Discussion.

Debate	Deliberation
Competitive in nature with the overall objective being to organize information and "win"	Cooperative in nature with the objective being to work together to examine documents and increase historical understanding
Begins with the belief that there are "right" and "wrong" positions	The purpose is to examine ideas and collectively increase historical understanding
Students listen and look for weaknesses in the ideas and positions of opponents	Students listen carefully and critically to others to look for their insights and to increase their understanding
Goal is to undermine ideas and positions of opponents based on the strengths of one's own arguments and personality	The goal is to encourage the participation of all students
Encourages students to conceal and ignore ideas that do not support their positions	Encourages students to examine a variety of sources and ideas including those that seem to challenge their initial beliefs
Students work to a conclusion that is consistent with their original beliefs	Students seek to understand the issue in more complex and meaningful terms

virtues that deliberation encompasses include veracity, nonviolence, practical judgment, civic integrity and magnanimity. By cultivating these and other deliberative skills and virtues, a democratic society helps secure both the basic opportunity of individuals and its collective capacity to pursue justice."[3]

John J. Patrick and Robert S. Leming, in promoting the use of deliberative discussion, made a very important point about teaching. They wrote that prospective teachers of history, the social sciences, and social studies should have the "disposition of a scholar" and "a depth of knowledge." When you as a teacher possess the scholar's disposition and knowledge in an academic discipline and its methods of inquiry, you can "generate new knowledge" with your students.[4] Patrick and Leming further pointed out the importance of deliberative discussion and its relationship to an academic discipline. They wrote, "Deliberative discussion should serve as the primary means by which students translate historical and social science knowledge into civic understanding. Deliberative discussions share characteristics that are consistent with democratic theory of practice."[5]

There are three additional reasons for emphasizing deliberative discussions in your teaching.[6] First, classrooms are flooded today with debates in which students do not reason together but are called on to choose sides and argue on issues, often superficially. The result is that students learn to talk past and outargue one another. They need a habit of mind that suspends judgments before making rash decisions. Deliberative discussions serve as an important and often overlooked intermediary step in decision making. History's habits of mind—its way of thinking—are developed through deliberative discussions.

Second, deliberative discussions can be framed around a discussion of a context-based historical issue. Your students can examine core documents. They can read, analyze, and discuss your first-order and second-order documents. They can find and read third-order documents that have particular meaning for them. And finally, they can synthesize these documents into a rich and meaningful interpretation of a historical event.

One of the great obstacles to student deliberation is that students frequently rush to evaluate a historical or contemporary issue and then spend the subsequent discussion period organizing evidence to support their initial positions. We suggest that you help your students suspend their evaluations of historical documents, artifacts, or incidents until they have had a chance to thoroughly examine the meaning of these sources.

Third, deliberative discussions are consistent with the expectations of students. Research concerning the New Social Studies movement of the 1960s and 1970s found that teaching methods that were radically different from the methods traditionally employed by teachers were quickly modified or abandoned.[7] Deliberative discussions are not a radical departure from traditional methods that are viewed as legitimate and fitting. Rather, they simply add depth and precision to those methods.

Deliberative discussions are an essential component of good teaching. They are a method for establishing the credibility of historical evidence and arguments and a means to develop historical understanding in students. Deliberation involves teachers and students in careful examination, reading, and extended discussion of historical sources (primary and secondary) and topics/issues.

You can engage your students in deliberative discussions using our approach of first-, second-, and third-order documents. You and your students begin by discussing the central ideas and issues in the first-order document. You ask students to suspend quick or present-minded judgments about past issues and points of view while trying to understand the context of the document. You then introduce additional related documents (second-order documents) so your students have a richer contextual understanding of the period. These documents corroborate or challenge your seminal, or core, first-order document. Your students are invited to find other documents that more fully illuminate their inquiries into the past.[8] This systematic inquiry offers students opportunities to understand ongoing ideas and issues that define who we are in space and time. This inquiry is structured while allowing your students to bring to bear their creative ideas in their choice of third-order documents. Once your students have determined their third-order document, they have a stronger command of the historical issue under consideration.

Doing Discussions in Your Classroom

There is no rigid pattern for leading deliberative discussions. Effective teachers vary instructional strategies to ensure that all students have an opportunity to learn. Effective teachers also vary the sources they bring to class, including such visuals and audios as photographs, art, campaign posters, literature, music, graphs, charts, maps, letters, speeches, diaries, and other artifacts to entice those students whose learning is embellished and enriched by such sources. Each one of these sources requires careful analysis prior to its introduction. Once you have decided which documents to bring to your classroom, your students need to analyze them with your help.

Initiating Inquiry

As an effective history teacher, you need to create a classroom environment conducive to discussion. You need to encourage students and build up their confidence so that they will contribute to a discussion. Establish a learning climate that lets students know that they are expected to learn once the classroom bell rings. To start your class effectively, you need a document—a short quote, a photograph, or an artifact—to focus your students' attention. Engage your students immediately so that every day your students enter your classroom they know that you are well prepared and that you expect their wholehearted engagement in the discussion.

A very effective teaching strategy to start discussions in an engaging way is a think-pair-share activity. This activity gives each student the confidence needed to participate in learning. It also helps you assess your students' initial ideas and misconceptions.

Let's consider a multi-day plan for a lesson on the Great Depression, which was the focus of Ben Stein's lesson. First, you could show a photograph, perhaps your first-order document, from the Dorothea Lange photograph collection, available online from the Library of Congress (see the Ideas for the History Classroom feature) as a way to introduce the Great Depression. Keep in mind that you must be careful not to analyze the source for students, but you should provide some structure for their inquiry. The primary source analysis guide for photographs/images on page 148 in Chapter 7 provides such a structure.

In place of the analysis guide, you might ask each student to take out a piece of paper and answer fundamental questions about the photograph, such as the following:

- List three adjectives that describe the individuals/objects/events in this photograph.
- What does this photograph tell you about these people's lives?
- When do you think this photograph was taken?
- Why do you think this photograph was taken?
- What title would you give this photograph?

These questions provide a framework for creative historical interpretation.

Your students' answers to your questions should not be confused with a discussion. Rather, as an artful teacher you will use these initial questions as a foundation for subsequent discussions. Quite obviously, some students will have misperceptions of the photograph. These misperceptions can be considered in your discussions. Remember that all students come to the discussion with varying amounts of intellectual capital to draw on.

Ideas for the History Classroom

Dorothea Lange Photograph

Courtesy of the Library of Congress.

After your students have independently considered the previous questions and written their answers on a piece of paper (a necessary step because it brings about ownership in the activity), ask them to join in small groups of two to four to share their answers. Tell them that if they like the answer of a colleague, to add it to their list of responses. (Or you can tell them to come to a consensus on answers.) In groups, your students should compare their answers and note areas of agreement and disagreement with others. Even the student who was initially ill prepared now has an opportunity to bring and take some intellectual capital to the discussion.

When you ask all students to share their responses, you invite even the shy and unprepared to participate. You also provide subtle encouragement for students to be better prepared for subsequent lessons. Because you have enabled your students to think about the questions on their own, then created an opportunity to share their answers, you can now call on individual students who will not feel the embarrassment of lacking preparation. Even the student who has the most difficulty learning has an opportunity to contribute to the discussion.

During this structured "share" segment of the activity, briefly record your students' responses on the chalkboard or an overhead projector. This action lets your students know that you respect them and take the activity and their ideas seriously.

When recording your students' responses, don't be too quick to make judgments at the time. Doing so stifles their enthusiasm. As you record your students' observations, you can make mental notes regarding their knowledge and dispositions to organize subsequent instruction. Once students have made contributions, you can transition to other documents, a lecture on the topic, or other activities. You can also tell your students that you want them to organize forthcoming information around the vital theme and narrative of values, beliefs, political ideas, and institutions.

As you introduce additional sources—your second-order documents—into the class discussion, have your students consult a secondary source to reinforce their knowledge of the Hawley-Smoot Tariff Act of 1930. For example, you could distribute an excerpt describing Hawley-Smoot (see Figure 8.3). In addition to a secondary source, you might introduce two additional second-order documents. For example, you can use two primary sources that describe life during the Depression. Teenagers were often forced to fend for themselves during the depression—sometimes because their parents could no longer provide for them. In this example, Peggy Eaton, a 15-year-old teenager chose to leave her ranch home in Wyoming in 1938 following an argument with her father. She describes her misadventures when running away from home. Peggy and a friend hopped a train, rode with hobos and dodged the railroad police while travelling the western states of Idaho, Oregon, and Washington in the hope of finding a job and making money. On more than one occasion she and her friend faced perils at railroad yards and on board freight cars. She recounts, for example, a decision she had to make as the train increased speed to forty miles per hour rather than slow down as it neared the La Grande, Oregon freight yard. "It looked like a trap," she writes, "especially since it was the same place where the bull [railroad police] had shot the man the day before." To avoid the bulls, Peggy leaped out of the freight car and tumbled over and over when she hit the ground. Some bulls were ruthless; others were friendly and even helpful, warning her of impending danger as she travelled the train. "[G]et off in Yakima," one

FIGURE 8.3 Secondary Source on Hawley-Smoot Tariff Act of 1930.

The crowning folly of the Hoover administration was the Smoot-Hawley Tariff, passed in June 1930. It came on top of the Fordney-McCumber Tariff of 1922, which had already put American agriculture in a tailspin during the preceding decade. The most protectionist legislation in U.S. history, Smoot-Hawley virtually closed the borders to foreign goods and ignited a vicious international trade war. Professor Barry Poulson notes that not only were 887 tariffs sharply increased, but the act broadened the list of dutiable commodities to 3,218 items as well. . . .

Foreign companies and their workers were flattened by Smoot-Hawley's steep tariff rates, and foreign governments soon retaliated with trade barriers of their own. With their ability to sell in the American market severely hampered, they curtailed their purchases of American goods. American agriculture was particularly hard hit. With a stroke of the presidential pen, farmers in this country lost nearly a third of their markets. Farm prices plummeted and tens of thousands of farmers went bankrupt. With the collapse of agriculture, rural banks failed in record numbers, dragging down hundreds of thousands of their customers.

Source: Excerpt from http://www.fee.org/publications/the-freeman/article.asp?aid=3489.

FIGURE 8.4 Ann Rivington: Living on Relief.

When I went to college I studied sociology. I was taught that hunger, squalor, dirt, and ignorance are the results of environment. Charity, therefore, is no solution. We must change the environment. In order to do this, we have settlement houses, playgrounds, and social workers in the slums.

In the past year and a half I have again revised my opinion. *I am no longer one of us* [italics added]. For all my education, my training in thrift and cleanliness, I am become one of them. My condition is shared by a large sector of the population. From my new place in society I regard the problems and misery of the poor with new eyes.

Two years ago I was living in comfort and apparent security. My husband had a good position in a well-known orchestra, and I was teaching a large and promising class of piano pupils. When the orchestra was disbanded, we started on a rapid downhill path. My husband was unable to secure another position. My class gradually dwindled away. We were forced to live on our savings.

In the early summer of 1933 I was eight months pregnant and we had just spent our last twelve dollars on one month's rent for an apartment. We found that such apartments really exist. They lack most elementary comforts. They are usually infested with mice and bedbugs. Ours was. Quite often the ceilings leak.

What, then, did we do for food when our last money was spent on rent? In vain we tried to borrow more. So strong was the influence of our training that my husband kept looking feverishly for work when there was no work, and blaming himself because he was unable to find it. An application to the Emergency Home Relief Bureau was the last act of our desperation. . . .

Source: Reprinted with the permission of Scribner, an imprint of Simon & Schuster Adult Publishing Group, from *Scribner's Magazine,* vol. 95, 1934. Copyright © 1934 by Charles Scribner's Sons; copyright renewed © 1962.

bull advised, "because after that there were low tunnels through the Cascade Mountains and he didn't want to see us get decapitated."[9]

Peggy Eaton's story illustrates the great difficulties facing individuals and families as they chased rumors hoping to find temporary jobs. Her experiences as a teenage runaway reflect the hardship of individuals seeking jobs and the difficulties people in towns had making ethical decisions regarding the treatment of large numbers of transients.

A second example can be found in Figure 8.4. Ann Rivington, an unemployed music teacher who was pregnant with her first child, recalls how the effects of the depression challenged her values.

For the artful history teacher, one question that must be considered is this: Is it more effective to focus on a primary source, such as "Ann Rivington: Living on Relief," or on the Hawley-Smoot Tariff of 1930 when drawing students into the drama of the Great Depression? Consider the fact that the individualism of the 19th century conditioned Ann Rivington to believe that poverty was a fate reserved to individuals possessing poor character. Her husband, who blamed himself for not being able to secure employment, also held this belief.

Primary sources invite your students to enter the past through a habit of mind—historical empathy. Encourage them to try to understand the world as Ann Rivington confronted it in 1933. Too easily students can dismiss the actions or beliefs of people living in the past as quaint or uninformed. You might hear students remark, "She was stupid to think it was her fault." Or, perhaps some of your students will observe, "Why didn't she and her husband leave and go somewhere else?" As an effective teacher you can tactfully move your students into the frame of mind of the time, encouraging them to understand the constraints of thought and practical circumstances facing Ann Rivington and her family in 1933.

The primary source analysis guide to historical thinking: print documents (see page 147 in Chapter 7) provides an organizing framework for your students to use when examining the lives of both Ann Rivington and Peggy Eaton and considering their motivations in the context of the Great Depression. Subsequently, your students can bring in their own documents (third-order) to expand the discussion to individuals experiencing the Depression in other parts of the United States and other countries.

Deliberating on Time and Place

Discussion, particularly deliberative discussion, offers an opportunity to examine people's ethics in a particular time and place. Students, when reading these documents, share the world of historical scholarship. They do not know all that they would like to know about Ann Rivington or Peggy Eaton; these sources reveal only partial information.

For example, even if we do not know Ann Rivington's exact age, we can guess that she was probably in her 20s or early 30s because she was recently married. That means that she was probably born in the first decade of the 20th century. Her worldview, her ethics, and the values that formed her perspective on the world

---

Ideas for the History Classroom

Promoting Discussion of Readings for All Students

Most teachers begin a discussion by asking their students to identify the main idea of a primary or secondary source. Students are intimidated when asked to discuss the main idea. To allay fears, we suggest the following three groupings of questions:

- Interesting?
- Puzzling, bothersome, or confusing?
- Question to ask the author?

Procedure

1. Write the three groups of questions on the board.
2. Ask your students to write on a piece of paper what they found in the primary or secondary source to be interesting; puzzling, bothersome, or confusing; and a question they would ask the author.
3. Give your students one or two minutes to write their responses.
4. Have students pair with another student to exchange what they found to be interesting; puzzling, bothersome, or confusing; and a question to ask the author. Encourage your students to add to their initial writing.
5. Ask your students to share their responses. Write student responses on the chalkboard. Make no judgments as you record their responses.
6. Lead your students into a discussion of the categories. For example, who else was puzzled by the statement/idea in the reading?

---

were shaped by parents born in the 19th century and teachers not only born but also educated in the 19th century. Her words express the conflict of an individual who was taught to believe in individual responsibility and initiative and then faced economic conditions beyond her control or the control of her husband.

Durable historical knowledge rests in her expression of the conflict she faced between individualism and the hope that an active government would relieve her conditions. As you use this strategy of encouraging discussions through the use of primary sources that draw students into a good story, you develop in your students durable knowledge of the issues of individualism versus government or the values of freedom and security. These key stories depict a turning point in history.

As a history teacher, you keep alive the open invitation to learning. The Dorothea Lange photograph, the Ann Rivington story, and the account of Peggy Eaton's travels are primary sources that contribute to each of your student's construction of historical understanding. The stories are not an end but a beginning. You and your students can weave together several stories and continue to develop a more nuanced understanding of the conditions of the Great Depression. As a history teacher, you have many opportunities to introduce primary sources that engage your students in the development of historical understanding by examining particular events and linking these events to larger historical contexts.

Generally speaking, you can be a successful history teacher by establishing an environment that invites and supports student involvement in the study of history. You want your students to deliberate together and to deliberate with you. Help your students connect particular ideas with larger themes of history (such as values, beliefs, political ideas, and institutions) and think about the past with one or more of historians' habits of mind (such as empathy). Your role in deliberative discussions is not to dominate informed conversation, but neither are you a mere "guide on the side."

Varying Sources to Engage Students in Discussion

As a reflective teacher, you recognize that students have different preferred learning styles. To motivate all of your students, vary the use of visual sources and written texts. On some occasions, you will use a visual as a first-order document and written texts as second-order documents. On other occasions, the procedure will be reversed.

Some students will enter the first-order deliberation more easily through a photograph or other visual document; some students will find the doorway into first-order deliberation more accessible through written texts. The third-order deliberation—when students find their own important documents—will

---

Ideas for the History Classroom
Modeling Historical Thinking

Modeling historical thinking for students is an important part of the teacher's role. As you engage your students in reading primary sources, you will want to ask questions that compel them to engage in sourcing, contextualization, and corroboration. Therefore, when you provide students with a document, before you have them read the text—and certainly before you ask them to determine the main idea—you should ask them questions to promote sourcing, contextualization, and corroboration.

For example, if you are teaching a lesson in which you use Franklin D. Roosevelt's October 5, 1937 "Quarantine the Aggressor" speech, your first question should be, "What do we know about FDR?" As you list students' responses on the board, you can then, as it becomes appropriate, utilize contextualization.

A second question might be, "Where are we in time? What does the United States look like in 1937? What does the world look like?"

Finally, you should ask students to consider what other documents—primary and secondary—they have read that might help them better understand FDR's speech at this time. Such a question might be, "What other sources have we encountered that will assist us in putting this document in perspective? What other ideas from the time or about the time should we consider?"

These types of questions should promote a discussion that will be grounded in historical context instead of being merely focused on a main idea.

demonstrate their understanding of the topic and indicate their preference for visual or written texts.

Deliberative discussion provides each individual with an opportunity to engage personally in an investigation of the past: to organize, share, and learn from the perspective of other students. The issues inherent in the documents and questions raised by you and your students in the course of inquiry shape your discussions. Your questions should be prefaced with *what, how,* and *why* as a catalyst to understanding multiple causation. This distinguishes deliberation from debate, which emphasizes *should.*

Evaluative judgment occurs as students gain greater expertise in situating documents within the appropriate time frame. Students learn historical inquiry by analyzing a number of documents that pertain to a particular historical issue or heuristic question. Ultimately, students engage in evaluation when they impart meaning to past and bind individual events into a larger framework of historical understanding (their narratives).

SUMMARY

We began this chapter with a discussion of *Ferris Bueller's Day Off* and Ben Stein's portrayal of an unfocused teacher who provides no opportunity to engage students in history. He was simply trying to involve students in "word-calling," that is, identifying a term, person, idea, or event. In the course of this chapter, we have suggested several steps to consider as you engage your students in learning history. Initially you decide on the sources that will intrigue your students. You take steps to ensure that all students feel as though they can contribute to discussions in an informed way. Ultimately, you are helping your students construct an informed meaning of the past.

Deliberative discussion engages students in the construction of historical knowledge. Students listen to one another, read and relate various documents, and build a historical understanding that persists long after the class is over. Deliberation pursues the truth while respecting the historical interpretations of others.

TRANSLATING HISTORY INTO CLASSROOM PRACTICE

Activity 8.1   Organizing a Deliberative Discussion

Suppose you observed a classroom teacher whose discussion replicated the Ben Stein scene in the movie *Ferris Bueller's Day Off.* What suggestions would you have to improve the teacher's instruction so he or she can avoid the "Anyone, Anyone" cry for help?

After reading this chapter, what suggestions do you have to reorganize Ben Stein's teaching into a deliberative discussion with students?

Activity 8.2   History and Effective Discussions

Consider the following list of important qualities of a good discussion. What is missing? How can history be part of good discussions?

1. Relevancy to a current topic
2. Student preparedness
3. Teacher asking provocative questions
4. Students asking questions of one another
5. Students challenging the ideas of classmates
6. Forms of classroom organization
7. Instructional methods

Activity 8.3 Marketing a Strategy for a Network Discussion Program

Deliberative discussions imply both thoughtful reason and choice with a suspension of judgment. Deliberation involves virtues that include veracity, nonviolence, practical judgment, civic integrity, and magnanimity. Deliberation offers an opportunity for people to reason together even if they are at extreme ends of an issue. Yet the media often presents programs that consist of 3- or 4-minute segments in which "experts" yell at each other or at best talk at each other to outdo their opponent in the time allotted.

Imagine that a broadcast network has put you in charge of its marketing campaign for a program that can emphasize either deliberation or debate. With three or four colleagues, prepare a presentation for the network's board of directors that demonstrates your marketing strategy and ideas. Your presentation should explain how the strategies you developed will make the program a success. Begin by naming the program and designing a promo. Then, explain to the board of directors the following:

1. How you will target television viewers
2. How you will determine the topics/issues/controversies
3. What you will emphasize in a 30-second advertising spot

REVIEWING THE CHAPTER

1. Describe the discussions you have experienced in middle and high school history classes. What historical issues were discussed? Did you need to be prepared to engage in these discussions?
2. What vital themes and narratives informed the discussions?
3. What habits of mind made you think in the context of the times?
4. What were your experiences with debates in middle and high school history classes? How carefully did you consider the ideas and arguments of the debate opponents?
5. Examine Figure 8.2 on debate and deliberation. What elements do debate and deliberation have in common? What elements are different?

9
Using Historical Images to Engage Your Students in the Past

It seems more probable that a teacher who presents material in an original manner is not necessarily highly creative but simply more willing to spend time thinking about how best to convey information to a specific audience.

— James C. Schott and Laurel R. Singleton, *Teaching the Social Sciences and History in Secondary Schools*, 2000

Consider the times you were inspired by someone or some event from history and how you can make that historical moment more meaningful for you and your students. . . . Though it can at times be tumultuous, enjoy the ride and reap the numerous rewards along the way. In short make history.

— James Percoco, *A Passion for the Past: Creative Teaching of U.S. History*, 1998

*I*n this chapter we provide three strategies for using images in your teaching to foster discussion. These three strategies engage your students in analyzing images and constructing meaning of the past.

Focus Questions

1. What teaching methods best support historical understanding and thinking?

2. How does your knowledge of content influence your decisions regarding teaching strategies?

3. How do these teaching methods support deliberation within your classroom?

4. How can images engage your students in discussion?

At Elgin High School we met with a U.S. history teacher whose students were male and female, white, black, and Hispanic. On the floor of his classroom were permanent chalk outlines of seven human torsos. We asked him why. He excitedly responded, "I want to make my classroom an alive experience. The lines on the floor are drawn to represent individuals who crossed the Atlantic on a slave ship. I want these outlines to be a constant reminder to my students of the hardships of the Middle Passage. And I want my students to get inside those lines, to feel what it was like to be a slave transported from one continent to another." This teacher wanted to emphasize both knowledge and empathy. The readings regarding slavery and the diagrams of the ship gave students the opportunity to understand and feel.

At Victor Andrew High School we observed a world history teacher using a slide depicting the trench warfare of World War I. The projection was displayed on a large wall. She asked her students to describe the features of a trench, as projected on to the wall, and what life must have been like for those soldiers. She then asked for volunteers to spend 15 minutes in the trench while they and their classmates read primary sources about the suffering of soldiers engaged in trench warfare. Toward the end of class, she and her students discussed a passage from Erich Maria Remarque's historical novel *All Quiet on the Western Front.*

Some of the ideas for both teachers came from the curriculum series *History Alive!* Both teachers took risks; they broke the stereotype of teaching history. In addition, both teachers gave their students brief writing assignments. They asked their students to write two paragraphs, one identifying a habit of mind that helped them think about their experiences and the second identifying key elements in primary sources that had meaning for them. The written assignment, the readings, and the class experiences were all integrated into discussions regarding the unique experiences of slavery and trench warfare, respectively.

In one class period, both teachers had made use of several meaningful teaching strategies. They used visuals, primary sources, role-playing, writing assignments, and integrative and focused deliberative discussions.

Variety of Teaching Methods

In your teaching situation, you can modify the technology involved. You might use the Internet to download images (the slave ship diagram or pictures of trenches) and display them with an LCD projector or an overhead projector. The technology can vary; however, your overarching purpose remains the same as that of the two teachers mentioned earlier: developing of historical understanding and empathy through the use of creative and interactive teaching–learning strategies.

Myriad methods are available to you as a history teacher. You can lecture, perhaps using an advance organizer such as an important concept, theme, or generalization. Advance organizers help lectures by providing an intellectual scaffold for your students to hang what otherwise might seem to be discrete bits of information.

"Jigsawing" strategies are associated with cooperative learning, wherein students divide up responsibilities, develop expertise, and share knowledge with each other. You can also organize your classroom into stations with your students rotating as if they were on a carousel from one station to the next. At each station your students discuss primary sources (single or multiple sources as mentioned in Chapter 7). Perhaps you want your students to role-play people from the past who have made life or death decisions or resolved everyday problems.

Maybe your teaching includes field trips to museums or walking tours of historic places in your community. Walking tours inform students of the ways human beings changed the landscape and interacted with the environment at different times. Perhaps you will enlist your students in oral history projects such as interviews with local members of your community whose life experiences and memories offer a wealth of perspectives regarding an event in their own past. Or perhaps your teaching includes using the Socratic method of discussion. Whatever methods you choose, we hope you use interactive teaching to create meaning of the past through informed understanding.

In-depth descriptions of the strategies just mentioned are beyond the scope of this text. You can easily access more information about these strategies elsewhere. We do ask you this question, however: If your department chair, your principal, or a member of the community were to walk into your classroom and observe your teaching at its best, what would they see you and your students doing?

Using Images to Engage Your Students in Discussions

There are numerous ways to use images in your classroom instruction. Some teachers display an image such as a photograph and then explain the meaning of the photograph to their students. If the teacher is an expert on the photograph and clearly analyzes its key aspects, the students will be informed in a meaningful way.

However, a lecture (or formal analysis of a photograph) does not provide for planned, systematic class discussions. Student involvement usually consists of students taking notes and thinking about your analysis of the image. You may ask them if they have any questions, or a student may ask a question, but either way, only a few students are participating. And during such a session, every answer relies heavily on you as the teacher.

What activities can you incorporate so your students will develop the skills of analysis? We suggest three strategies to help engage your students in analyzing an image and constructing meaning of the past: people, space, and time; similarities and differences; and quadrantal-hemispheric analysis. For all three strategies we suggest you use the think-pair-share structure (described in Chapter 8) as a means to support any discussion you initiate. The *think* component involves your students in ownership. *Pair* lets them discuss ideas with a classroom colleague, giving them confidence that they can *share* and contribute to the discussion with the class as a whole.

Strategy 1: Analyzing an Image for Discussion: The People, Space, and Time Strategy

The **people, space, and time strategy** consists of asking your students to examine an image (such as the image on page 177). Display this image and ask students to take out a sheet of paper and answer the following questions:

1. Was this person living east or west of the Appalachian Mountains? (history, geography)
2. Speculate on three present-day cities where this person may have lived. (geography, history, sociology, economics)
3. Was this portrait painted before or after the Civil War? (history—time)
4. Speculate a century and a decade when the portrait was made. (history—time)
5. Write down five adjectives to describe this person and/or this person's way of living. (history, sociology, economics, geography)
6. Speculate as to the motives of the creator of this portrait. (history)
7. What title would you give this portrait?

anticipatory

add to it

note it

Notice that these questions immediately cause your students to examine the painting. For example, the first question has a geographic quality. Your students will need to infer from the clothing where the person might have lived. Depending on the image you choose, you can modify your reference to a geographic feature. For example, you can decide whether your question should focus on the cardinal points of east–west or north–south. You may also choose to emphasize other physical or cultural features.

Your second, third, and fourth questions refer to the dimension of time. Each student at this point is looking for clues in the clothing, clothing style, furniture, and other artifacts. Notice too that the questions begin with the present day, relate to a specific important event in history, and then call on students to think historically about a specific century and decade.

Question 5 is intended to give life to the human being in the portrait. Students must use their historical imaginations as they describe the person and artifacts in the image. They have to notice cleanliness, sloppiness, formality, and informality as well as the objects in the photograph.

Question 6 suggests to your students that images have a purpose and that the painter or photographer is attempting to convey a story or idea in visual form. The painter/photographer stages the image just as the historian conveys an interpretation in written form.

Question 7 allows for creativity and the application of knowledge. It is a good measure of students' sophistication.

This people, space, and time strategy has a hidden purpose—to find out what your students already know. You support their participation in a discussion by allowing them a comfortable learning environment in which to extend their knowledge (when they pair with another classmate) and to exchange ideas.

Ideas for the History Classroom

People, Space, and Time Image Analysis Strategy

Paul Revere

1. Was this person living east or west of the Appalachian Mountains? (history, geography)
2. Speculate on three present-day cities where this person may have lived. (geography, history, sociology, economics)
3. Was this portrait painted before or after the Civil War? (history—time)
4. Speculate a century and a decade when the portrait was made. (history—time)
5. Write down five adjectives to describe this person and/or this person's way of living. (history, sociology, economics, geography)
6. Speculate as to the motives of the creator of this portrait. (history)
7. What title would you give this portrait?

Photograph © 2008 Museum of Fine Arts, Boston. John Singleton Copley, American, 1738–1815. *Paul Revere*, 1768. Oil on canvas. 89.22 × 72.39 cm (35 1/8 × 28 1/2 in.). Museum of Fine Arts, Boston. Gift of Joseph W. Revere, William B. Revere and Edward H. R. Revere, 30.781.

Give your students a time limit (such as 5 minutes) to discuss what they believe are the geographic, social, economic, and political themes defining the image. Finally, during the share segment (when you ask students as a class the questions provided) you can call on your students, knowing that they have a foundation from which to contribute to the discussion. In essence, they are confident that they can succeed because they have thought about your questions and recorded responses, and then found out what another classmate thinks, which they can then add to their own knowledge.

This people, space, and time strategy can take 10 to 20 minutes. You can extend the discussion even further based on your abilities to nurture your students' ability to think. Of course, the time required will also depend on the composition of your class; students' knowledge and enthusiasm will be a major factor in determining the length of your discussion, as any veteran teacher will tell you. But what is important is that you have laid the foundation for your students to be successful. Your questioning does not have to be rote. You can use an impromptu Socratic method of discussion that invites students to think and listen to their classmates.

To extend your discussion, you can pose an eighth question: In addition to Paul Revere, what other people should we be looking for as we think about this time period in history?

In the case of our example, we used John Singleton Copley's portrait of Paul Revere, which was most likely painted in 1770. Copley used a technique of *portrait d'apparat* in his paintings. He surrounded his subjects with objects that had meaning in their everyday lives. Notice in this portrait that Revere was a silversmith. Copley also used reflections in this portrait. The three reflections provide a subtle clue to the meaning of this portrait. First, we see a reflection on Revere's working table, probably made of mahogany. Second, we see a reflection of his fingertips on the teapot, which symbolizes his craftsmanship. And third, Copley provided a rectangular reflection on the teapot, perhaps of a window toward which Revere is looking.[1] What is Revere looking toward? Who else will be involved? These are questions of inquiry that engage your students in social, economic, and political events.

Finally, you and your students can connect the image of Revere (or any other image) to one of history's vital themes and narratives and habits of mind. What vital theme organizes the content of this image for you? Is it values, beliefs, political ideas, and institutions? Paul Revere may have been looking out the window with a steady gaze waiting for the inevitable war with the British. Will your theme serve as a window to the past for those thinking about classical liberalism (individual rights) and classical republicanism (common good)? Let your students determine a vital theme and habit of mind that is important for them.

Strategy 2: Analyzing an Image for Discussion: Similarities and Differences

don't necessary need to be buildings

The second strategy, **similarities and differences**, also uses the think-pair-share structure. In the similarities and differences strategy, you can display two images (such as those shown on page 179.) This example shows both the Parthenon and the Lincoln Memorial. Ask your students to take out a sheet of paper and identify three characteristics that are similar and three characteristics that are different between the two buildings. Give them 1 minute to list the similarities and differences they can identify. Then, give them 1 minute to pair with another classmate. After the think and pair opportunities, call on your students to share their comparative characteristics. Record their descriptions to use as a basis for subsequent discussions or for further activities that relate to the theme, era, or period of history you are studying.

Ideas for the History Classroom

Similarities and Differences Image Analysis Strategy

Strategy 3: Analyzing an Image for Discussion: Quadrantal/Hemispheric Analysis

A third strategy, **quadrantal/hemispheric analysis,** prepares students to be careful observers of images. Display an image such as the one on page 181. Tell your students they have 20 seconds to remember what they see in the photograph. Then cover the photograph and ask them to describe what they observed. Write down their observations on the chalkboard or overhead projector. Your students may have much to describe or very little to describe, depending on their experiences with photos and their historical knowledge.

Then, tell your students that you have divided the photograph into four quadrants and that they can see only one quadrant at a time. (You may choose to divide the photograph into two hemispheres instead, depending on the details of your photograph and the ability levels of your students. The hemisphere approach is a helpful way to accommodate students with special needs and younger students in the analysis of images.)

Ask your students which quadrant they want to see. Reveal this quadrant and tell them they have 30 seconds to list the objects and people in this section of the photograph. Cover the quadrant and repeat this procedure until the students have viewed the entire photograph one section at a time.

Once all four quadrants have been revealed, ask your students to pair and share the details they observed in each quadrant. Then ask them these questions:

1. Where was this photograph taken?
2. When was this photograph taken?
3. What does this photograph tell us about people's lives?
4. What were the motivations of the photographer?
5. How does this photograph relate to one of history's vital themes and narratives? Habits of mind?

Notice that these questions establish the foundations of geography and time. They also encourage students to think about the conditions in which people lived. They allow them to speculate about the purposes of the photographer, whose photograph is much like a historical interpretation. Finally, ask your students to relate the photograph to one of history's vital themes and narratives and/or to one of the 10 themes of the National Social Studies Standards.

Of course, throughout this process you are taking steps to reinforce student discussion. Ask your students to explain how they identified a place, a time, or a motive and connected these to a vital theme and narrative. You can also ask them to react to the explanations of their classmates and to elaborate on these ideas.

You can continue this discussion of a photograph by providing your students with additional written primary sources. Organize your class into small groups of two to four students with each group responsible for creating a museum exhibit. Using this example of the Vietnam War, you can provide 13 photographs for students to analyze. In addition, you can provide several written primary sources, and perhaps three or four sources of a secondary nature.

Then, and this is a key point, inform your students that they are museum curators with limited space in their facility. As curators, they can select only six images and/or print documents. Which of the six will they choose and why? Furthermore, tell your students that to organize the content of their museum exhibit they should relate each artifact to one of the vital themes and narratives and to one of history's habits of mind.[2]

Your students should prepare a written and oral presentation for those who enter their exhibit. Adjacent to each artifact should be a placard that describes

Ideas for the History Classroom

Quadrantal/Hemispheric Image Analysis Strategy

1. Where was this photograph taken?
2. When was this photograph taken?
3. What does this photograph tell us about people's lives?
4. What were the motivations of the photographer?
5. How does this photograph relate to one of history's vital themes and narratives?

the details of the image or written document and an explanation of how the document relates to their vital theme and narrative as well as a habit of mind.

SUMMARY

We began this chapter by emphasizing the importance of making an impression on students with images. The Elgin teacher drew outlines of torsos on his classroom floor to leave an indelible impression of slavery, slave ships, and the Middle Passage in the minds of his students. The Victor Andrew teacher displayed an image on the wall of her classroom. The image was large enough for students to approach the projection and imagine soldiers "getting into a World War I trench." Both teachers also used other sources to complement the images.

We suggested three additional strategies you can use to generate discussions in your class. We provided questions to ask your students to think about as they analyze images. When your students can analyze images, they draw on their content knowledge and ask further questions, the mark of historical inquiry. In the next chapter we continue with ways to further develop in your students the adventure of history through writing.

TRANSLATING HISTORY INTO CLASSROOM PRACTICE

Activity 9.1   Creating Your Own People, Space, and Time Image Analysis Strategy

Review the people, space, and time image analysis strategy. What image (portrait, sketch, drawing, or photograph) would you use to engage your students in a period of U.S. history or an era of world history? Consider, for example, an image north or south of the Yellow River (or the Yangtze River) in China or a photograph of the Ganges and Indus rivers in India. Keep in mind that you can modify the geographic features (Appalachian Mountains) and key events (before or after the Civil War) in your seven basic questions.

Activity 9.2   Creating Your Own Similarities and Differences Image Analysis Strategy

Review the similarities and differences image analysis strategy. What two images (portraits, sketches, drawings, or photographs) would you use to engage your students in a period of U.S. history or an era of world history? For example, display a theater of ancient Greece (theater at Delphi) and a modern performance auditorium. What similarities and differences do you anticipate your students will find in the images you have selected?

Activity 9.3   Creating Your Own Quadrantal/Hemispheric Image Analysis Strategy

Review the quadrantal/hemispheric image analysis strategy. What image (portrait, sketch, drawing, or photograph) is best adapted to engage your students in a period of U.S. history or an era of world history? Would you use a quadrantal or hemispheric strategy to analyze, for example, a 1602 painting by Jan Brueghel of the Battle of Gaugamela (331 BCE) when Alexander the Great and Darius' forces met? In what way is the image you have chosen well suited for this image analysis strategy?

REVIEWING THE CHAPTER

1. If your cooperating teacher, university supervisor, department chair, or principal were to walk into you classroom and observe your teaching at its best, what would they see you and your students doing?

2. Three strategies to analyze images are described in this chapter. Which of the strategies will you most likely use immediately in your teaching? Why?

3. Do photographers' pictures capture the truth? Why is it fair to describe photographers as having motives? Give an example in history.

10

Using Writing to Engage Your Students in the Past

Writing history is a perpetual exercise in judgment.

— Cushing Strout

[W]riting has been as much a part of the history of democratic self-government as reading, and is essential to public speaking. In the course of American history, as local self-government developed, so too did the kind and amount of writing that people needed to do as citizens.

— Sandra Stotsky, 1990

*T*his chapter is about writing as an important auxiliary to history and as a way to engage students in history and historical thinking. We offer some examples of how to use writing as an important tool to engage your students in the study of the past. One example is from world history—the French Revolution—and two examples are from U.S. history—the colonial period and the 20th century.

Focus Questions

1. What strategies can you use to encourage writing in your history teaching?

2. How does writing improve your students' knowledge and understanding of historical content?

3. What writing strategies best support your students' historical understanding and thinking?

4. How do writing strategies support deliberation within your classroom?

At Normal Community High School we observed a geography/history/social studies teacher who engaged his students in local history. He gave his 25 students a first-hand experience by using a road, Route 66, as a primary source.

Route 66, a once-famous highway in the United States, was born, so to speak, in 1926. It was a cross-country road spanning eight states between Chicago, Illinois, and Santa Monica, California. Originally a two-lane road, it was expanded to four lanes after World War II (and renamed an interstate). It stretched nearly 2,500 miles from the Midwest to the Pacific coast. Some of the road was originally paved with concrete, but many sections were gravel and dirt. By the late 1930s it was all paved with concrete or asphalt.

The Normal Community High School teacher engaged his students with a real-life primary source—a road. His students researched the origins of Route 66 as it passed by a nearby town, Towanda, in Central Illinois. His students investigated Dead Man's Curve, a dangerous stretch of the road known for its many accidents during the 1930s, 1940s, and 1950s. They interviewed state troopers and people who worked at Fern's Café, where people of all ages gathered. They found out about Henderson's Dairy, a Standard Oil Station, and a Texaco station that had been built to serve travelers on Route 66. They also learned about such advertisements as Burma Shave signs and other products displayed on billboards and the sides of barns.

The Normal Community High School teacher helped his students learn about how a road is a primary source and how the artifacts that accompany a road offer us opportunities to write a narrative about the past. His students learned about local history and tied local experiences to national experiences. They were involved in converting two and a half miles of Route 66 into a linear parkway. They also saved the Money Creek Bridge, which was built in the 1950s. Their petition—their actions as citizens—saved a historic site that otherwise would have been destroyed. Finally, students wrote reflective essays about what they learned, and they created brochures titled, "Historic Route 66: A Geographic Journey." Then, they translated their brochures from English into French, German, Japanese, Spanish, and Russian. They could now view Route 66 from a local, national, and international perspective.[1]

Before we describe several strategies to integrate the content of history and writing, let's examine the importance of writing.

Writing and Historical Knowledge

Effective history teaching takes into account the cognitive revolution that challenged the behaviorist model, which dominated the first half of the 20th century. Harvard psychologist Howard Gardner was one of the first to identify the cognitive revolution. In the mid-1980s Gardner described how cognitive theory casts a wary eye on the behavioral proxies used as stand-ins for learning. Gardner emphasized that students possess "multiple intelligences."[2] He pointed out that effective history teaching combines content knowledge and an understanding of the various ways students learn. Your aim as a history teacher is to invigorate such intelligences as visual intelligence, logical intelligence, kinesthetic intelligence, and verbal intelligence.

Writing strongly relates to verbal/linguistic intelligence. All students have this intelligence to a degree. Your purpose is to hone their intelligence. Scaffolding is important. Like historians, students need "to build their thinking on secure scaffolding."[3] To stimulate writing, you can give significant assignments that allow your students opportunities to think about the subject at hand. Writing is a process involving preparation, drafting, revising, and publishing. As such, it is best to have your students write "real" texts for "real" purposes and audiences.[4]

Because we live in a world of language, your students need to be able to express themselves both privately and publicly. Knowledge is a foundation. As your students write, they will quickly find out what they know and do not know. In other words, if your students do not know the subject, they will have difficulty writing and expressing their thoughts in a critical, analytical, and insightful manner.

Writing can take many forms, such as daily journals; poems; captions for cartoons (with explanations of their meaning); charts and tables; reports; notes; book reviews; scripts for a PowerPoint presentation, slide show, or video; newsletters; and advertisements. As your students write, they are simultaneously learning more content, learning what they need to know, and learning to become better writers.

The activities in which you engage your students (such as living histories, oral histories, simulation exercises, and service learning) also give them opportunities to write about history.[5] For example, the questions your students write prior to interviewing a member of the community (for an oral history project) cause them to think historically. Your students' knowledge of content feeds their abilities to write meaningful questions. During and after such activities, your students should reflect on what they have learned. Thoughtful reflection requires students to organize the content and to explain the relationship the content had with their experiences. They should be able to organize their knowledge around larger ideas. Encourage them to communicate clearly what they know and what they think.

For your students to write daily journals, essays, research papers, and other assignments, they must have knowledge. Writing specialists tell us that writing is a process that requires your students to think about what to write, to choose what information to use as evidence, and to order the information so as to articulate meaningfully a clear message.[6] Writing is thinking; it causes your students to classify, infer, discern relevant from irrelevant information, and identify whole and partial relationships. Moreover, writing leads to metacognition and refines students' thinking.

Whether your students are studying the landscape forms of Africa or Australia, African folktales, the religions of China, or the origins of the American Revolution, writing can and should take place. As a history, social science, or social studies teacher you can set an ambiance for writing by doing the following:

- Communicate to your students a belief that writing is fun, nonthreatening, and part of learning.
- Have students write many times throughout the year rather than once or twice.

- Have students prepare short papers (one to two pages in length) that they repeatedly revise or expand.
- Give students immediate feedback or have their student colleagues give feedback on what they have written.

Feedback and grading should not be confused. The purpose of feedback is to clarify portions of your students' writing and to help them rethink what they have written, generate new insights or arguments, and uncover new information. Either you or their student colleagues can provide feedback. Feedback is most helpful when it is positive, includes brief remarks in the form of questions rather than long judgmental statements, and focuses on a limited number of errors rather than pointing out every grammatical mistake.[7]

Guidelines for Writing Assignments

As a history and social studies teacher, you might consider the following guidelines when making writing assignments:

1. Write to different audiences from varying points of view.
2. Write to specific assertions rather than general topics.
3. Rewrite and refine assignments from feedback you and other students provide.
4. Use writing to advance the study of content.

Ideas for the History Classroom

Writing to Different Audiences

Audiences for student writing might include the following:

- The writer of a primary or secondary source
- A student younger and less knowledgeable
- A trusted adult
- A foreigner who has little knowledge and understanding of the culture, history, and geography
- A teacher as partner in a dialogue
- A teacher as reviewer
- A peer
- A defined section of the public
- The public at large

Writing to Different Audiences and from Varying Points of View

Have your students write to different audiences from varying points of view (see the Ideas for the History Classroom feature). Your students who are at higher levels may be able to use the complex language and structure of such disciplines as history, political science, economics, sociology, and geography. Sometimes you will want your students to write to an expert such as you or other historians, or to a leading figure (also an expert) from a particular time period. For example, your students might write to Black Hawk about settlement and expansion in Illinois, or they might write to Frederick Douglass about the Dred Scott decision. You can also have your students write as a slave, slave owner, or abolitionist, or as a factory worker, corporate executive, or small business owner during a particular period. Writing to an expert compels your students to reshape information, to empathize, and to understand how a point of view is cast by frame of reference.

You don't always have to have your students write to an expert, though. Instead, they can write to an audience that has less knowledge about a topic or period of time. Rather than writing *to* an expert, your students *become the experts*. For example, you can have your students write a letter to an Inuit describing the geographical and cultural features of Africa. Or you can have your high school students write a letter about a historical event (such as the development of the Federalist and Democratic-Republican parties) to a student in the seventh grade. Writing as experts, your students must carefully break down ideas and organize information so that it has meaning to someone less knowledgeable.

Making Specific Assertions

Another option you have is to have your students address specific assertions rather than general topics. Your writing assignments should be purposeful, and assertions provide an avenue to teach your students to generate their own interpretations. Addressing specific assertions causes your students to concentrate on a topic and collect information relevant to the issue or the problem. Students must classify information into groups and infer how groups of information relate to each other. Furthermore, as your students react to an assertion, they are forced to define the relationships of groups of information into a sentence, which often becomes a topic sentence or organizing idea. You can help your students generate a body of information through brainstorming, reading a primary source, viewing a film, analyzing an image such as a photograph or painting, taking notes from a lecture, or discussing a simulation or role-playing exercise. The key is to have students write for a purpose.[8]

Rewriting and Refining

Rewriting and refining are important steps in the writing process. Students can rewrite their assignments from feedback you and other students provide. Students are capable of checking for clarity of presentation, accuracy, and logic, and shaping and refining the final product.[9]

Your students can provide feedback to each other regarding whether the main idea is communicated and whether the evidence appropriately contributes to the main idea. Moreover, students learn when they give feedback. They learn from what the writer has written and consider alternative perspectives and ideas that will contribute to their own writing.

Writing to Advance the Study of Content

An important purpose of writing is to advance the study of content.[10] Historian J. G. A. Pocock asserted that the creation of historical accounts implies that the "task of learning to think draws very close to the task of learning to write."[11] As a history teacher, you should coach your students in their writing and discuss their thinking with them. Whether you are working with advanced placement (AP) students or slower learners, coaching is part of your task as a classroom teacher.

AP teachers coach their students in preparation for document-based questions and free-response questions on the AP U.S. history and European history tests. Students are often required to write a reaction to an assertion, and starting an essay is sometimes difficult even for students who have an extensive knowledge base. The following is a typical AP U.S. history question:

> The Kansas-Nebraska Act was the single most important step on the road to the Civil War. React to this assertion. In your reaction, provide examples that support or refute this assertion.

As a teacher, you can help all of your students by suggesting a prototype opening statement, such as, Historians do not accept monocausal explanations (or one explanation) for the outbreak of the Civil War. Of course, your students must be capable of identifying and analyzing various causes of the war and be capable of analyzing such elements as the impact of the Kansas-Nebraska Act on the second party system. However, the stem—Historians do not accept monocausal explanations—provides an initial opening line for your students' essays.[12]

You can also coach students who might complain that they do not know how to begin. For these students, you need to phrase questions so they can "turn the words around" to formulate clear opening statements. For example, you can ask this question: How was the North able to win the Civil War? A question asked in this manner allows your students to respond, "The North won the Civil War by. . . ."

Three Types of Writing

Generally speaking, your students have an understanding of three types of writing when they enter your class: persuasive, expository, and narrative (see Figure 10.1). They were perhaps introduced to all three types of writing in elementary and middle school. Each type of writing has its own distinctive qualities. Persuasive writing, for example, asks students to convince a reader that their point of view is valid or to convince a reader to take a specific action.

FIGURE 10.1   Familiar Types of Writing for Students.

1. **Persuasive writing**—Students attempt to convince a reader of the credibility of their view or to take a specific action.
2. **Expository writing**—Students give information or explain or define the meaning of something.
3. **Narrative writing**—Students tell a story or describe a series of events, usually arranged in chronological order.

FIGURE 10.2   Types of Writing: The Writing Generator.

Advertisement	Diary	Personal
Autobiography	Editorial	Poetry
Cartoon	Log	Resume
Biography	Invitation	Postcard
Charter	Lyric	Script
Constitution	Obituary	

Source: Excerpted from Stephen Parker, *The Craft of Writing* (London: Paul Chapman, 1993), 192–193.

Expository writing calls on students to give information, explain something, or define the meaning of something. An example of expository writing is explaining the meaning of imperialism. Expository writing, usually in the form of an essay, is developed with facts, statistics, examples, cause and effect, and definitions. An expository essay is often unemotional and written in the third person.

Narrative writing asks your students to tell a story or to describe a series of events, which are usually arranged in chronological order. Narrative writings may be personal, allowing students to tell about something they experienced.

Each of the three writing types requires that students use focus, supporting evidence, elaboration, organization, writing conventions, and integration. Many teachers rely on only a single form of writing—transactional report writing[13]— which requires students to present facts in the form of reporting, arguing, persuading, convincing, and analyzing. Students often collect information from a single resource such as a textbook, a primary source, a film, or the teacher. To teach effectively, you will want to expand the opportunities for students to write using multiple sources (perhaps using the first-, second-, and third-order documents approach). A wide array of writing opportunities exists. Writing experiences may include diaries, personal letters, advertisements, autobiographies, biographies, scripts, posters, obituaries, and even poetry (see Figure 10.2).

The Importance of Paragraphs

Some of your students may need help to understand the paragraph's importance and structure. Students who have problems in writing may appreciate the comparison of a paragraph to a sandwich. The top slice of bread (topic sentence) should not be stale but should be fresh and state the main idea. The meat and condiments in the center of the sandwich provide the information and examples related to the topic sentence. The bottom slice of the bread (concluding sentence) explains the importance of the main idea relative to the arguments presented. As a history teacher you can help students who lack confidence in writing by providing them with the sandwich (or hamburger) model for writing paragraphs.[14] Such a model provides a picture in your students' minds of the structure of a paragraph.

Once your students recognize the importance of knowing the structure of a paragraph, you can emphasize its importance relative to content. You can have all your students, for example, write a paragraph but write a concluding sentence on a separate page. Your students can then exchange paragraphs and read the paragraph of a colleague in class. Based on what they read, students write concluding sentences to their classmates' paragraphs. The author of the paragraph then compares his or her own concluding sentence with the one written by a classmate.

In history, writing best occurs when a thesis organizes the content. Generally speaking, writing involves a sequence of stages:

1. The teacher poses a problem for students, usually beginning with *how* or *why*.
2. Students collect and classify information.
3. Students formulate a central idea for their paragraph or essay.
4. Students create an outline, or at minimum identify ideas that are of lesser importance to major ideas.
5. Students write and then revise what they have written.

Usually the most frustrating part of writing is formulating a central idea, or thesis. But don't let that discourage you or your students. Students do not have to be profound. They need to look back at their notes, study the details, and ask questions. Remind them to explain, in a limited way, how or why something happened.

One of the best ways to organize a history paragraph, or essay, is to organize the information around one of history's vital themes and narratives. A narrative tells a story. A theme provides an opportunity to analyze and synthesize content. Your students will have to decide what knowledge they will include to support the central idea of their writing. With your help, students should also embed within their writing at least one of history's habits of mind. The ability to discriminate important from unimportant information drives historical thinking.[15] You can encourage your students to think as someone else in the context of the past through writing and other teaching strategies such as role-playing.

Effective Writing Assignments

As a history teacher you can help your students construct their knowledge through various writing strategies. The following sections include examples of writing-to-learn strategies. Keep in mind that all of the examples can help you as a teacher lead discussions about history. Writing-to-learn assignments are an effective way to engage your students in history. When you integrate writing activities into your history and social studies teaching, you provide opportunities for your students to explore, expand, and refine their historical ideas.

The following examples of ways to organize your writing activities are based on Bloom's taxonomy (a fancy word for classification), multiple intelligences, and writing as a way to prepare for a test.

The French Revolution and Bloom's Taxonomy Approach

The first level of Bloom's taxonomy, the knowledge level, asks students to recall information. Let's take an example in world history. During a study of the French Revolution, you and your students discuss the "Declaration of the Rights of Man and the Citizen," adopted by the French National Assembly on August 26, 1789. You and your students will discuss, no doubt, the admiration the marquis de Lafayette, who helped the Americans during the American Revolution, had for the Declaration of Independence. Although the French held a high regard for the American Declaration of Independence and were familiar with its text, they were also familiar with the American revolutionary state constitutions and bills of rights. These documents had been translated into French and published in France several times. The duc de La Rochefoucauld d'Enville, for example, held a seat in the 1789 National Assembly. With the help of Benjamin Franklin, he translated and distributed the *Constitutions des treize États-Unis de l'Amerique* (1783).

This translated document included the American state constitutions and bills of rights, a series of charters, the American Declaration of Independence, and the Articles of Confederation. Among the American documents, the only document to include the words "all men are created equal" was the Declaration of Independence. None of the American state bills of rights used the exact words "all men are created equal." Nor did the French Declaration.[16] In particular, the French Declaration echoed George Mason's phrase, "Men are born and remain free and equal in rights," which Thomas Jefferson had changed and revised in the American Declaration of Independence to "all men are created equal." Thus, the French Declaration was more closely modeled after the bills of rights in the American state constitutions.[17]

Even compared to the state bills of rights, however, the French Declaration was distinctive to France's very different historical experience and situation. American bills of rights, like the English Bill of Rights, were expressed in phrases that limited the government. Americans, as well their English counterparts, had a long tradition of understanding rights. The French Declaration, on the other hand, served as a "national catechism" intended to enlighten French citizens as to their rights and duties. Thus, the French "Declaration of the Rights of Man and the Citizen" had four purposes: to educate French citizens in their rights and duties; to set forth principles on which the entire constitution of France was to be founded; to outlaw specific practices of the Old Regime in France; and to serve as a preamble for the completed constitution in 1791.

During your study of the French Revolution, you can have your students write a simulated news article that reports the events that took place at the National

Assembly and the fruits of the Assembly's deliberation, namely, the "Declaration of the Rights of Man and the Citizen." At the knowledge level, your students' writing is aimed toward the factual elements of the event; they should create a report that lists the significant social and political changes in France.

The second level of Bloom's taxonomy, comprehension, requires your students to translate ideas they have learned. At this level, you might have your students explain, discuss, describe, or summarize what they have learned about the "Declaration of the Rights of Man and the Citizen." During your study of the French Revolution, you can have your students write a summary of the causes of the revolution. After observing and reading about the "Declaration of the Rights of Man and the Citizen," your students can prepare a readers' theater script to share with others in the class. The script provides an excellent opportunity for discussion regarding the Declaration.

At the third level of the taxonomy, application, your students use what they have learned in a new situation. For example, using what they know about the French Declaration and the influence of American state bills of rights, your students can write the duc de La Rochefoucauld d'Enville's journal entry regarding the rise of Jacobin clubs.

At the fourth level of the taxonomy, analysis, your students must separate information into parts and determine their connections. Making comparisons engages students in analysis. Your students might compare, for example, the 1789 French Declaration to the 1776 Virginia Declaration of Rights (or another state's bill of rights). They might also compare the ideas of the French Declaration to a key paragraph from the Declaration of Independence and/or the Bill of Rights, which was added to the U.S. Constitution in 1791. (Note that many people mistakenly believe that the U.S. Bill of Rights, proposed in 1789 and ratified in 1791, influenced the French Declaration of Rights.) In writing a comparison essay, students must establish a baseline from which to make comparisons. Your students can use one of the documents previously mentioned as their baseline and compare the purposes of the French Declaration with the purposes of the American documents.

Synthesis and evaluation are the next levels of the taxonomy. (In Bloom's taxonomy, evaluation is higher synthesis. Some educators argue that synthesis, which is an act of creative thinking, may be higher than evaluation, which is a judgment.) At the synthesis level, your students put information together in new ways. They combine ideas, beliefs, and principles, which can involve writing an essay based on a prediction of how the French Revolution would affect French society. Or they might write a play depicting a Frenchman's experiences following the Napoleonic Wars and the ideals expressed in the French "Declaration of the Rights of Man and the Citizen."

At the evaluation level, your students make judgments about the French Revolution and the "Declaration of the Rights of Man and the Citizen." You can create a writing activity in which students select, recommend, justify, critique, or debate the merits of the French Revolution. You might ask them to write an editorial for an 1815 newspaper discussing what they view as the most influential factor of the French Revolution. In preparation for a debate, your students can write opening or rebuttal statements in support of or rejecting the proposition that liberty was the key pursuit of French revolutionaries.

Work with your students in developing the various levels of thinking. You will need to lead focused discussions so they can deliberate when there are disagreements with classmates over the "Declaration of the Rights of Man and the Citizen" and the legacy of the French Revolution.

We suggest that in deliberative discussions you postpone the evaluative level until students have had ample opportunities for thoughtful discussion. Encourage students not to rush to judgment too soon, as is so often the unfortunate practice.

Massachusetts Bay and the Chesapeake Bay Colonies, and Multiple Intelligences

As a history teacher you can generate writing activities that take into account Howard Gardner's multiple intelligences theory. For example, suppose you and your students have been studying colonial America. You have determined that you want your students to know and think about the Massachusetts Bay and the Chesapeake Bay colonies. In the end, you want them to be able to compare life in the two colonies. You have discussed with your students images of life in both geographic regions and have studied several written sources that relate to each region's political, economic, and social conditions. Your sources include, for example, tables depicting the ratio of women to men in both colonies.

After having your students analyze visuals and read descriptions that portray life in both regions, you assign a writing activity that reads as follows:

> Imagine you are an Englishman living in the 1600s. You have visited both the Massachusetts Bay and Chesapeake Bay colonies in America. Indeed, you have gained a reputation as an expert on these colonies. One family in England, whom you know well, has decided to let their daughter travel to America. The parents cannot decide if she should live in the Massachusetts Bay colony or the Chesapeake Bay colony. They have asked for your advice; they want to know the advantages of one of the colonies over the other.

> Create a postcard you might send to the family. On the front side of the postcard, draw a scene of what the daughter might see in America. On the left side draw a scene of Massachusetts Bay. On the right side draw a scene of Chesapeake Bay. On the back side of the postcard, write a message describing both scenes. You should present a few facts about each colony and explain why you drew these objects in the scenes. Then tell the family which colony you believe is the better choice for their daughter.

Note several key points about this writing assignment. First, you are asking your students to write from the perspective of an authority; therefore, your students must be clear and assume that their readers are less informed than they are. Second, this writing assignment provides multiple opportunities for your students to communicate what they know about both geographic regions and the daily lives in each. You can coach your students in discussions that encourage them to provide details and to draw informed conclusions.

In a discussion with your students, encourage them to consider what would best suit the daughter of a family who knows little about the Massachusetts Bay or Chesapeake Bay regions. What are the climatic conditions? What disparities are there in sexual roles and status? What are the economic and social advantages and disadvantages this young female has compared to males? How are these regions organized politically and will their political organizations have an effect on her? What role does religion play in these colonies? What are the religious, political, and economic motives of immigrants coming from different parts of Europe to the Americas? How did English settlers interact with Native Americans in the two regions? What importance did the rise of individualism have on the development of the two regions?

How your students portray life in Massachusetts Bay and Chesapeake Bay allows them to express what they know and think about life in the past. The elaboration of each one of your students depends on your coaching and their depth of understanding.

Reviewing for a Test on the 20th Century

Writing prior to a test on a unit of study can also be an effective way to increase your students' knowledge. After you and your students have investigated a unit on the 20th century, you may want to know how much they know *before* they take a test. A rotation essay involves the entire class *and you* in writing.[18] The procedure is simple:

1. Write a focus or topic sentence on the board and tell your students to write the focus sentence at the top of a sheet of paper. (Examples: Americans have had to adapt to numerous changes in the 20th century. Or, The threat of nuclear war has impeded social progress. Or, The two main events of the 20th century were the two great world wars, twin mountain ranges in the shadows of which we have lived.)

2. Tell your students to write for 2 minutes. (You must also write for 2 minutes.)

3. After 2 minutes, tell your students to rotate their papers; that is, pass their papers to a student on the left. (Your paper is also passed to a student, and you receive one of your student's papers.)

4. Tell your students to read the essay they have been given and then pick up where the writing stopped. They can either add to it or bring in a new idea. Along with your students, read silently, then write for an additional 2 minutes.

5. Follow this procedure for three rotations. For each rotation, your students and you should read what has been written and then write for 2 minutes.

6. Share the results. Read the last paper you received aloud. Your students may also read papers aloud.

The rotation essay may show that your students know a great deal or not much at all. If the latter is the case, you should not be disappointed. Instead, capitalize on the opportunity to revisit key ideas that students should consider as they write about the focus sentence. Because you wrote with your students during the rotation, you have modeled for your students that writing is important. Your students are now aware of what they already know as well as what they need to know to organize their knowledge for an essay test.

SUMMARY

Writing helps your students clarify their understanding of the past. Writing history requires asking questions about information, collecting information, organizing information, and presenting ideas based on historical questions and issues. As the noted historian Cushing Strout once remarked, "Writing history is a perpetual exercise in judgment."

We suggested a number of writing strategies throughout this chapter. You can have your students write about primary and secondary sources and write to audiences, contemporary or historical. We concluded with a writing strategy that helps students review a unit of study. The opportunities for you to draw out the human propensity to create meaning—to make sense of the world—are numerous. Writing will help your students draw their information from sources, interpret factual data, organize it chronologically, and develop some literary style. Be patient as your students "do history" and develop their capacity to think historically.

TRANSLATING HISTORY INTO CLASSROOM PRACTICE

Activity 10.1   Creating Your Own Writing Assignment

Review the Various audiences to which studentd can write (see page 189) the type of writing in Figure 10.2 (see page 191).

Create an assignment appropriate to a period or era of history that uses one or more of the items from each category.

Explain the criteria you used when selecting the type of writing assignment and the audience for whom students will write.

Activity 10.2   Devising a Writing Assignment Related to a Period or Era of History

Read and think about one of the suggested effective writing strategies presented in this chapter. Devise a writing assignment that is related to a period or era of history that you want to emphasize. Prepare the following for your students:

- An open-ended question
- Sources you think students should draw from to respond to the question
- A rubric to assess your students' knowledge, reasoning, and ability to communicate what they know and think (see Chapter 6, pages 118–119)

Activity 10.3   Adapting Sample Writing Assignment Prompts to Your History Class

Consider one of the following prompts as a writing assignment in your history class. Then modify the example for a period or era of history you will teach.

- Create a magazine for children in the 1660s and the 1860s.
- Create a briefing to a board of directors that plans to develop a property site. The site contains archaeological remnants.
- Decide which five items from the 1580s, 1680s, 1780s (or whenever you would choose) to place in a time capsule to be opened in 1,000 years. Explain to people in the year 2580, 2680, or 2780 what the items were used for and why they are valuable.
- Produce a guidebook to a local museum or historic site for very young children, tourists, or very old people.
- Write an obituary with two classmates for Liu Chi, 206–195 bce, (later called Liu Pang or his dynastic title, Kao Tsu). One will write an obituary just after his death, another after the accession of Wu Ti, 140–87 BCE (the "Martial Emperor"), and another after the accession of Wang Mang, 45 BCE–AD 23.
- Explain to a group of elementary students what you think the technology or machinery in a diagram was for, and draw a sequence of diagrams to illustrate how it worked. Why was it designed?

  Source: The preceding six items are from Chris Husbands, *What Is History Teaching?* (Philadelphia: Open University Press, 2003), 110–111.

- Students write a narrative history of themselves in third person.

REVIEWING THE CHAPTER

1. Describe the writing assignments you experienced in a middle- and high-school history class. How often did you write in history classes? What were your most meaningful writing experiences?

2. Several strategies for writing are described in this chapter. Which of the strategies will you most likely use immediately in your teaching? Why?

3. Create a writing assignment prompt for your students in a U.S. history or world history course. Write a response to the prompt. Then apply the rubric presented in chapter 6 of this book. Identify the criteria you will look for in the three dimensions—knowledge, reasoning, and communication—of the rubric.

Conclusion

Numerous individuals as well as curricular programs and institutions have influenced what you think students should know and be able to do with that knowledge. We hope you believe that all students have the ability to learn.

In this text we bring to bear theory, teaching models, and practical experience. We offer a history-centered civic education that stresses context-based inquiry as an antidote to presentism in thinking about public issues. Historical thinking is essential in the preparation of citizens who possess a sense of justice that regulates individual actions to secure the rights of individuals equally throughout society. We emphasize deliberation about primary documents and secondary narratives as a method of teaching and learning civic knowledge through the study of history. Our first-, second-, and third-order document approach to teaching history should be revisited at times throughout the school year when you deem it appropriate.

Teaching with primary sources and narrative interpretations has much potential. Our systematic approach of using first-, second-, and third-order documents helps you identify your intellectual direction. It initiates inquiry with a foundation of knowledge, and then allows students to construct meaning to the past. Our approach helps students of all age levels and abilities bond their own seminal document to a historical period, issue, or event and to link their narratives to core documents. Research shows that students are not blank slates when they enter the classroom. Our approach encourages students to rethink their narratives as they discuss core documents in an informed way.

Teaching, Philip W. Jackson reminds us, is humbling. A teacher is required to decide what to do *and* what not to do in the classroom.[1] Once you know the experiences of your students, you must use your own preparation and experience to create an effective learning environment. Students want to learn from their teacher, and they feel confident when their teacher is knowledgeable. At times, then, a teacher must demonstrate that he or she is in firm command of an academic discipline. At other times, however, a teacher needs to work with a student on the same level and from the same perspective to understand what is causing the student to struggle. Jackson claims that two traditions dominate our teaching: mimetic and transformative.[2] He prefers the latter, as do we. Our hope is that through the study of history, all students can experience an important change in the way they think about the past and their own lives.

In this book we suggest that you use both constructivism and reflective thinking in your teaching. Although the two are not identical, they are not in conflict.

They are separated as psychological and philosophical dimensions of the practicing teacher. Constructivism is the psychological dimension that informs us how students learn and how knowledge comes into long-term memory. Reflective teaching is more philosophical.

Reflective practice requires you to look at the consequences of knowledge for liberal and civic education purposes. Historical knowledge and thinking help us understand the past and the world around us, and help us act in an informed way.

John Dewey made an early distinction between unreflective and reflective teaching. The former, dominated by impulse and the authority of traditions, embraces the everyday reality in schools, presuming undiscriminatingly that only the technical practices of pedagogy should be considered when planning for instruction.[3] Reflective teaching is distinguished from technical teaching. The reflective practitioner thinks systematically about how to integrate significant content with sound pedagogical practices, about how best to adapt content and methodology according to the experiential levels and interests of students, and about how to exercise collateral responsibilities toward students and the community. The history teacher who practices reflectively recognizes that history is an integrative discipline that informs the reflective thinking of students as they construct meaning to the past.

History allows students to understand events and historical debates in the context of their times. It enables each student and citizen, as a lifelong learner, to argue for the continuation of warranted political, economic, and social policies and traditions, as well as for necessary political, economic, and social change.

The study of history must extend beyond the acquisition of discrete pieces of information. As a teacher of history, you need to help students master the contours of a given narrative and know about significant individuals, their ideas, and key political and social events that reflect continuity and change in a society. History is concerned with the attempt to understand the past. Knowledge of the past is far from simple. There is plainly too much history for any student to learn unless you carefully select what to teach.

Students should also know about universal themes and ideas that cut across the human experience. These themes and ideas serve as filters that help them differentiate between what is significant and what is insignificant in the historical record.

History instruction within the reflective practice framework considers the worth of knowledge both now and in the future. As a reflective teacher of history, you must know and understand the structure of history. That is, you must know that history is organized around seminal vital themes and narratives that are punctuated by key turning points in the story of the human adventure (see Figure 1). You must have command of historical content, both the main ideas and supporting details, and understand history's pivotal role as an integrative discipline among other school subjects. History's power of synthesis enables you and your students to draw on ideas contributed by a number of disciplines to develop an understanding of the actions of people and the importance of events over a period of time.

To be a reflective teacher of history, you should possess knowledge of content and pedagogy, be able to implement knowledge in the classroom, and want to be a lifelong learner about both the past and the present. You must also recognize the importance of having an open spirit of inquiry and curiosity about the past.

FIGURE 1: Qualities in a Well-Prepared History Teacher

	The Reflective Practitioner and The Teaching and Learning of History	
Knowledge of Content and Pedagogy	**Performance in the Classroom**	**Disposition towards the Profession**

Knowledge about the Structure of History	**Knowledge** about Teaching	**Knowledge** about the three dimensions of professional growth: as a teacher, scholar, and person
• Vital themes and narratives • Turning points in history people, space, and time • Inquiry: "Doing" history and understanding ways historians think • Standards for teachers and students of history	• Teaching strategies • Relationship of planning, instruction, and assessment • Lessons and assessments that help students meet national, state, or local standards	• Values the idea of lifelong learning of content and pedagogy

Reasoning	**Reasoning**	**Reasoning**
• Research base for teaching • Reflective thinking • Understands the changing place of history and the social sciences in the curriculum	• Philosophy of teaching: mimetic and transformative traditions of teaching • Understands history's role as an integrative discipline in the curriculum • Understands history's power to develop students' ability to make informed decisions	• Values the idea of continual reflection on teaching and thinking about history

Communication	**Communication**	**Communication**
• Spirit of inquiry	• Implements classroom activities based on knowledge and reflection on content, pedagogy, and the role of the teacher/scholar	• Values the idea of modeling for students' and others' best personal and professional practice

Source: Adapted from Frederick D. Drake and Lawrence W. McBride, "The Summative Teaching Portfolio and the Reflective Practitioner of History," *The History Teacher* 34, no. 1 (November 2000): 41–60. Used with permission.

Understanding the past is also about looking for evidence and understanding how the evidence might be interpreted, what limitations the evidence has, and how historical events might be explained differently by different historians.[4] Thus, as a reflective teacher, you should encourage students' inquiry and questioning of sources and ideas.

Dewey defined reflective thought as "active, persistent, and careful consideration of any belief or supposed form of knowledge in the light of the grounds that support it and the further conclusions to which it tends."[5] Alan F. Griffin, who mentored numerous teachers in reflective thinking from the 1930s until his death in the 1960s, wrote that the practice of reflective teaching means that "we need to know what we mean by democracy, and we need to ground that knowledge as widely and richly as possible. We need not merely to get acquainted with our culture, but to make judgments about it in terms of the democratic ideal."[6]

In our judgment no one is more important than the citizen who understands and practices the democratic ideal. A liberal mind requires the citizen, or teacher, to possess moral and intellectual virtues. A liberal education requires an academic discipline, such as history, to provide a "furniture of the mind" from which we can understand our culture, the democratic experience, and ourselves. Self-discipline is an important quality that our students, as citizens, must possess so they do not act solely on impulse. As students construct a meaning of the past, the warehouse of knowledge they have should be broad in its scope with the teacher helping students identify key turning points in the past.

Teaching history should stress pluralistic integration. Social historian John Higham suggested that pluralistic integration assumes and understands that the fundamental compatibilities and continuing tensions of civic unity with social and cultural diversity are possible. Thus, enjoy the challenges of bringing into the classroom others' ideas so that all students can examine primary sources, the revisions of past interpretations, the engagement of an open mind, and the ideas of others that differ from our own. Engagement in historical revisionism and ideas that challenge students' accepted assumptions cause them to rearrange the "furniture of the mind" and to create their own knowledge of the past so that it becomes meaningful in their own lives. The teacher, we believe, initiates the student's inquiries into knowledge and its meaning; the student, through informed questions, pursues the inquiry to arrive at an understanding of others as well as self.

We have a reasoned commitment to the cross-fertilizing of civic unity with social and cultural diversity. Ideas may vary concerning culture, democracy, and the importance of the citizen. At the heart of our democratic dream is that none of us is stuck inside our own skin.[7] Our identities are not reducible to our membership in a race, ethnic group, or gender. We hope that students who are involved in your classroom community feel that the world is opened up to them, that they are not imprisoned by terminology and identities that prohibit free discussion and deliberations about themselves and their social affiliations.

We often think of Henry Adams' time-honored passage, written in *The Education of Henry Adams*, "A teacher affects eternity; he can never tell where his influence stops." These 12 words may serve as a gentle reminder of your importance. Adams' statement (even though written in the context of disgruntlement as he taught medieval history at Harvard College in 1870) provides a dignified reason for teaching. His sentiments imply noble, inspiring, exact, and succinct purposes for teaching. Adams wanted so desperately to motivate his students to love history as he did and to involve them more actively in its study. Adams believed that his efforts in discussion, lecture, and the use of the "historical method" were illusory pleasures at best. He had little hope in his students, speculating that "the number of students whose minds were above the average was . . . barely one in ten; the rest could not be much stimulated by any inducements a teacher could suggest." Adams therefore decided to "try to cultivate the tenth mind, though necessarily at the expense of the other nine."

Although we confess that Adams' conclusion may be a temptation, we encourage you to believe that engaging *all* students in an understanding of the past and of themselves is an important endeavor. Try to use the broad range of your students' abilities, namely, to develop their multiple intelligences. There is much reciprocity in the teacher–student relationship. Perhaps you will learn more from your students and colleagues each day and appreciate the transformations that have evolved because of your interactions with them.

We hope that your instruction contributes to students' critical analysis of the cultural, intellectual, institutional, and ethical contexts of the past. And we hope that your teaching results in durable knowledge and skills that students can draw on as informed, active citizens. History's durable knowledge rests in doing history and understanding the ways historians think. Engage your students in primary and secondary sources and deliberate with your students as fellow lifelong learners on the meaning of the past, the present, and the future.

TRANSLATING HISTORY INTO CLASSROOM PRACTICE

Activity 1   Using a Visual Synectic Model to Reflect on Your Teaching

In this activity we use a visual synectic method of teaching. With two classmates, reach a consensus regarding whether teaching history is similar to picture 1, 2, or 3 on page 206. Provide at least three reasons why teaching history is represented by the image you have selected. What other images represent the teaching of history?

Activity 2   Incorporating Vital Themes and Habits of Mind

This activity provides you with an opportunity to link vital themes and narratives, habits of mind, and primary sources through a PowerPoint presentation.

1. Select one of the vital themes and narratives from Figure 1.2 (in Chapter 1, page 16).
2. Find an image (photograph, painting, sketch, or map) that you consider to be historically significant.
3. Select two or three habits of mind from Figure 1.1 (in chapter 1, page 15) that help your students enter the past.

Teaching history is like . . . .

because . . . .

You can start from any one of the three points. For example, you may want to begin with a vital theme and narrative and find an image as well as habits of mind that illustrate this vital theme. Or you may develop your presentation around an image or based on a habit of mind. Regardless of your starting point, your presentation should demonstrate your ability to connect vital themes and narratives, habits of mind, secondary sources, and primary sources.

Endnotes

Preface

1. David M. Kennedy, "The Art of the Table: Story-Telling and History Teaching," *The History Teacher* 31 (May 1998):318.

2. Michael Whelan, "No Need to Apologize: A Good Lecture Can Stimulate Student Interest," *History Matters* 5 (December 1992).

Chapter 1

1. Sam Wineburg, *Historical Thinking and Other Natural Acts: Charting the Future of Teaching the Past* (Philadelphia: Temple University Press, 2001), 10, and Sam Wineburg, "Making Historical Sense," in *Knowing, Teaching, and Learning History*, Peter N. Stearns, Peter Sexias, and Sam Wineburg, eds. (New York: New York University Press, 2000), 312.

2. Sarah Drake Brown, "The Citizen as Historical Being: History's Role in Education for Democracy," *Illinois Council for the Social Studies* 65 (Fall 2005): 17–28.

3. Bernard Lewis, *The Middle East: A Brief History of the Last 2,000 Years* (New York: Simon & Schuster, 1995) and Bernard Lewis, *What Went Wrong? Western Impact and Middle Eastern Response* (New York: Oxford University Press, 2001).

4. Gaillard Hunt, ed., *The Writings of James Madison,* 9 vols. (New York, 1906), VI, 83–85; Louis Henkin, *Foreign Affairs and the Constitution* (Mineola, NY, 1972), vii; and Walter LaFeber, "The Constitution and United States Foreign Policy," *Journal of American History* 74 (December 1987): 695.

5. James Madison to Thomas Jefferson, April 2, 1798, in *The Writings of James Madison.*

6. Robert A. Divine, *Perpetual War for Perpetual Peace* (College Station: Texas A&M University Press, 2000), 85.

7. You will need to consider your own narrative, which has been influenced by courses you have taken in your preparation to be a history, social science, or social studies teacher and books you have read. Perhaps, for example, your narrative is similar to those of the realists who regard U.S. involvement in the world as naive and that American foreign policy should be based on balance of power relations. Or perhaps your narrative shares the views of the revisionists/corporatists, who believe that U.S. involvement in world events is not naive, but shaped by economic interests and access to open markets overseas. Or possibly postrevisionists shaped your narrative, an interpretation that the United States has had a coherent and persistent national strategy of security in the 20th century. Democracy, most frequently manifest in

republican government, and security complement each other. The more democracies there are in the New World Order, the more secure is the United States. The downside of this security strategy is that a "garrison state" may result in an overzealous pursuit of safety and security at home. For a realist interpretation, see as examples George F. Kennan, *American Diplomacy: 1900–1950* (Chicago: University of Chicago Press, 1951); Marc Trachtenberg, *History and Strategy* (Princeton: Princeton University Press, 1991); and Marc Trachtenberg, *A Constructed Peace: The Making of the European Settlement, 1945–1963* (Princeton: Princeton University Press, 1999). For revisionist/corporatist interpretations, see William Appleman Williams, *The Tragedy of American Diplomacy* (New York: Norton, 1988 [first published in 1959]) and Michael J. Hogan, *The Marshall Plan: America, Britain, and the Reconstruction of Western Europe, 1947–1952* (Cambridge: Cambridge University Press, 1987). For postrevisionists, see John Lewis Gaddis, *The United States and the Origins of the Cold War, 1941–1947* (New York: Columbia University Press, 1972) and *We Now Know: Rethinking Cold War History* (Oxford: Clarendon Press, 1997); Melvyn Leffler, *A Preponderance of Power: National Security, the Truman Administration, and the Cold War* (Stanford, CA: Stanford University Press, 1992); and *The Specter of Communism: The United States and the Origins of the Cold War, 1917–1953* (New York: Hill and Wang, 1994). Among postrevisionists, Gaddis and Leffler's perspectives differ.

8. John Dewey, *Experience and Education* (New York: Simon & Schuster, 1997, 1938).

9. We model our questions after the very thoughtful questions historian Eric Foner raised in his book, *The Story of American Freedom* (New York: Norton, 1998), xvi.

10. Robert Kagan, *Of Paradise and Power: America and Europe in the New World Order* (New York: Knopf, 2003), 3.

11. Lee S. Shulman, "Those Who Understand: Knowledge Growth in Teaching," *Educational Researcher* 15, no. 2 (1986); Lee S. Schulman, "Knowledge and Teaching: Foundations of the New Reform," *Harvard Educational Review* 57, no. 1 (1987).

12. Bruce VanSledright, *In Search of America's Past: Learning to Read History in Elementary School*, with a foreword by Larry Cuban (New York: Teachers College Press, 2002), 8.

13. National Center for History in the Schools, *National Standards for History: Basic Edition* (Los Angeles: National Center for History in the Schools, 1996), 1, 41.

14. Paul Gagnon and the Bradley Commission on History in Schools, eds., *Historical Literacy: The Case for History in American Education* (Boston: Houghton Mifflin, 1989), 25–26. The Bradley Commission on History in the Schools also presents the six vital themes and narratives in its indispensable pamphlet, *Building a History Curriculum: Guidelines for Teaching History in Schools* (Educational Excellence Network: 1988, 1989), 9.

15. Gagnon, *Historical Literacy*, 26–27 and the Bradley Commission, *Building a History Curriculum, Guidelines for Teaching History in Schools*, 10–11.

16. NAEP U.S. History Consensus Project, *U.S. History Framework for the 1994 National Assessment of Educational Progress* (Washington, D.C.: National Assessment Governing Board, 1994), and National Assesment of Educational Progress in U.S. History, *Assessment and Exercise Specifications: Revised for the 2006 NAEP U.S. History Assessment Based on the National Governing Board* (2006 NAEP U.S. History Framework, September 2003). An NAEP World History Framework has yet to be developed and published at the time

of the writing of this book. The first NAEP assessment of world history is scheduled to be administered in 2010 to students in the twelfth grade.

17. William H. McNeill, "Why Study History? Three Historians Respond," in *Historical Literacy: The Case for History in American Education,* Paul Gagnon and the Bradley Commission on History in Schools, eds. (New York: Macmillan, 1989), 103.

18. Carl Becker, *Dial 59* (September 2, 1915): 148.

19. William H. McNeill, Symposium at the Library of Congress, March 1–2, 1996, as reported in *Occasional Papers of the National Council for History Education, Inc.* (September 1996): 1.

20. Paul Gagnon, "History's Role in Civic Education: The Precondition for Political Intelligence," in *Educating the Democratic Mind,* Walter Parker, ed. (Albany: State University of New York, 1996), 241–262.

21. Peter N. Stearns, "Why Study History?" American Historical Association, http://www.historians.org/PUBS/Free/WhyStudyHistory.htm

22. Peter Novick, *That Noble Dream: The "Objectivity Question" and the American Historical Profession* (Cambridge: Cambridge University Press, 1995). Also see Joyce Appleby, Lynn Hunt, and Margaret Jacob, *Telling the Truth about History* (New York: Norton, 1994).

23. Peter N. Stearns, "Getting Specific about Training in Historical Analysis: A Case Study in World History," in *Knowing, Teaching, and Learning History: National and International Perspectives,* Peter N. Stearns, Peter Seixas, and Sam Wineburg, eds. (New York: New York University Press, 2000), 429.

24. Ross E. Dunn and David Vigilante, *Bring History Alive! A Sourcebook for Teaching World History* (Los Angeles: National Center for History in the Schools, 1996), 7.

25. Edward Hallett Carr, *What Is History?* (New York: Vintage Books, 1961) and Georg G. Iggers, *Historiography in the Twentieth Century: From Scientific Objectivity to the Postmodern Challenge* (Hanover, NH: Wesleyan University Press, 1997).

26. This point has been firmly emphasized by historians, including Richard J. Evans, *In Defense of History* (New York: Norton, 1999), chs. 3 and 4; R. G. Collingwood, *The Idea of History* (New York: Oxford University Press, 1956), 192, 246; and John Lewis Gaddis, *The Landscape of History: How Historians Map the Past* (New York: Oxford University Press, 2002), 17–18.

27. Gerald Danzer and Mark Newman, "Primary Sources in the Teaching of History," in *Bring History Alive! A Sourcebook for Teaching United States History,* Kirk Ankey, Richard Del Rio, Gary B. Nash, and David Vigilante, eds. (Los Angeles: National Center for History in Schools, 1996), 22.

28. Robert B. Bain, "Into the Breach: Using Research and Theory to Shape History Instruction," in *Knowing, Teaching, and Learning History: National and International Perspectives,* Peter N. Stearns, Peter Seixas, and Sam Wineburg, eds. (New York: New York University Press, 2000), 332.

29. Arthur Herman, *The Idea of Decline in Western History* (New York: Free Press), 194–198.

30. We borrow from Bernard Murchland, whose essay "Civic Education: Parsing the Problem" summarizes David Mathews' four levels of civic intelligence, in *Civic Learning for Teachers: Capstone for Educational Reform, Proceedings of the Seminar on Civic Learning in*

the Education of the Teaching Profession, Alan H. Jones, ed. (Ann Arbor, MI: Prakken Publications, 1985), 34–35. Also see David Mathews, "Civic Intelligence," *Social Education* 49 (1985): 678–681.

31. See David Mathews, "The Liberal Arts and the Civic Arts," *Liberal Education* 68 (1982): 269–275, and Mark H. Curtis, "The Liberal Arts as Civic Arts: A Historical Perspective," *Liberal Education* 68 (1982): 277–280. This entire volume of *Liberal Education* was devoted to "civic purposes of liberal learning."

32. Sam Wineburg, *Historical Thinking and Other Unnatural Acts: Charting the Future of Teaching the Past* (Philadelphia: Temple University Press, 2001), 170.

33. George Mason University, Center for History and New Media: History News Network. Available from the World Wide Web: http://hnn.us/.

Chapter 2

1. As quoted in Dagobert D. Runes, ed., *The Selected Writings of Benjamin Rush* (New York: Philosophical Library, 1947), 92.

2. Carl F. Kaestle, *Pillars of the Republic: Common Schools and American Society, 1780–1860* (New York: Hill and Wang, 1983), 7–8.

3. *Ibid.,* 7.

4. Noah Webster, *An American Selection of Lessons in Reading and Speaking* (Philadelphia: Young and M'Culloch, 1787) and Mason Locke Weems, *The Life of George Washington,* Marcus Cunliffe, ed. (Cambridge: Harvard University Press, 1962), 141–159. The text of Washington's farewell address follows the ninth edition of 1809. For further reference, see Gerald A. Danzer and Mark Newman, *Tuning In: Primary Sources in the Teaching of History* (Chicago: The World History Project, 1991), 5.

5. Hazel Whitman Hertzberg, *Social Studies Reform, 1880–1980* (Boulder, CO: Social Science Education Consortium, 1981), 4–5.

6. Philip W. Jackson, *The Practice of Teaching* (New York: Teachers College Press, 1986), 115–145.

7. We draw from David B. Tyack, *The One Best System: A History of American Urban Education* (Cambridge, MA: Harvard University Press, 1974) and Herbert M. Kliebard, *The Struggle for the American Curriculum* (New York: Routledge, 1995), who analyze the various strands of Progressive education.

8. Diane Ravitch, *Left Back: A Century of Battles Over School Reform* (New York: Simon and Schuster, 2000), 84.

9. Kliebard, *American Curriculum,* 84.

10. Herbert M. Kliebard, *Schooled to Work* (New York: Teachers College Press, 1999), 171, 231.

11. George S. Counts, *Dare the School Build a New Social Order* (Carbondale, IL: Southern Illinois University Press, 1978), 4.

12. See, for example, Paul Gagnon and the Bradley Commission on History in Schools, eds., *Historical Literacy: The Case for History in American Education* (Boston: Houghton Mifflin, 1989); the Bradley Commission on History in the Schools, *Building a History Curriculum: Guidelines for Teaching History in Schools* (Washington, D.C.: Educational

Excellence Network 1988, 1989); and Diane Ravitch, *Left Back: A Century of Battles Over School Reform* (New York: Simon and Schuster, 2000).

13. Leopold von Ranke, *The Theory and Practice of History,* Georg G. Iggers and Konrad Von Moltke, eds. (Indianapolis: Bobbs-Merrill, 1973), xix–xx. Also, see Leopold von Ranke, *The Secret of World History: Selected Writings of the Art and Science of History,* Roger Wines, ed. (New York: Fordham University Press, 1981), 21; Stephen Bann, *The Clothing of Clio: A Study of the Representation of History in Nineteenth-Century Britain and France* (New York: Cambridge University Press, 1984), 8–10; Joyce Appleby, Lynn Hunt, and Margaret Jacob, *Telling the Truth about History* (New York: Norton, 1994), 74, 234; Peter Novick, *That Noble Dream: The "Objectivity Question" and the American Historical Profession* (Cambridge: Cambridge University Press, 1988 and 1995), 28–31; Keith Windschuttle, *The Killing of History: Literary Critics and Social Theorists Are Murdering Our Past* (San Francisco: Encounter Books, 1996), 322–324; Georg G. Iggers, *Historiography in the Twentieth Century: From Scientific Objectivity to the Postmodern Challenge* (Hanover, NH: Wesleyan University Press, 1997); and Richard J. Evans, *In Defense of History* (New York: Norton, 1997 and 2000), 14–20.

14. Henry Johnson, *Teaching of History in Elementary and Secondary Schools* (New York: Macmillan, 1916), 159–160.

15. Herbert M. Kliebard, *Changing Course: American Curriculum Reform in the Twentieth Century* (New York: Teachers College Press, 2002), 24–38. Chapter Two, "That Evil Genius of the Negro Race: Thomas Jesse Jones and Educational Reform," addresses specifically the role of social studies origins and Thomas Jesse Jones. See additionally Sarah Drake Brown, "A Comparative Analysis of Historical Thinking Skills in the History Standards of Seven States: California, Idaho, Illinois, Indiana, Massachusetts, Texas, Virginia" (Ph.D. diss., Indiana University, 2004), Chapter II.

16. Gary B. Nash, Charlotte Crabtree, and Ross E. Dunn, *History on Trial: Culture Wars and the Teaching of the Past* (New York: Knopf, 1997), 65–66. Also see Allan Nevins, "American History for Americans," *New York Times Magazine,* May 3, 1942; *New York Times,* April 4, 1943; and Hazel Whitman Hertzberg, *Social Studies Reform, 1880–1980* (Boulder: Social Science Education Consortium, 1981), 67.

17. Arthur E. Bestor, *Educational Wastelands: The Retreat from Learning in Our Public Schools* (Urbana: University of Illinois Press, 1953) and Richard Hofstadter, *Anti-Intellectualism in American Life* (New York: Vintage Books, 1962).

18. Jerome Bruner, *The Process of Education* (Cambridge: Harvard University Press, 1960).

19. Shirley H. Engle, "Decision Making: The Heart of Social Studies Instruction," *Social Education* (November 1960): 301–304, 306; Shirley H. Engle, "Thoughts in Regard to Revision," *Social Education* 27 (April 1963): 182–184, 196; and Shirley H. Engle and Anna S. Ochoa, *Education for Democratic Citizenship: Decision Making in the Social Studies* (New York: Teachers College Press, 1988), 139–141.

20. Peter N. Stearns, "Getting Specific about Training in Historical Analysis: A Case Study in World History," in *Knowing, Teaching, and Learning History: National and International Perspectives,* Peter N. Stearns, Peter Seixas, and Sam Wineburg, eds. (New York: New York University Press, 2000).

21. Sam Wineburg, *Historical Thinking and Other Unnatural Acts: Charting the Future of Teaching the Past* (Philadelphia: Temple University Press, 2001), 7.

22. David Jenness, *Making Sense of Social Studies* (New York: Macmillan Publishing Company, 1990), 153–154 and Lynn R. Nelson and Frederick D. Drake, "Secondary Teachers'

Reactions to the New Social Studies," *Theory and Research in Social Education* 22, no. 1 (Winter 1994): 69–70.

23. Linda Symcox, *Whose History: The Struggle for National Standards in American Classrooms* (New York: Teachers College Press, 2002), 72.

24. Charlotte Crabtree, "Returning History to the Elementary Schools," in *Historical Literacy: The Case for History in American Education,* Paul Gagnon and the Bradley Commission on History in Schools, eds. (New York: Macmillan, 1989), 173–187.

25. Ibid., 25–27 and Bradley Commission, *Building a History Curriculum.*

26. Lynne V. Cheney, *American Memory: A Report on the Humanities in the Nation's Public Schools* (Washington, D.C.: Superintendent of Documents, Government Printing Office, 1987).

27. http://www.socialstudies.org/standards/execsummary/.

28. Lawrence W. McBride, "Could This Be the End of History? Point of View," *Social Education* 57, no. 6 (October 1993): 282–283.

29. Sarah Drake Brown and John J. Patrick, *History Education in the Fifty States: A Survey of Teacher Certification and State-Based Standards and Assessments for Teachers and Students.* Paper presented at Innovations in Collaboration: A School-University Model to Enhance History Teaching, K–16, Alexandria, VA, June 28, 2003. Also see Sarah Drake Brown, "History Standards in the Fifty States," ERIC *Digest* (November 2003), EDO-SO-2003-13; Sarah Drake Brown, "State Certification Requirements for History Teachers," ERIC *Digest* (December 2003), EDO-SO-2003-14; and Sarah Drake Brown, "A Comparative Analysis."

30. Stephen J. Thornton, "From Content to Subject Matter," *Social Studies* 92, no. 6. (2001): 237–243.

Chapter 3

1. American Historical Association Committee of Seven, *The Study of History in Schools* (New York: Macmillan, 1899).

2. National Center for History in the Schools, *National Standards for History: Basic Edition* (Los Angeles: National Center for History in the Schools, 1996), 59–72.

3. Sarah Drake Brown and John J. Patrick, *History Education in the Fifty States: A Survey of Teacher Certification and State-Based Standards and Assessments for Teachers and Students.* Paper presented at Innovations in Collaboration: A School-University Model to Enhance History Teaching, K–16, Alexandria, VA, June 28, 2003. Also see Sarah Drake Brown, "History Standards in the Fifty States," ERIC *Digest* (November 2003), EDO-SO-2003-13, and Sarah Drake Brown, "A Comparative Analysis of Historical Thinking Skills in the History Standards of Seven States: California, Idaho, Illinois, Indiana, Massachusetts, Texas, Virginia" (Ph.D. diss., Indiana University, 2004).

4. "Benchmarks for Professional Development in Teaching of History as a Discipline," *Perspectives* (May 2003): 41–44.

5. The Bradley Commission on History in Schools, *Building a History Curriculum: Guidelines for Teaching History in Schools* (Washington, D.C.: Educational Excellence Network, 1988, 1989), 9.

6. Keith Windschuttle, *The Killing of History: How Literary Critics and Social Theorists Are Murdering Our Past* (San Francisco: Encounter Books, 2000), 12. Karl Popper, *The Open Society and Its Enemies* (Princeton: Princeton University Press, 1950) and *The Poverty of Historicism* (New York: Harper & Row, 1964) changed the meaning of historicism to imply larger laws of historical development. For a critique of Popper's change in meaning through "falsifiability," see Windschuttle's commentary, 209–214. Austrian philosopher Karl Popper challenged utopian thinking and those who claimed to know the historical laws of change (historicism), which he criticized as false dogma and a threat to open society. Popper challenged Marxist (and Nazi) narratives in the 20th century. He disliked, for example, the tendencies of Marxists to interpret every event as a validation of their theories. Popper sought to improve society by determining if problems have social solutions. He advocated free institutions, open-mindedness, and individual liberties in a marketplace of ideas.

7. Richard Pipes, *Three "Whys" of the Russian Revolution* (New York: Vintage Books, 1997), 3 and 9–10, and Alexander Rabinowitch, *The Bolsheviks Come to Power: The Revolution of 1917 in Petrograd* (New York: W. W. Norton, 1976). Pipes outlines causation in his book using the analogy of an apple tree. See also, for the distinctions in time and causation, Fernand Braudel, *On History,* trans. Sarah Matthews (Chicago: University of Chicago Press, 1980), and David Hackett Fischer, *Historians' Fallacies: Toward a Logic of Historical Thought* (New York: Harper and Row, 1970).

8. *Ibid.,* 11–14.

9. Bruce A. VanSledright, "On the Importance of Historical Positionality to Thinking about and Teaching History," *International Journal of Social Education* 12, no. 2 (Fall/Winter 1997–98): 1–18.

10. Linda S. Levstik, "Articulating the Silences: Teachers' and Adolescents' Conceptions of Historical Significance," in *Knowing, Teaching, and Learning History: National and International Perspectives,* Peter N. Stearns, Peter Seixas, and Sam Wineburg, eds. (New York: New York University Press, 2000), 284–305. Levstik strongly suggests alternative narratives should be provided or otherwise the national narrative will be regarded with cynicism.

11. Sam Wineburg, *Historical Thinking and Other Unnatural Acts: Charting the Future of Teaching the Past* (Philadelphia: Temple University Press, 2001), and Frederick D. Drake and Sarah Drake Brown, "A Systematic Approach to Improve Students' Historical Thinking," *The History Teacher* 36, no. 4 (August 2003): 465–489.

12. Wineburg, *Historical Thinking,* 7.

13. Peter J. Lee, "Putting Principles into Practice: Understanding History," in *How Students Learn: History in the Classroom*, M. Suzanne Donovan and John D. Bransford, eds. (Washington, D.C.: The National Academics Press, 2005), 31–77.

14. Samuel S. Wineburg, "Probing the Depths of Students' Historical Knowledge," *Perspectives* (March 1992): 19–24 and Wineburg, *Historical Thinking.*

15. Frederick D. Drake, "Teaching Historical Thinking," ERIC *Digest* (August 2002), EDO-SO-2002-6. Also see Gaca Leinhardt and Kathleen McCarthy Young, "Two Texts, Three Readers: Distance and Expertise in Reading History," *Cognition and Instruction* 14, no. 4 (1996): 441–486.

16. Robert B. Bain, "Into the Breach: Using Research and Theory to Shape History Instruction," in *Knowing, Teaching, and Learning History: National and International Perspectives,*

Peter N. Stearns, Peter Seixas, and Sam Wineburg, eds. (New York: New York University Press, 2000), 333.

17. We do not believe that those in the Piaget-Peel-Hallam tradition are necessarily opponents of history and historical thinking. We believe that they (Hallam in particular) were suggesting that historical thinking is difficult. Since their writings, we have tried to read a more current body of literature that includes Peter Lee's work, which softens the harsh criticisms of Hallam regarding students' capabilities of historical thinking. See Peter Lee, "History Across the Water: A U.K. Perspective on History Education Research," *Issues in Education: Contributions from Educational Psychology* 4 (1998): 211–220.

18. William G. Perry, Jr., *Forms of Intellectual and Ethical Development in the College Years: A Scheme* (San Francisco: Jossey-Bass, 1999), xxxi–xxxv.

19. Lev Semenovich Vygotsky, *Mind in Society* (Cambridge: Harvard University Press, 1978). See also Jerome S. Bruner, *Toward a Theory of Instruction* (Cambridge: Harvard University Press, 1974); Jerome S. Bruner, *Actual Minds, Possible Worlds* (Cambridge: Harvard University Press, 1986); David J. Wood, *How Children Think and Learn: The Social Contexts of Cognitive Development* (Malden, MA.: Blackwell, 1998); Paul Cooper and Donald McIntyre, *Effective Teaching and Learning: Teachers and Students' Perspectives* (Philadelphia: Open University Press, 1996); and Chris Husbands and Anna Pendry, "Thinking and Feeling: Pupils' Preconceptions about the Past and Historical Understanding," in *Issues in History Teaching,* James Arthur and Robert Phillips, eds. (New York: Routledge, 2000), 125–134.

20. Richard C. Anderson, "The Notion of Schemata and the Educational Enterprise," in *Schooling and the Acquisition of Knowledge,* Richard C. Anderson, Rand J. Spiro, and William E. Montague, eds. (Hillsdale, NJ: Erlbaum, 1977) and Wood, *How Children Think and Learn.*

21. David Ausubel, "The Use of Advance Organizers in the Learning and Retention of Meaningful Verbal Material," *Journal of Educational Psychology* 51 (1960): 267–272, and David Ausubel, *The Psychology of Meaningful Verbal Learning* (New York: Grune and Stratton, 1963).

22. Jerome Bruner, *The Study of Thinking* (New York: Wiley, 1956); Jerome Bruner, *The Process of Education* (New York: Vintage Books, 1960); and Jerome Bruner, *The Culture of Education* (Cambridge: Harvard University Press, 1996).

23. See Georg G. Iggers, *Historiography in the Twentieth Century: From Scientific Objectivity to the Postmodern Challenge* (Hanover, NH: Wesleyan University Press, 1997), 101–105.

24. Jerome Bruner, *Toward a Theory of Instruction* (Cambridge: Harvard University Press, 1966).

25. Stuart J. Foster, John D. Hogue, and Richard H. Rosch, "Thinking Aloud about History: Children's and Adolescents' Responses to Historical Photographs, *Theory and Research in Social Education* 27 (Spring 1999): 179–214.

Chapter 4

1. Peter N. Stearns, "Getting Specific about Training in Historical Analysis: A Case Study in World History," in *Knowing, Teaching, and Learning History: National and International Perspectives,* Peter N. Stearns, Peter Seixas, and Sam Wineburg, eds. (New York: New York University Press, 2000), 429.

2. Ross E. Dunn and David Vigilante, *Bring History Alive! A Sourcebook for Teaching World History* (Los Angeles: National Center for History in Schools, 1996), 7.

3. See Walter La Feber, "The Constitution and United States Foreign Policy," *The Journal of American History* 74, no. 3 (December 1987): 695–717.

4. National Assessment Governing Board, *U.S. History Framework for the 1994 National Assessment of Educational Progress: NAEP U.S. History Consensus Project* (Washington, D.C.: National Assessment Governing Board, 1994, 2001).

5. Richard W. Slatta, "The Whys and Wherefores of Comparative Frontier History," October 2003, http://www.usembassy.at/en/download/pdf/slatta.pdf; CEU-HESP Comparative History Projects, http://www.hist.ceu.hu/?q=node/27; and Comparative History Failures: Feudalism, http://www.umass.edu/wsp/comparative/failures/feudalism.html.

6. These documents may be found in Eugene V. Debs, "A Call to the People," August 23, 1897, http://www.marxists.org/history/usa/parties/spusa/1897/0823-debs-calltothepeople.pdf and Vladimir Lenin, "What is to be Done?" 1902, http://www.marxists.org/archive/lenin/works/download/what-itd.pdf.

7. David A. Shannon, "Eugene V. Debs," in *Encyclopedia of American Biography*, John A. Garraty and Jerome L. Sternstein, eds. (New York: Harper & Row, 1974), 266–267.

8. Robert Service, *Comrades! A History of World Communism* (Cambridge, MA.: Harvard University Press, 2006), 39–40 and 49–50.

9. Further information regarding the Civics Mosaic program and Comparative Civics lessons may be obtained at http://civicsmosaic.com/.

10. Simone Aria, Marilyn Hitchens, and Heidi Roupp, "Teaching World History: The Global Human Experience through Time," ERIC *Digest.*

11. Ross E. Dunn, "Constructing World History in the Classroom," in *Knowing, Teaching, and Learning History,* 121–140.

12. *Ibid.,* 124–125.

13. J. M. Roberts, *The Triumph of the West: The Origin, Rise, and Legacy of Western Civilization* (London: British Broadcasting Organization, 1985), and J. M. Roberts, *A Concise History of the World* (New York: Oxford University Press, 1995).

14. Stearns, "Getting Specific," 420, 429.

15. Richard Hofstadter, *The American Political Tradition and the Men Who Made It* (New York: Knopf, 1948).

16. Eric Foner, *The Story of American Freedom* (New York: Norton, 1998).

17. Gary B. Nash, *Red, White, and Black: The Peoples of Early North America* (Upper Saddle River, NJ: Prentice Hall, 1974, 2000).

18. Thomas Bender, *La Pietra Report: Project on Internationalizing the Study of American History* (2000). See also on the Internet: http://www.nyu.edu/gsas/dept/icas/internationalizing.htm.

19. Denis Shemilt, "The Caliph's Coin: The Currency of Narrative Frameworks in History Teaching," in *Knowing, Teaching, and Learning History,* 85.

20. James V. Wertsch, "Is It Possible to Teach Beliefs, as Well as Knowledge about History?," in *Knowing, Teaching, and Learning History,* 45–46.

Chapter 5

1. Frances Fitzgerald, *America Revised: History Schoolbooks in the Twentieth Century* (Boston: Little, Brown, 1979) and James W. Loewen, *Lies My Teacher Told Me: Everything Your American History Textbook Got Wrong* (New York: Touchstone, 1995).

2. Avon Crismore, "The Rhetoric of Textbooks: Metadiscourse," *Journal of Curriculum Studies* 16 (1984): 279–296, and Sam Wineburg, *Historical Thinking and Other Unnatural Acts: Charting the Future of Teaching the Past* (Philadelphia: Temple University Press, 2001), 12, 47.

3. Sarah Drake Brown and John J. Patrick, *History Education in the Fifty States: A Survey of Teacher Certification and State-Based Standards and Assessments for Teachers and Students.* Paper presented at Innovations in Collaboration: A School-University Model to Enhance History Teaching, K–16, Alexandria, VA, June 28, 2003. Also see Sarah Drake Brown, "History Standards in the Fifty States," ERIC *Digest* (November 2003), EDO-SO-2003-13 and Sarah Drake Brown, "State Certification Requirements for History Teachers," ERIC *Digest* (December 2003), EDO-SO-2003-14.

4. Paul Gagnon suggests that "good history standards . . . lay before students, parents, teachers, and the teachers-of-teachers the lean, essential, common core of history learning that all high school graduates in a modern democracy have the right to confront." See Paul A. Gagnon, "How a Standard Becomes a Lesson," *History Matters* 7, no. 3 (November 1994): 1.

5. Elliot W. Eisner, *The Educational Imagination: On the Design and Evaluation of School Programs* (New York: Macmillan, 1994).

6. Two very helpful sources that will assist you in accommodating students with special needs are Beverly H. Johns and E. Paula Crowley, *Students with Disabilities and General Education: A Desktop Reference for School Personnel—Practical Approaches and Sound Procedures* (Danvers, MA: LRP Publications, 2003), and E. Paula Crowley and Frederick D. Drake, *Teaching History in Inclusive Settings* (unpublished handbook, 2001).

Chapter 6

1. Numerous educators have written about alternative assessment. For basic information, see J. L. Herman, P. R. Aschbacher, and L. Winters, *A Practical Guide to Alternative Assessment* (Alexandria, VA: Association for Supervision and Curriculum Development, 1992); Robert J. Marzano, Debra Pickering, and Jay McTighe, *Assessing Student Outcomes* (Alexandria, VA: Association for Supervision and Curriculum Development, 1993); Lorrie Shephard, "Why We Need Better Assessments," *Educational Leadership* 46 (April 1989): 4–9; Grant Wiggins, "Teaching to the (Authentic Test)," *Educational Leadership* 46 (April 1989): 41–47; Grant Wiggins, "A True Test: Toward More Authentic and Equitable Assessment," *Phi Delta Kappan* (May 1989): 703–713; and Grant Wiggins, "Assessment: Authenticity, Context, and Validity," *Phi Delta Kappan* (November 1993): 200–214.

2. Frederick D. Drake, "Using Alternative Assessments to Improve the Teaching and Learning of History," ERIC *Digest* (June 1997), EDO-SO-97-9.

3. Howard Gardner, *The Unschooled Mind: How Children Think and How Schools Should Teach* (New York: Basic Books, 1991), and Howard Gardner, *Multiple Intelligences: The Theory in Practice* (New York: Basic Books, 1993).

4. Paul Gagnon and the Bradley Commission on History in Schools, eds., *Historical Literacy: The Case for History in American Education* (Boston: Houghton Mifflin, 1989), 26–27. The Bradley Commission on History in the Schools also presents the six vital themes and narratives in their indispensable pamphlet, *Building a History Curriculum: Guidelines for Teaching History in Schools* (Westlake, OH: Educational Excellence Network, 1988, 1989), 10–11.

5. Paul Gagnon, ed., *Historical Literacy,* 25–26, and the Bradley Commission on History in Schools, *Building a History Curriculum,* 9.

6. *National Standards for History* (Los Angeles: National Center for History in the Schools, 1996), 14.

7. *National Standards for History,* 15–16.

8. This rubric was developed by Lawrence W. McBride, Frederick D. Drake, and Marcel Lewinski as part of an alternative assessment project published as *Alternative Assessment in the Social Sciences* (Illinois State Board of Education, 1996). For information concerning availability, write to John Craig, Illinois State Board of Education, School and Student Assessment Division, 100 N. First Street, Springfield, IL 62777-0001.

9. Between April and May of 1995, approximately 2,000 students completed one or more of 37 different activities, and 125 teachers applied the rubric to assess their students' work. For examples of student work and how teachers used the rubric, see McBride, Drake, and Lewinski, *Alternative Assessment in the Social Sciences,* 1996.

10. The examples in this chapter were drawn from a publication in *The History Teacher.* See Frederick D. Drake and Lawrence W. McBride, "Reinvigorating the Teaching of History through Alternative Assessment," *The History Teacher 30,* no. 2 (February 1997): 145–173.

11. Frederick D. Drake, "Using Alternative Assessments to Improve the Teaching and Learning of History," *ERIC Digest* (June 1997), EDO-SO-97-9.

12. For a discussion of the wider implications of the failure of students to improve their knowledge and understanding of history, see Lewis H. Lapham, "The Republic Is in Trouble," in *History Matters* 8, no. 5 (January 1996): 1, 5.

Chapter 7

1. Much of this chapter is from Frederick D. Drake and Sarah Drake Brown, "A Systematic Approach to Improve Students' Historical Thinking," *The History Teacher* 36, no. 4 (August 2003): 465–489.

2. Gerald Danzer and Mark Newman, "Primary Sources in the Teaching of History," in *Bring History Alive! A Sourcebook for Teaching United States History,* Kirk Ankey, Richard Del Rio, Gary B. Nash, and David Vigilante, eds. (Los Angeles: National Center for History in Schools, 1996), 21–25.

3. Joan W. Musbach, "Using Primary Sources in the Secondary Classroom," *OAH Magazine of History* (Fall 2001): 30–32.

4. A number of books provide a plethora of web sites for history and social studies teachers. For example, see Dennis A. Trinkle and Scott A. Merriman, eds., *The History Highway 3.0: A Guide to Internet Resources* (Armonk, NY: M. E. Sharpe, 2002) and Michael J. Berson, Barbara C. Cruz, James A. Duplass, and J. Howard Johnston, *Social Studies on the Internet* (Columbus: Pearson Merrill Prentice Hall, 2004). Also an excellent curriculum

entitled *Choices,* a program of the Watson Institute for International Studies, provides primary sources for teachers interested in an international perspective. See http://www.choices.edu/index.cfm for information.

5. Kenneth M. Jensen, *Origins of the Cold War: The Novikov, Kennan, and Roberts' "Long Telegrams" of 1946* (Washington, D.C.: United States Institute of Peace, 1995), 28.

6. See Sean Greenwood, "Frank Roberts and the 'Other' Long Telegram: The View from the British Embassy in Moscow, March 1946," *Journal of Contemporary History* 25 (London: Sage, 1990), 103–122.

7. Peter N. Stearns, *Meaning Over Memory: Recasting the Teaching of Culture and History* (Chapel Hill, NC: University of North Carolina Press, 1993).

8. Robert B. Bain, "Into the Breach: Using Research and Theory to Shape History Instruction," in *Knowing, Teaching, and Learning History,* 332.

9. Following the public release of the Novikov "Long Telegram" and a symposium prepared by the United States Institute of Peace, the editors of the journal *Diplomatic History* made the documents available. Kenneth M. Jensen's revised edition of *Origins of the Cold War* provides excellent commentaries regarding historians' views of the three documents and their significance.

10. We realize that comparison is very difficult and that it must be taught with great care and nurturing. Peter N. Stearns' excellent essay, "Getting Specific about Training in Historical Analysis: A Case Study in World History," suggests ways to help students "grasp comparative fundamentals" and view history in a "comparative context." See Peter N. Stearns, "Getting Specific about Training in Historical Analysis: A Case Study in World History," in *Knowing, Teaching, and Learning History,* 419–436.

11. Kathleen Medina, Jeffrey Pollard, Debra Schneider, and Camille Leonhardt, *How Do Students Understand the Discipline of History as an Outcome of Teachers' Professional Development?* (Oakland, CA: Regents of the University of California, 2000).

12. Jerome Bruner, *The Study of Thinking* (New York: Wiley, 1956); Jerome Bruner, *The Process of Education* (New York: Vintage Books, 1960); and Jerome Bruner, *The Culture of Education* (Cambridge: Harvard University Press, 1996).

13. The Historical Context section of the analysis guide draws students to consider the document in the context of local/regional, national, and world views. The importance of internationalizing U.S. history has been emphasized in several articles. See David Thelen, "Of Audiences, Borderlands, and Comparisons: Toward the Internationalization of American History," *The Journal of American History* 79 (September 1992): 432–462; Pauline Maier, "Nationhood and Citizenship: What Difference Did the American Revolution Make?" in *Diversity and Citizenship: Rediscovering American Nationhood,* Gary Jeffrey Jacobsohn and Susan Dunns, eds. (Lanham, MD: Rowman and Littlefield, 1996), 45–64; Stearns, Seixas, and Wineburg, eds., *Knowing, Teaching, and Learning History,* and Thomas Bender, *La Pietra Report: Project on Internationalizing the Study of American History* (2000) on the Internet http://www.nyu.edu/gass/dept/icas/internationalizing.htm.

Chapter 8

1. *Ferris Bueller's Day Off,* Paramount Pictures, 1986.

2. Linda M. McNeil, *Contradictions of Control: School Structure and School Knowledge* (New York: Routledge, 1988); Larry Cuban, *How Teachers Taught: Constancy and Change in*

American Classrooms, 1890–1990 (New York: Teachers College Press, 1993); and Theodore Sizer, *Horace's Compromise: The Dilemma of the American High School* (Boston: Houghton Mifflin, 1992).

3. Amy Gutmann, *Democratic Education* (Princeton: Princeton University Press, 1999), xiii.

4. John J. Patrick and Robert S. Leming, "Conclusion: Recommendations and Reactions," in *Principles and Practices of Democracy in the Education of Social Studies Teachers: Civic Learning in Teacher Education*, John J. Patrick and Robert S. Leming, eds., vol. 1 (Bloomington, IN: The ERIC Clearinghouse for Social Studies/Social Science Education, 2001), 247.

5. *Ibid.*, 248.

6. For further discussion of the importance of deliberative discussion, see Walter C. Parker, *Teaching Democracy: Unity and Diversity in Public Life* (New York: Teachers College Press, 2003). Parker provides a rationale for discussion in public settings. He advocates deliberation for public policy issues. Our purpose is to foster students' understanding. Deliberative discussion is important for the rumination of ideas and documents. Listening to ideas is a complement to reading ideas. Historical understanding provides an elaborate foundation for deliberation concerning historical issues and present-day policy issues. Also see Diana E. Hess, "Teaching Controversial Public Issues Discussions: Learning from Skilled Teachers," *Theory and Research in Social Education* 30, no. 1 (Winter 2002): 10–41 and Lynn Brice, "Deliberative Discourse Enacted: Task, Text, and Talk," *Theory and Research in Social Education* 30, no. 1 (Winter 2002): 66–87.

7. John D. Haas, *The Era of the New Social Studies* (Boulder, CO: Social Science Educational Consortium, 1977); Hazel W. Hertzberg, *Social Studies Reform 1880–1980* (Boulder, CO: Social Science Education Consortium, 1981); and Lynn R. Nelson and Frederick D. Drake, "Secondary Teachers' Reaction to the New Social Studies," *Theory and Research in Social Education* 22 (Winter 1994): 44–73.

8. Frederick D. Drake, "Teaching Historical Thinking," ERIC *Digest.* (Bloomington, IN: Clearinghouse for Social Studies/Social Science Education, EDO-SO-2002-5).

9. Phillip Hoose, *We Were There, Too! Young People in U.S. History* (New York: Farrar Straus Giroux, 2001), 198-200. Hoose's book provides primary sources that may appeal to students because they originated with young people's involvement in U.S. history. Other books that may prove include Susan Campbell Bartoletti, *Kids on Strike* (Boston: Houghton Mifflin Company, 1999) and Russell Freedman, *Kids At Work: Lewis Hine and the Crusade Against Child Labor* (New York: Clarion Books, 1994).

Chapter 9

1. For an intriguing analysis of John Singleton Copley's portrait, *Paul Revere,* see historian David Hacket Fischer's *Paul Revere's Ride* (New York: Oxford University Press, 1994), 3–6.

2. We are indebted to Art Pease of New Hampshire, Earl Bell of the University of Chicago Laboratory School, and Fred Walk of Normal Community High School in Illinois for the interdisciplinary approach to the people, space, and time image analysis strategy. Since the late 1980s we have been using people, space, and time with modifications to introduce students to images. We have used the similarities and differences approach as well since the early 1990s and have watched Dennis Schnierle of Lincoln-Way East High School in Illinois use the similarities and differences

approach with preservice teachers. We are indebted to Linda Clark, a history teacher from Padua High School, who created much of Vietnam photo activity and the analysis approach that we call quadrantal/hemispheric analysis. Linda Clark is a member of the National Council for History Education and has received numerous teaching awards. She created much of this activity for the U.S. National Archives and Records Administration (NARA). Her photographs and a description of her activity can be found in NARA's Digital Classroom: Teaching with Documents Lesson Plan: The War in Vietnam—A Story in Photographs. See http://www.archives.gov/digitalclassroom/lessons/vietnamphotographs/vietnam_photos.html.

Chapter 10

1. We want to thank Fred Walk, an excellent teacher at Normal Community High School in Normal, Illinois. Mr. Walk has published his experiences using a road (Route 66) as a primary source in "Towanda's Historic Route 66," *Historic Illinois* 21, no. 6 (April 2002): 10–12. Mr. Walk has received numerous teaching awards over a career that spans 30 years at Normal Community High School.

2. Howard Gardner, *The Mind's New Science: A History of the Cognitive Revolution* (New York: Basic Books, 1985) and Howard Gardner, *Multiple Intelligences: The Theory in Practice* (New York: Basic Books, 1993). These multiple intelligences include visual/spatial, logical/mathematical, verbal/linguistic, musical/rhythmic, bodily/kinesthetic, interpersonal/social, and intrapersonal/introspective intelligences.

3. Chris Husbands, *What Is History Teaching?* (Philadelphia: Open University Press, 2003), 106.

4. *Ibid.*, 100.

5. William C. Kashatus, *Past, Present & Personal: Teaching Writing in U.S. History* (Portsmouth, NH: Heinemann, 2002).

6. Barry K. Beyer, "Using Writing to Learn in History," *The History Teacher* 13, no. 2 (1980): 167–178; Mary M. Dupuis et al., *Teaching Reading and Writing in the Content Areas* (Glenview, IL: Scott, Foresman and Company, 1989); and Henry A. Giroux, "Teaching Content and Thinking through Writing," *Social Education* 43, no. 3 (1979): 190–193.

7. Dupuis et al., *Teaching Reading and Writing* and B. C. Mallonee and J. R. Breihan, "Responding to Students' Drafts: Interdisciplinary Consensus," *College Composition and Communication* 36, no. 2 (1985): 213–231.

8. Beyer, "Using Writing to Learn in History," and Dupuis et al., *Teaching Reading and Writing*.

9. Husbands, *What Is History Teaching?*, 107.

10. Beyer, "Using Writing to Learn in History," 167–178; Henry A. Giroux, "Teaching Content and Thinking through Writing"; Dupuis et al., *Teaching Reading and Writing;* and Judith A. Langer and Arthur N. Applebee, *How Writing Shapes Thinking: A Study of Teaching and Learning* (Urbana, IL: National Council of Teachers of English, 1987).

11. J. G. A. Pocock, "Working on Ideas in Time," in *The Historian's Workshop,* ed. L. Perry Curtis (New York: Knopf, 1970), 161.

12. Frederick D. Drake, "Ideas for Writing to Learn in the Social Studies," *Issues Current in the Social Studies* 2, no. 2 (1993): 4–7.

13. Husbands, *What Is History Teaching?,* 101.

14. Barry K. Beyer, *Teaching Thinking in Social Studies* (Columbus: Charles E. Merrill, 1979), 252–253.

15. In Chapter 7 we described the use of a systematic approach, which we label the first-, second-, and third-order approach.

16. Pauline Maier, *American Scripture: Making the Declaration of Independence* (New York: Knopf, 1997), 167.

17. *Ibid.,* 168.

18. J. H. Hedberg, "Writing and Thinking about the English Industrial Revolution," *Social Education* 52, no. 4 (1988): 260–263.

Conclusion

1. Philip W. Jackson, *The Practice of Teaching* (New York: Teachers College Press, 1986).

2. *Ibid.,* 115–145.

3. John Dewey, *Experience and Education* (New York: Kappa Delta Pi, 1938).

4. Chris Husbands, *What Is History Teaching?* (Philadelphia: Open University Press, 2003), 133.

5. John Dewey, *How We Think* (Boston: D.C. Heath, 1910, 1933), 6.

6. Alan F. Griffin, *A Philosophical Approach to the Subject-Matter Preparation of Teachers of History* (Washington, D.C.: National Council for the Social Studies, 1992), 17.

7. Jean Bethke Elshtain, *Democracy on Trial* (New York: Basic Books, 1995), 86.

Glossary

Chronological Thinking—More than the order of facts and events. It involves an understanding of cause and effect relationships and change over time.

Comparative Thinking—In historical thinking, historians describe conditions in other parts of the world at the time. A baseline is needed for comparisons to be made.

Contextualization—In historical thinking, historians describe the time frame and conditions both locally and nationally.

Corroboration Heuristic—In historical thinking, what historians do to relate one document to another document.

Deliberation—Deliberation cultivates reasoning and choice. It fosters virtues that are necessary for a democratic society. These virtues include "veracity, nonviolence, practical judgment, civic integrity, and magnanimity" (Amy Gutmann).

Deliberative Discussion—A method of discussion to develop both liberal and civic knowledge. Deliberation implies both reason and choice; judgments are suspended. In a deliberative discussion students and teacher are not in a contest or debate to be won.

Diachronic Organization—An approach that takes one theme and traces it from its inception to the present.

Durable Knowledge—Knowledge that informs the ideas individuals bring to their conversations as citizens.

Electronic Media—A type of **primary source** such as videotapes, audiotapes, and film clips.

Expressive Objectives—Objectives that describe a situation or problem with which students must cope. Diverse interpretations and solutions are expected among students.

First-Order Document—The most essential primary source for the teacher on a particular period, era, or topic in history.

Folklore, Folkways, and Mythology—A type of **primary source** passed through oral tradition.

Habits of Mind—The insights, perspectives, and understandings that are a principal aim of historical study. These thoughtful judgments extend students beyond the formal skills of critical thinking. The National Council for History Education (formerly the Bradley Commission on History in Schools) suggests 13 of history's habits of mind to illuminate continuing themes and significant questions of history.

Heuristic—Exploratory problem-solving technique that uses self-educating strategies in historical investigation. Questions historians use as they probe a **primary source** or **secondary source.**

Historiography—The history of writing history. A study of how history has been written and how and why historian's interpretations (giving meaning) of the past change.

Images—A type of **primary source** such as paintings, photographs, political cartoons, photographs, charts, graphs, and posters.

Instructional Objectives—Objectives that specify unambiguously a particular behavior, skill, or item of knowledge that all students should acquire after a learning activity.

Mimetic Tradition of Teaching—The conceptualization of teaching as transmitting an identifiable body of knowledge that belongs to the teacher and that should be passed on to the student.

People, Space, and Time Questioning Strategy—A strategy in which teachers ask their students to analyze an image. Questions a teacher asks establish the foundations of geography and time.

Performance Assessment—Also known as alternative or authentic assessment, it requires students to perform a task rather than select an answer from a multiple-choice test or related bubble test. Performance assessment creates situations in which students actively communicate through writing or demonstrate what they know and understand.

Physical Environment and Material Culture—A type of primary source such as architecture, landscaping, and household artifacts.

Positionality—A frame of reference for historical thinking about the past. It emanates from an array of cultural experiences to inform ontological (worldview), existential (who am I?), and epistemological (how do I know?) questions/stances.

Primary Sources—Direct records left behind from the period or by the people who are the subject of the historian's study. They may be a document in print (e.g., a letter, diary, speech, official correspondence, newspaper, or magazine article); an image (e.g., a photograph, painting, political cartoon, map, chart, graph); broadcast media (e.g., movie or television show clip, radio broadcast); or an artifact (e.g., tool, apparatus).

Print (or Textual) Documents—Written **primary sources** such as letters, diaries, telegrams, and speeches.

Quadrantal/Hemispheric Analysis—A form of analysis in which a teacher divides an image into quadrants or hemispheres and asks students to analyze parts of an image (such as a photograph) in greater detail. The teacher's questions establish the foundations of geography and time.

Rubric—A scoring guide to assess a student's performance. A three-dimensional, analytic rubric, shared with students, assesses simultaneously a students' performance in the dimensions of knowledge, reasoning, and communication. It can be used as a diagnostic and instructional tool.

Second-Order Documents—Three to five **primary sources** or **secondary sources** that challenge or corroborate the central idea in the first-order document. These documents, selected by the teacher, provide a nuanced understanding of the topic by offering multiple perspectives.

Secondary Sources—Books, essays, and articles historians write that are accounts of a period or a topic after an event has taken place. They offer a narrative of the subject studied by the historian. Depending on the focus of a particular study, a secondary source can serve as a primary source. For example, although a textbook is typically considered a secondary source, a work such as David Saville Muzzey's *History of the American People* (1927) becomes a primary source when studying textbooks written in the 1920s.

Similarities and Differences Strategy—An analytical strategy in which a teacher displays two images and students identify characteristics that are similar and different between the two images. The teacher's questions establish the foundations of geography and time.

Sourcing Heuristic—In historical thinking, what historians do before reading for content comprehension.

Synchronic Organization—An approach that examines several themes within a particular time period. This approach considers the relationship of multiple political, economic, and social phenomena within a short period of time. The synchronic approach investigates the uniqueness of past society.

Third-Order Documents—Additional **primary sources** or **secondary sources** that students find to challenge or corroborate the **first-order document.** Ultimately, students should select a third-order document to serve as their first-order document.

Transformative Tradition of Teaching—The conceptualization of teaching as creating a qualitative change within students. Transformative teachers emphasize helping students make meaning of the past.

Vital Themes and Narratives—The National Council for History Education (formerly the Bradley Commission on History in Schools) suggests six vital themes and narratives that illustrate universal historical themes. Themes serve as a larger idea around which to organize the content of the past meaningfully for students. The themes provide opportunities for analytic and synthetic thinking. Narratives provide interesting stories that help students remember the past.

Index